Lang
Poems and plays

Other Books by Alison Lurie

*Love and Friendship*
*The Nowhere City*
*Imaginary Friends*
*Real People*
*The War Between the Tates*

# V.R. LANG
# Poems & Plays

*with a Memoir by*

*ALISON LURIE*

*Random House*  *New York*

# V.R. LANG
# Poems & Plays

*with a Memoir by*
*ALISON LURIE*

 Published in the United States by Random House, Inc., New York, and simultaneously in Canada by Random House of Canada Limited, Toronto.

Since this page cannot legibly accommodate the necessary acknowledgments, they can be found on the facing page.

Library of Congress Cataloging in Publication Data
Lang, V R 1924–1956.
Poems & plays.
I. Lurie, Alison
PS3562.A4848P6 1975 811'.5'4 75-10258
ISBN 0-394-49904-2

*Manufactured in the United States of America*

2 4 6 8 9 7 5 3

FIRST EDITION

ACKNOWLEDGMENTS

V. R. Lang's poems and plays were previously published in the collection entitled *The Pitch* in 1962 and prior to that as follows: "The Suicide," "At the Meeting of Two Families," "25 Years," "The Pitch," "Pique-Dame," "Death of Another Swan: Miami," "Lately by Language," from "Poems to Preserve the Years at Home," "Then all the listening cries of nature," "I Too Have Lived in Arcadia" (abridged edition), "The Elizabethans and Illusion," "Incantation to the Age of Stone," and "Already Ripening Barberries are Red" originally appeared in *Poetry*; "Lyric for the Father of a Girl," "Suicide Note," "Who Is the Real Oscar Mole?," "Born Old," "After Perigot and Willie," "Argument," and "How to Tell a Diamond from a Burning Baby" first appeared in *Quarterly Review of Literature*; "Dummy in the Crowd" published in *Folder*; "Address to the Redcoats" published in *Cambridge Review*; and "Waiting and Peeking" published in *The New Pocket Anthology of Modern Verse*.

"To Violet Lang" by Frank O'Hara used by permission of Donald Allen, Literary Executor of the Estate of Frank O'Hara.

*Part title illustrations by Edward Gorey.*

# To Violet Lang

*My darling*
*it would have been no sacrifice*
*to give my life*
*for yours*
*I wish, I am, waiting for you*
*on the "other side"*
*offering you a bath*
*and my new poems to read in it*
*everything is gone*
*except you, really you, you are always with me*

Frank O'Hara
March 10, 1959

# *Foreword*

I cannot think of a better introduction to Bunny's work than Alison's memoir. I knew Bunny through most of the period described and was married to her at the end; in almost every particular that I can recognize, it is an accurate and perceptive account of a life whose detailed inner workings I knew very well. Above all, it records, with great precision, Bunny's extraordinary style of speech and behavior, and this makes it a document more valuable to me now than all the photographs and souvenirs combined. Its publication here gives the reader what one would have thought only Bunny herself, alive, could have provided: that is, a projection of the spirit from which her work sprang.

I would like to thank the following for helping me edit Bunny's poetry: Lawrence Osgood, Julia Randall, Helen Wells, Mac Hammond, and Sarah Braveman.

BRADLEY PHILLIPS
*New York, March 1975*

# *Contents*

# *Introduction*

This memoir was written almost twenty years ago, not for publication but in an attempt to record and save part of my world which had just disappeared. For me, and many of her friends, Bunny's death was a first serious experience of mortality. It wasn't just elderly relatives who died, newspaper casualties and the pawns of war. One of ourselves, even the queen, could be lifted off the board as succinctly as a jumped piece in chess.

It was hard for us to get used to the idea. For months afterwards we would find ourselves imagining that we saw Bunny at the end of a street, starting to dial her telephone number, setting aside some story to tell her; thinking how she would laugh when she heard that Gregory Corso had actually— and then remembering that she couldn't laugh, because her mouth was full of earth.

For years I used to dream about her: I would go on longer and longer journeys by bus and train and on foot to find her in some large strange house, oddly dressed. "I've been very ill," she would tell me, "but I'm getting better now." In my last dream, she was upstairs in bed in a boarding house by the sea on a cold winter day. The room had gray pink-sprigged wallpaper and a view of the empty ocean. Bunny spoke to me; she moved her lips, but no sounds came out, so I don't know what she was trying to say.

All of us tried to keep Bunny alive by referring current events to her opinion, quoting lines from her letters and poems, guessing and even arguing about what she would have said of this or that film, marriage, poem, or person. David Jackson and James Merrill attempted to get in touch with her spirit through their ouija board, producing long transcriptions in which Bunny's views and conversational style were oddly like their own. (In their defense it must be admitted that when she was in the mood Bunny could and did alter her views and style to suit her audience.)

Of course whenever someone dies, each of the survivors is left with a slightly different image. With Bunny, who had so many moods and roles, these images were perhaps more different than usual. It is quite likely that there are people who will recognize almost nothing in this portrait, or at least feel that my emphasis is all wrong.

Persons who have read the earlier, privately printed version of the memoir will also notice some changes. As far as possible I have kept to the original text. But I have altered the names and descriptions of some of the characters and made certain cuts to avoid causing embarrassment or legal action, and I have corrected a few factual errors. I should like to thank everyone who helped point out such errors, and especially those who did not ask to have their part in the story disguised or tidied up.

Time alters the meaning of the past as well as our memory of it. I wrote about a private matter and private persons—some young writers and a provincial little-theatre group. Now a long scholarly study is being made of the Poets' Theatre, and the names and subsequent adventures of many of its members are literary history. It is only accident that the name V. R. Lang is not among them. If she had lived she would certainly have taken her place in the so-called New York School of poets, along with her friends John Ashbery, Kenneth Koch, and Frank O'Hara. (Her poems are occasionally so much like O'Hara's that one which was found among his papers, "To Frank's Guardian Angel," was printed as his in the recent collected edition.)

Indeed, I think that if she were still alive Bunny would now be better known than any of us, not because she was a better writer, but because she was a woman, and a special kind of woman—one who combined literary talent with great organizational ability, driving energy, and a gift for publicity. Many of her poems are what would now be called feminist. Her two last plays, *Fire Exit* and *I Too Have Lived in Arcadia*, both have central female characters who prefer a lonely independence to the emotional deceits and defeats of failed romantic love.

Bunny was a feminist before the movement was reinvented, in the dark ages of the early 1950's when it was much less popular to be a single female of independent mind and professional ambition than it is now; when any girl who didn't really want to stay home and keep house for a man and a lot of children was apt to be told by her friends and psychiatrists that she had not Accepted Herself as a Woman. Considering what she was able to accomplish in that hostile climate, it seems only logical that she would have been even more successful after the weather changed. My hope in publishing this book is to take advantage of the good weather, and give V. R. Lang, and her work, some of the attention that she loved and deserved.

ALISON LURIE
*Ithaca, New York*
*January 1975*

V. R. LANG
A Memoir
ALISON LURIE

She was of medium height and rather heavy, with firm, fair, heavy flesh. Her hands were broad, with short fingers; her face molded in low relief like a face made in clay by a child. There was something childish too in the full pout of the mouth and the placing of the rather round eyes. On this simple base Bunny built her many appearances. Her drawers were filled with extra attachments: long golden switches of hair, bunches of curls every shade from peroxide to henna; pink sponge-rubber breasts; thick false black eyelashes; artificial fingernails like fragments of seashell. A green tin box of theatrical make-up stood always open on her dressing table. She had trunks and closets of clothes put away all over the house, and never threw anything out that could be worn: what was no longer a dress would become a costume. Whole poetic plays were often clothed out of these trunks and closets. After the play had closed, Bunny always went round and took her things back, and sometimes other people's things as well. What was no longer a costume would become a dress—if the distinction can be made. Since her weight varied from season to season and year to year, from about 125 to 150, at any one time she could only wear part of her collection. She would pull something out of a closet and use it until it was filthy. Then it would go to the cleaners—unless Bunny happened to be broke—and back into the closet, perhaps for five years.

A few things were constant year after year: men's navy cotton jerseys or sweat shirts; torn blue sneakers, showing her painted toenails; and an old trenchcoat faded to white and soiled to brown which did not keep off rain. (When she wanted to keep off rain Bunny used one of half a dozen family umbrellas from the stand in her front hall.) This was the costume in which for six years Bunny attended Poets' Theatre meetings and rehearsals; she also usually wore it when writing, although not always. I remember in May 1951 finding her before her typewriter in an old starched and stained cook's uniform, about size 42. But ordinarily she liked to have appropriate dress for every activity. I saw her in this uniform again only when she was down in the basement kitchen cooking or, during a later phase, mixing cosmetics.

I remember what Bunny wore when we met, in June 1949, at a party on Beacon Hill: a white strapless piqué dress, very tight on top, up over which bulged brown shoulders. Apparently growing out of the cleft between her breasts was a large mauve orchid. She talked seriously about poetry and little magazines. Otherwise I remember only how her escort, a morose-looking individual with a bad complexion, perfectly demonstrated the wish not to be present. Throughout the party he sat on the window sill at one end of the room, facing outwards into the evening, dangling his legs over a drop of four stories to Pinckney Street. Almost everyone there except Bunny tried to make him come in, but he would not.

This man, Roger Jackson, was a determined yet defeated character, a brilliant actor who later appeared in almost every Poets' Theatre production, sometimes doubling three or more parts. He was Bunny's oldest, indeed her childhood friend. His father owned a small factory which made artificial limbs. During most of 1949 Roger and Bunny were writing an historical novel which was intended to make them very rich. It was typed entirely on the stationery of Roger's father's firm, which they used because it was free: every page was printed with NEW ENGLAND ARTIFICIAL LIMB CO. and a small picture of a mechanical leg in the top left-hand corner. Perhaps because of this influence, perhaps because they failed to get a publisher's advance when they submitted the first hundred pages, the story eventually became morbidly fantastic, a joke: the heroine, for example, was made to give birth to twin monsters.

Roger's own history was morose. A graduate of Harvard, he was injured during the war in a laboratory explosion in Iowa. His convalescence in Army hospitals was protracted; finally discharged, he became a hospital orderly at the Massachusetts General Hospital. So stubbornly did he cling to this degradation, however, that he rose by 1952 to be head of all operating-room orderlies at Massachusetts General, and eventually became the "Nurse" in charge of a large clinic. He lived in Cambridge, boarding in the house of Bunny's eldest sister. He was always around, waiting somewhere in the background of every large party. Bunny remarked once that if nothing else happened to her she supposed finally she would marry Roger Jackson.

Perhaps this was what he was waiting for: but it was hopeless, since something always happened to Bunny; if it was slow in coming, she encouraged it. She told me, for instance, how one dull day she was driving home from a rehearsal in her car along Mount Auburn Street in Cambridge, when she saw a terribly attractive young man. As she drove on, she wondered if he had really been all that attractive, so she went round the block and passed him again. He was, so she drove up to the curb, stopped, leaned out, and said: "Who are you?"

"And what happened then?" I asked, for the story seemed to be over.

"Oh, we had a fling, but he was very stupid really, so I passed him on to Butch."

I knew Bunny first as hostess and party girl, perhaps her most superficial role: "Miss Violet Ranney Lang, daughter of Malcolm Lang, graduate of Hannah More Academy, presented to Society in 1941, member of the Vincent Club, the Charlotte Cushman Club," etc. She gave wonderful parties where everyone enjoyed themselves; she also gave hopeless, terrible parties at which she alone had the strength to grit her teeth and imitate a good time. Usually her parties were held on the first floor of the four-story brownstone house at 209 Bay State Road. There were always the same props: dim yellow lamps or candles or a Christmas tree glittering with artificial golden icicles and snow; rugs rolled back, phonograph playing; flowers; and later there was always lobster newburg and champagne—though sometimes not even faintly enough of either—laid out on the family lace and silver. Through the dining-room window neon lights, red and blue, blinked across the wet, black river. Behind, someone was always dancing in the hall, someone sulking or reading in the library, someone confessing or making love—or simply waiting for the bathroom—on the back stairs. And however well you got to know Bunny you would always be introduced to someone you had never seen or heard of, yet who seemed completely intimate there, completely at home.

It was no use to ask about these people then or later: Bunny would not explain them. In the same way, in conversation, she would mention names I had never heard of as if they were well-known to me. For example, I remember her complaining during a quarrel she was having with Lyon Phelps, the president of the Poets' Theatre: "That Lyon. Why, do you know, he's actually beginning to be asked out to dinner. People are actually inviting him around as an extra man. People like Lee Gardner."

It was afternoon. We were up in Bunny's bedroom, doing nothing in particular. "Who is Lee Gardner?" I asked, although I hardly hoped to learn.

"Oh, you know Lee Gardner."

"No, who is he?"

"She." Bunny took a pot of black cold cream out of a drawer and began to spread it on her face.

"All right, who is she?"

"Oh, you must have met her. She's been around forever."

"No. Is she interesting?"

A long pause, while Bunny put cold cream on. "Not terribly."

The conversation was finished: if I insisted on pushing it further it would have gone something like this:

I: "Well, but who is she? When did you meet her?"

Bunny: "Oh, years ago. We used to go to school together."

I: "What does she do now?"

Bunny: "Oh, she married Bob Gardner," or "She lives over on Storey Street," or even "She's Belle Gardner's sister-in-law," this leading inevitably to:

"Who is Belle Gardner?"

"Oh, you know Belle Gardner."

Why did Bunny do this? Her friends and lovers claimed that it was because of her angry loyalty to everyone she accepted for her friends and lovers: her enemies, that she had no conception of anyone's individuality or even existence and therefore could not describe them. Perhaps it was a residue of her background and training: Bunny had been brought up in a society so small and stable that to give someone's name was a sufficient description. She was unique only in that she extended the rule to people from outside this society.

Bunny liked her parties to have an occasion: New Year's Eve, Thanksgiving, Bastille Day; she liked elaborate picnics and masquerades. Every year, in May, she gave herself a large birthday party at which she received presents. I especially remember a house party in New Boston, New Hampshire, just before her father sold the old family summer home. It was at the end of nowhere down a dirt road beside a river, a large dilapidated frame house full of broken wicker furniture, old photograph albums, and phonograph records, with the hand-cranked Victrola playing day and night:

*I've got money in marbles and chalk, sweetheart,*
*But I still feel like I was poor:*
*For my money won't spend and my marbles won't roll*
*And my chalk won't write any more.*

It rained the first day. Next morning it cleared, and after breakfast everyone went outside. Bunny, Larry Osgood, and I explored down the little river in an old rowboat with cracked white paint, broken oarlocks, and bottom awash with lukewarm water. Bunny rowed most of the way, in a long white nightgown and bare feet, her recently dyed hair golden orange. I can see her setting her pink mouth, with a rim of last night's lipstick still on it, stretching her legs and plump dirty toes for the stroke, pulling the boat down through the water, between meadows and marshes just becoming yellow-green. Larry, who was then twenty-one and a sophomore at Harvard, was complaining as we went that he wished he were more strange; if only everyone would not say all the time: "Larry is so nice and ordinary."

"Just let yourself go, dear," Bunny advised him in her Irish charwoman voice, pulling on the oars.

She said: "Once someone at a party asked me, 'And What

Do You Do?' So I told him, 'What I like. Well, let's see. I wake up about noon; I have breakfast in bed, and I read magazines and the papers, and then I write letters or something. Then about four I get up and have a lovely long bath and dress and go and have cocktails with friends at the Ritz, or they come to my house or I go to theirs; then dinner somewhere; and then, if I'm not going out that evening, I come home and read a novel, or maybe I play old records over.' 'That's wonderful,' he said, 'that's marvellous. But now tell me; what do you Really do?' "

The grandest party Bunny ever gave, except for her wedding, was the Charlotte Cushman Club 1954 Theatrical Ball, of which she was chairman. How smoothly she slipped into the part, how right she looked in the picture which appeared in the papers under the line "Working for Charity Ball." From out of nowhere, but as if they had always been there, she turned up a committee of twelve respectable society women, all of whom seemed to know her intimately, but as "Violet." Balloons, gilt chairs, caterers, orchestra leaders, press photographers, and society editors appeared around her. At committee meetings (I was the fourteenth member, although I did not belong to the Charlotte Cushman Club) she wore pearls and a hat indistinguishable from the other indistinguishable Newbury Street hats. She greeted the other "girls" with nasal Boston cries and enthusiastic embraces of the type peculiar to well-bred women, where one grips hands and rubs powdered cheeks together, making kissing noises into the air.

Since I knew that Bunny had just had a violent affair with an abstract painter named Mike Goldberg in a loft on the Lower East Side, and been told by a series of doctors that she probably had Hodgkins' disease, a form of cancer, I found all this incongruous. But when I made some ironic remark about the mutual affection of these society women, she lost her temper. "They like each other a lot better than anyone you know," she almost shouted as we stood in the lobby waiting for the Cushman Club maid to let us out of the heavy gold-barred door onto Beacon Street. "And if they don't, at least they're civilized about it."

It was like Bunny that she did not care to hear criticism of any of her roles, much as she mocked them herself in word or act. She liked her audience to be passive, sympathetic to whatever came on the boards: comedy, tragedy, burlesque, operetta. She might want you to see her, for instance, as a Michael Arlen or Ronald Fairbank heroine, all frantic, fantastic, tragic wit, and glamour, and the next moment she would turn around and undercut it. So she wrote to me (November 1954):

*Sorry to get this into the mail so late, tra la la, but my social obligations are just going to be the DEATH of me. I'm wearing out my poor little party slippers and shall have to have dear Fritz make me some new ones before the season is half over, why doesn't someone take pity on us poor debutantes? when all I would really like to do would be just to sit and think in some quiet, meditative place like maybe a convent. like YOU. I think of you in those divinely becoming garments and the pretty white cowl and know that you are ever so much happier than wicked us. I think the things of the spirit are just marvellous, anyway, they really stay with you unlike the worldly things which get so boring and all those creditors. I am sure you will never be sorry you took your Vows and now where did I put that invitation to tea at the Ritz with that dear black governor from Barbados, let me see . . .*

But if Bunny's audience had really let itself go, so much the worse for them. They were in the position of someone who has kissed Daisy Miller and then sees her take off her rubber mask and become Diamond Lil. Or vice versa—it could be equally disturbing.

In life, as well as on stage, Bunny was the kind of actress who sincerely and passionately maintains that she can play any role ever written better than any other actress. Perhaps this was just the demand of the youngest of many daughters for her father's attention: I can do anything any of them can do, and better.

Bunny's father, Malcolm Lang, was a Boston musician, seventy years old when I met him in 1949 and already five years retired. Like his more famous father, B. J. Lang, he was a choral conductor and a well-known organist. He played regularly at King's Chapel for many years, until he became involved in an obscure quarrel, and after that at a fashionable church in Brookline. Before his marriage he had composed choral and other works, including an oratorio, *Medea*, which was sung by the Cecilia Society. It was during the performance of this work in Philadelphia that he met his wife, who was singing in it. They were married in 1910. After this date Mr. Lang continued teaching and conducting, but he did not compose any more.

Bunny's mother, Ethel Ranney, was rather rich and—according to Bunny—a great beauty. She died when Bunny was twenty-five, in 1949, after an illness of many years. Bunny always spoke of her in superlatives. "Everyone loved her, she had such utter charm. Dogs loved her, horses loved her, the servants we had all loved her, they would do anything for her. Pa simply worshipped her," she said one day at tea. I only see now, copying the statement from my diary, that animals were mentioned first and children omitted from this list.

Bunny was the last of seven children, all girls, to their parents' disappointment. Before she was born one sister had died in infancy. When I met Bunny all the others were married and except for Margie, the eldest, lived in distant parts of the country. Before the war, before the Depression, Bunny told me, there had been twelve people in the house at 209 Bay State Road: Mr. and Mrs. Lang, the children, a maid, a cook, and two nurses or governesses (depending on the girls' ages)—eleven women and one man. By 1949 there were only three: Bunny, her father, and an old cook named Della.

Mr. Lang lived on the second floor; never as far as I knew climbing to the two stories above, never descending to the ground floor except to eat meals or go out. When he wished to communicate with the basement he went to the dumbwaiter, opened the door, and shouted. Aged, yet reverberating, his voice emerged on every floor. "Vi! Vi! are you there?" "Yes, Pa!" Bunny would shout back. "Coming!" Sometimes Bunny would not answer or would not come soon enough, and when this happened her father would pound on the shelves of the dumbwaiter, or if it was not on his floor at the time he would shake the cords, producing an unusual noise. So I heard him, long before I saw him; it was not until I had known Bunny for a year that she introduced me when we met accidentally one day in the hall, and another year after that before my husband and I were invited to dinner to meet Mr. Lang formally.

We went up to the second floor for sherry first. Mr. Lang's bedroom faced the street; his sitting room looked out over the Charles River, where since his marriage he had seen factories, warehouses, and billboards replace the trees and frame houses of Cambridge. More recently the City of Boston had appropriated his backyard and cut off his access to the water in order to build Storrow Drive, appreciated since by thousands of motorists. He had not forgiven them. Mr. Lang's rooms and the bathroom between them dated from 1930, with faded figured carpets, little mirrors, framed etchings, and glass-fronted bookcases full of worn-looking books. This was due partly to his wish to keep everything unchanged, partly to lack of money. According to Bunny, it was the misfortune of the Lang family to have passed rather rapidly through a slow-moving society. In 1900 they were rich, but not yet quite genteel; in 1925 they were both genteel and rich; but by 1950, as a result of their high family birth rate and standard of living, as well as the Depression, they were genteel but no longer quite rich.

Bay State Road, too, had risen and fallen rapidly. Before the Civil War it was nothing but a narrow spit of land out beyond the Reservoir, overgrown with coarse grass and scrub. The street was first laid out during the end-of-the-century prosperity. The ugly, imposing four-story brownstone houses built along both sides were equipped with every 1900 convenience and luxury. On the water side their gardens ran down towards the river, where some of the residents kept a boat tied up to a dock.

In 1924, when Bunny was born, Bay State Road was still an elegant address, but the fortunes of the families who lived there were less firmly based than those of Beacon Hill. Gradually debts and taxes drove them out. By 1950 the street was much changed. On the water side the houses were still well-kept, but now most of them belonged to institutions: schools, clubs, charities. Flags of a South American consulate hung between the beeches at one end of the street, the banners of Boston University fraternities at the other. The inland or "wrong" side had definitely fallen off in appearance. Some of the buildings had become rooming houses; others showed the brass plates of doctors and dentists, even of chiropodists, orthopedists, and correspondence schools. Mr. Lang's house, with its polished stone steps and brass rail, remained outwardly unchanged; but inside everything slid very slowly downhill. The curtains and slipcovers were still washed and ironed, but they were not mended or replaced; the wallpaper hung loose and faded in the hall, the cream-colored paint wore thin on the woodwork.

Mr. Lang's sitting room, especially in the late afternoon light, still had a certain pale elegance. There were silver objects on little tables, music and magazine stands, and a grand piano, which I never heard played. One of Bunny's lovers, a high-fidelity addict, later tried to interest Mr. Lang in a phonograph, but he refused it: he preferred to read scores. I only once heard him discuss music: he compared the playing of two violinists, praising neither. He read books from the Boston Public Library in Copley Square, and two daily newspapers; he listened to his radio (also circa 1930, with a case in the shape of a Gothic arch). He liked to hear the news and descriptions of local events, parades, ceremonies, and in the spring the Marathon and boat races.

Physically Mr. Lang was a small man, of dry, gray, stiff, and increasingly elderly appearance. He resembled his daughter not at all. He seemed to regard her friends with a consistent faint irony, occasionally rising to dislike; he spoke to them, when at all, on topics which interested him at the time, regardless of their interests. He never asked them how they or their families were or were feeling. That day at dinner he was at first silent, and then began to speak of the peculiarities of Boston architecture. He knew stories about the construction and remodeling of the State House, and had been up inside the dome, where he was once nearly locked in overnight. He described a double house on Beacon Street which in order to conform with the pattern of the street had been built with one set of false front steps and a false front door which opened only on a brick wall. He became quite animated over this, and then fell silent when dessert came in. It was a kind of involved pudding, quivering on the plate, pale, impossible to eat. When Bunny did not do the cooking herself meals at her house were long and tasteless. I later found that they were composed mainly by opening a great many red S. S. Pierce cans and heating or chilling the contents, which were never combined or seasoned but served very hot or very cold in individual silver dishes with covers. Mr. Lang liked sliced head of iceberg lettuce with S. S. Pierce mayonnaise, and this item was served once a day.

In spite of this dinner party, I was never sure Mr. Lang knew me afterwards. Sometimes I thought that he only pretended to; sometimes that he only pretended not to. We used to nod in the hall if we passed. One day when I was visiting Bunny my husband came to pick me up in the car. The cook opened the door.

"Miss Vi said for you to go upstairs, Mr. Bishop," she told him. On the second floor landing Mr. Lang suddenly jumped at him out of the bathroom, waving a toothbrush mug.

"Who are you, sir?" he said, or shouted, and then stood watching Jonathan suspiciously for a long while as he passed on up the stairs.

The Poets' Theatre of Cambridge was founded in the fall of 1950 when, as they were in the habit of remarking on the back of their yearly prospectus, "several of New England's outstanding poets joined forces with a group of younger writers in an effort to revive poetic drama." Richard Wilbur (who never came to meetings), John Ciardi, and Richard Eberhart were the several outstanding poets. Bunny (under her professional name, V. R. Lang) was one of the younger writers: the others were Hugh Amory, John Ashbery, Edward Gorey, Donald Hall, William Matchett, George Montgomery, Frank O'Hara, and Lyon Phelps. They were all attending Harvard or had recently graduated from it, and none of them had been published except in the *Harvard Advocate*. This gave Bunny, whose work had appeared in *Poetry* and *The Chicago Review*, an immediate prominence.

Dick Eberhart was elected president of the organization; Bunny became secretary. She and her friends did the real work; Eberhart and Ciardi had other jobs and were already established Young American Poets (aged forty-six and thirty-four). At this point they kept their social distance from the unestablished poets, most of whom were under twenty-five. The emotional temperature of the Poets' Theatre in the early days was high, for most of the younger writers and their friends were in love with Bunny and with each other. There were secrets, confidences, collaborations, poems, and dramas *à clef* passed from hand to hand, public quarrels and reconciliations, and the best scenes were not always played on stage.

From 1950 to 1955, while I was observing it, the Poets' Theatre passed through three stages or incarnations: bohemian, academic, and social. Through it all a certain aura of art and amateurism clung to it: an aura that people like me found delightful, but that used to make other people (and sometimes Bunny) scream because it was so inefficient and unprofessional. Always there was the theatrical atmosphere of rehearsals, feuds, affairs, debts, and parties. And as the organization rose (or some would say, fell) it was always surrounded by patrons, protégés, parasites, paramours, flatterers, and hangers-on.

The early productions of the Poets' Theatre were free, and ran one or two nights in the parish house of Christ Church, Cambridge. The first budget, for four one-act plays with a total cast of twenty, was forty-five dollars. Luckily, a collection taken up at the door in intermission produced forty-eight dollars. After that, somehow, each show cost more than the last one until in December 1952 Bunny's *Fire Exit* contracted a debt of fifteen hundred dollars which nearly wrecked the organization. But kind friends saved it: throughout the years the Poets' Theatre always depended on presents; unexpected bills were discharged by someone's unexpected generosity—at first that of students who could give fifty cents, later that of patrons of the arts who could give five or five hundred dollars, finally that of foundations, the Croesuses of our age.

The Poets' Theatre's increasing need for money was one of the things that pushed it (not without violent internal struggles) up the social hill towards where money was. Another factor was that as time passed the original members of the theatre grew older. They graduated from Harvard and lost their undergraduate freedom to be all things at once. Economic necessity closed in. Those who cared most about being social or cultural deviants sooner or later went to New York or to Europe, where this life can be lived without interference. Those who stayed on changed as the theatre changed, and allied themselves with the academic system of Harvard or the social systems of Boston and Cambridge into which it eventually leads.

In its early days the Poets' Theatre was shunned by respectable Harvard and Cambridge society. Only the furthest avant-garde of the faculty attended its productions. This was also true of the students. There was once an incident when a freshman just up from Andover who had been cast in a play came to Bunny and told her he would have to drop out. He was terribly sorry, frightfully sorry really, but he wanted to make a final club and he had found out that the Poets' Theatre was N.G., No Good. He thought Bunny might like to know this, for she was a nice Boston girl, a distant cousin of his.

Later all this changed. The first to come round was the Harvard faculty, a group for which Bunny had little use. She was the only member of the Poets' Theatre who had never had any connection with Harvard University as an institution, and she felt, besides, a settled spitefulness towards academia in general.

> *Who are all these old horrors that are whipping out their plays?* [*she wrote*]. *I always dreaded the moment this would happen and I always knew it would come. Professors, by definition, always have a play in their bureau drawer. Until the MacLeish, they scorned us. We were not* GOOD ENOUGH TO DO THEIR PLAYS. *Now everything is changed. If we don't do them, they will tell their classes and all of their influential friends that we are capricious and undergraduate and Not Serious. If we do them, we will all die of boredom.*

The next step towards financial security was the creation of two specially privileged classes of audience called Members and

Sponsors. Members paid ten dollars a year, Sponsors twenty-five and up—as high up as they could be persuaded to go. They were rewarded with reserved seats and advance notice of shows. Sponsors were also invited to private readings of poetry and poetic plays; if they were especially helpful they had their names printed in the program.

The custom arose of giving every script under serious consideration a private reading to the Sponsors, usually at the home of some important Sponsor. Elaborate refreshments would be provided by the hostesses, who were of course encouraged to take a competitive attitude in the matter. The Sponsors had no legal voice in deciding which scripts were to be given public performance, but such is the force of public opinion and caterers' cakes that plays which they strongly disliked did not get produced. Not only the poetic play, but the poet, would be judged at these parties. If he was "possible," there would be quite a stampede for him, and a series of fund-raising parties, cocktail parties, and dinner-and-theatre parties would begin, sometimes carried to such an extent that the actual production seemed only an annex.

What the Sponsors liked best was celebrities, especially English celebrities. They were delighted when the Poets' Theatre began to rent imported poets from John Malcolm Brinnin, the well-known importer. They liked us to get the most expensive kinds, and then they would give enormous parties with domestic celebrities and ourselves and all their friends who would die of envy. There was quite a bitter competition for ones like T. S. Eliot and Dylan Thomas. The more the poets cost (and the really celebrated ones would never think of settling for a percentage of the gross, they wanted a flat thousand dollars or more and paid in advance) the bigger the reading had to be, in bigger auditoriums. The height of all this came in 1955, when Dame Edith and Sir Osbert Sitwell appeared in Sanders Theatre. I was not there, but Bunny described it to me:

*. . . the most outrageous exhibit you can possibly imagine . . . In Sanders Eddy and others had dropped a vast antique tapestry to simulate a back wall. Against it towered about 12 trees, birches, poplars and cypresses that they had picked up at the*

*close of the flower show, about 15 feet tall, and out of their pots sprawled ivy and whatnot. Up by the lectern were 2 tapestried antique chairs and nearby an ancient iron candelabra. Just behind at the center a stone fountain cupid carrying a basin . . . Roger Shattuck was Captain of the Parquets (honestly) and under his supervision worked about 20 girls in black dresses with silk ribbons dramatically across the front shoulder to waist ambassador style. Stacy Grandin was in full command and I worked under her, on the floor. I seated the Amorys and the Perkinses and May Sarton and two questionable friends, ladies with moustaches. Also the Kennedys and the Puseys and the Coxes and Mrs. McCormick (reaper) who was wearing a great vast mink bell . . . Every seat was sold and we the ushers had to stand or sit on the dirty steps in our party dresses. Well, sir, when people were admitted to the House at ten to 8 this earsplitting trumpeting music started which obtained till 8:40, when Lyon appeared theatrically from behind the tapestry, spotlit, and wearing a waiter suit, and carrying a five page typewritten address about the history of Sanders and acting at Harvard and English poetry and the contribution of the noble Sitwells to this art. Then he ducked back under the tapestry to fetch those aged parties, that poor old man with his palsy and both of them with canes, simply agonizing to watch. He led Dame Edith in on his bony arm like a waiter's towel, and behind hobbled and swayed Sir Osbert. There was a terrible moment that Sir O would not make his chair so enfeebled is he but he did. Then Lyon bowed gracefully off and Dame E gave the sold-out house a swift cold look of appraisal . . . Sir O tottered to the stand where, with this dreadful palsy trying to find his pages, he announced he would read and then she would read and then he would read, etc., which is about the last word I really understood what inspired mumblers they are. The floor kept laughing appreciatively but everybody else just strained irritably and kept a morose silence.*

From the beginning Bunny was involved in every Poets' Theatre show, as actress, director, writer, designer, and producer. She was not a good actress, though it was marvellous to watch her on the stage. She could save a bad play sometimes simply by walking out and smiling at the audience: the less the lines meant, the more she could put into them. But though offstage she played so many parts, onstage it was always one part: the tough, warm-hearted but disillusioned, grown-up little girl. She liked to wear her hair hanging long, heavy make-up and a pout. She liked white—draggled white evening gowns circa 1920 or 1935, long flannel nightgowns, preferably torn here and there, cocoons wound of sheeting even; her favorite costume was a white cotton camisole and petticoat and bare feet. If a play she was in ran more than one night she would change her costume every night. This of course irritated the rest of the cast and drove an unsympathetic designer or director frantic: they considered it a form of upstaging. She used to arrive backstage early and spend up to an hour inventing a new version of her costume, snatching things out of drawers with a glad cry, or off the racks where other actors had hung their street clothes, putting on and taking off and pinning things together until it was time for her cue. "It throws me; I never know what's coming until she walks on stage, and it just *throws* me!" an actor who played with her used to scream.

Left to herself, Bunny had wonderful comedy timing, a beautiful slow comic grace, and a nice husky voice. She knew how to make a good entrance, and she could ad-lib perfectly in any emergency, an important gift in amateur theatre. But in every sense of the word she could not *take* direction. She refused to do as she was told, or did not understand, and when a director got tough with her she began to move stiffly and sound stifled. It was awful to see her in her single professional appearance, as Maria in *Love's Labours Lost* at the Brattle Theatre. She wore a too-elaborate purple costume and headdress and spoke in a choked ingénue's voice, hugging her elbows to her sides as if she had been told not to move her arms. "Every rehearsal that pig Alby Marre took another one of my lines away from me." But you could see why: when the play opened Bunny's own stage character was still struggling to break through, to be, to say whatever it was she so much wanted to say, against the impediment of Shakespeare.

Bunny wished to use the Poets' Theatre to further her own

ends. She was hardly alone in this. Among the original members as well as those that joined later not one was single-mindedly anxious to "revive poetic drama." Her motives were less worldly than most, for she did not principally hope to rise in society, to go on the professional stage, to get her poetry published, to become locally famous, or to meet possible lovers. Each of these ends was attained by some member of the theatre; all except the first were realized by Bunny, but in her case they came by the way, however much she might enjoy them. What she really wanted was to express herself, to present herself, and she used whatever means came to hand with admirable unscrupulousness.

It was in this spirit that she undertook to direct a play. First, there was a conference with the author, at which she convinced him of her view of the work in an atmosphere of intense significance, often late at night with quantities of black coffee or beer. In the early days of the theatre most authors were already Bunny's friends or lovers or hoped to be. If sometimes on opening night they had a fleeting feeling that this was not quite what they had meant, they kept it to themselves.

In the spring of 1952, however, the Poets' Theatre decided to produce a one-act play by Cid Corman, a Boston poet with a local avant-garde reputation. He owned a magazine (*Origin, the Quarterly for the Creative*), and a weekly radio program on which he interviewed poets he liked at the time and read from their works. His play, *The Circle*, was tragic and symbolic: the characters had names like "The Old Man," "Second Philosopher," and "A Child." The plot concerned the discovery and worship of an imaginary circle which the characters believed to be hanging prominently in the center of the stage; it ended with the death of a brave character called "A Stranger" who refused to see the imaginary object.

On hearing that his play had been accepted, Mr. Corman declined to confer with the director. His letter to Bunny expressed an avuncular detachment: "I'll be interested to see what you make of it." Bunny did not care much for this. She was further irritated when Cid Corman did not turn up for casting. Poets' Theatre authors usually loved to help with casting and rehearsals: the previous year Paul Goodman had come up from New York especially for this purpose.

I did not realize how angry she was until I went over to her house to consult about the costumes one Sunday afternoon. Bunny and Ted Gorey, a member of the Poets' Theatre who had graduated from Harvard and now worked in a Boston bookstore, were down in the basement kitchen. It was the maid's day out and Bunny was cooking dinner. As I came in she had just opened the oven door; a blast of hot air came out into the room, and the smell of gas and burning jam. She carried four pie tins over to the window and set them on the sill.

"That smells nice," said Ted without expression from the wicker sofa where he was lying.

"You can have a piece as soon as it's cool."

"I can hardly wait."

We talked a little; finally I asked Bunny if she had been able to borrow costumes from the Brattle Theatre. It had been tentatively decided that all the characters should wear some form of tights and leotard, and we had asked at rehearsal if anyone owned dancing costume or long underwear which could be dyed.

"Dickie Baldridge is being slippery as usual," she said. "But it doesn't matter, I've found a box of stuff here, almost all we'll need." She dragged out a carton from under the kitchen table. "Here we are. Six perfectly good union suits." She began to lay them out over Ted's feet and legs. "One, two, three. That's a little one. Well, maybe that girl Sonia Grant could fit into it. We have to have a big one for Arnie. Four, five." She held up a union suit with gaping holes in the stomach and legs. "These two are a little torn, but you can mend them so it won't show from the stage. And six. That's a large one. It might fit Arnie, or you may have to get him one from the Morgan Memorial. You can try it on tonight. And these are some hats and things I think we can use." She pulled out a mauve satin turban with red cherries and veiling and tried it on askew, making a face at her reflection in the glass of the kitchen cupboard.

"Devastating, my dear," Ted said.

"You know, Bunny, I was talking to some of the cast, and

they are very upset about the costumes. They want us to rent leotards. They said they felt embarrassed about wearing underwear on stage. You know it might be rather revealing."

"Anyone who feels modest can wear some more underwear underneath," Bunny siad. "The union suits will look better after we dye them."

"What color are you going to dye them?"

"Pink."

"I thought *The Circle* was supposed to be a serious play full of deep significance," Ted said.

Bunny took up another hat, a crushed straw cartwheel with chiffon streamers, and began to flatten out the brim.

"Listen, Bunny," I told her, "some of the cast said they wouldn't wear union suits."

"Who said that?"

I gave the names.

"If they want to be in *The Circle*, they'll wear union suits. Here, try this one." She put the hat with the streamers on my head and tied a bow under my chin. "Becoming. No, don't take it off, let me look at it. Here's a good one for you, pal." She held up a broken blue cloche of about 1925 to Ted, and then crammed it down on his head. "Perfect. Maybe Arnie could wear that."

Ted climbed up off the couch, shaking the six union suits from his long thin legs, to look at his reflection in the cupboard door.

"Adorable with my mustache," he said. "I suppose Mr. Corman specified these costumes in his stage directions. Or did he tell you about them personally?"

"Cid Corman hasn't taken the trouble to come to rehearsal. I've sent him postcards notifying him about the times and places and he hasn't showed once. He didn't even bother to answer my last letter."

"Not very cooperative."

"I'll fix him," Bunny muttered. "I guess he'll have to come to the performance."

*The Circle* opened on May 21 in Fogg Museum Court. It was last on a program of three one-act plays. During the preceding intermission Lyon Phelps, who was then vice-president of the theatre, rushed into the dressing room. "Cid Corman is out front!" he announced.

The cast stopped, halfway into their costumes. "Oh, is he? Where is he?"

"Sitting in the second row, over by the pillar. He's talking to John Brinnin."

Half dressed, or nearly undressed, the casts of *The Circle* and the other plays hurried on stage and applied their faces to the curtain. Bunny and Lyon were left nearly alone in the dressing room. "Well, Cid Corman is here," he repeated.

"Oh, he is, is he," Bunny said. She sat before the mirror dressed in the bottom half of her pink union suit, the top hanging down over the black net corset which she always wore on stage. On her head was a red hat with feathers.

"Can't you tone it down a little just for tonight?" Lyon asked.

"No." Unlike most people, Bunny habitually used this simple word.

"Listen, Cid Corman could do a lot for the Poets' Theatre if he felt like it."

Carefully, Bunny went on with her make-up, sticking on her false eyelashes with white glue.

"Really, Bunny—"

"You mind your own business. This play is going to get the performance it deserves." Fully made up, she stood and put her arms into the union suit, buttoned it, and stepped into her high-heeled shoes. "All right, two minutes!" she cried. The cast of *The Circle* poured back into the dressing room.

"This is going to be awful," Lyon said to me.

The music began for *The Circle*; it was Stravinsky, but during the last weeks it had been changed from one of the symphonies to the Elephant Polka. We were out front in time to see the curtain part. When the first characters came on in their salmon-pink union suits there was a muffled roar from the front of the audience. Lyon began to walk nervously around in the gallery at the back of the crowd.

The play went very well. The audience began to laugh when The Philosopher (I think it was) came on in a sunbonnet, and soon they were laughing continually so that it was impossible to hear what Cid Corman said, if anything. In the mob scene Bunny had used an old stage trick for creating the effect of an angrily muttering crowd; she had half the mob continually repeat "rhubarb, rhubarb," while the other half murmured "vichyssoise, vichyssoise." This time, however, the actual words were clearly audible, at least to me.

Finally The Stranger was killed. The rest of the cast, in comic pantomime, began to tiptoe off, leaving him lying on his back with his legs sticking up in the air. Suddenly there was a tumultuous event at the front of the theatre; murmurs, curses, someone trying to rise and being pulled down. But Cid Corman, who was unusually large, fat, and strong, stood up again, shaking off his friends with a loud violence which caused two folding chairs to fold, and pushed his way out of the audience. He passed us on his way out, his face red with anger, shouting and waving his heavy hands, surrounded by a collection of friends of all sexes, none of whom I had ever seen before, in their bohemian hair and cheap suits. Behind him the curtain came down amid roars of applause and laughter, and he pushed out through the doors, never to be seen again at any Poets' Theatre performance.

Inevitably Bunny grew tired of trying to make over other people's plays. Why should she not write one herself? She was a published poet, and had been editor of the *Chicago Review* at college. Besides her historical novel she had written short stories, a novel about life in Greenwich Village, several surrealistic prose pieces, and a parody of poetic drama, all unpublished, though the last had been a great success on stage. When she worked at all, she worked intensely, writing and rewriting, not always for the better. Everything she wrote contained wonderful lines and fragments; almost nothing was complete:

*A stranger bathing in the sea survived a snail*
*The real could not compete with the original . . .*

*A dog I patted bit me in the leg.*
*The people with me burst out laughing.*
*Nothing since to write that is amusing.*

And then would come lines like: "Things go on anyway, arranging everything that happens." There were often a lot of personal images and references irritating and baffling to outsiders. This was deliberate: Bunny liked to think of the world as made up of We and They:

> *What we are is known by some.*
> *The others need not guess.*

Bunny spent the summer of 1952 writing *Fire Exit: A Vaudeville for Eurydice.* She sat up long hot nights over her typewriter, and long wet afternoons when the lightning flashed over the river, with her telephone off the hook for hours. Everything went into it. *Fire Exit* was based somewhat on the legend of Orpheus. Eurydice, an innocent orphan girl brought up by warm-hearted circus people (Act I) falls in love with Orpheus, a selfish classical musician (Act II). They marry, but he treats her with egotistical coldness, and she finally leaves him (Act III). After ten years, Orpheus finds Eurydice working in a burlesque show in Union City, New Jersey (Epilogue). He tries to persuade her to come back, but loses her forever when he demonstrates that he still does not love or trust her. (The Hell in which she is left, a Freudian might notice, is populated by six sister-figures and a father-figure.)

When *Fire Exit* opened on December 1, 1952, it was a completely Bunny production. Not only had she written the play, she directed it, produced it, and starred in it. She also chose the cast, designed the costumes and sets, arranged the music and lighting, did the publicity, and managed the theatre.

At first, of course, this was not the arrangement. The Poets' Theatre made gestures towards finding a director, but none of the available directors dared to deal with Bunny. Bunny herself went through a complicated and sincere pretense of finding a star—sincere in that she did not admit to herself that she was looking for her double. She found every available candidate lacking in something. Previously, no Poets' Theatre production had run for more than three performances; Bunny went privately to the Brattle Theatre and arranged to rent it for two weeks at a large price, more than the total funds then in the Poets' Theatre bank account. When this became known, the other board members called a special meeting at Molly Howe's house, the declared purpose of which was to Stop Bunny. She arrived very late, perhaps on purpose, perhaps because Molly had told her a later time than other people. We had all agreed that Bunny must be stopped from running the theatre into bankruptcy when she walked in on us, stamping into the dim, faded Victorian décor of Molly's drawing room. She was wearing black rubber boots and an old Daisy-Mae cotton blouse, and looked as if she had been crying for weeks. She sat down: Bill Matchett, our treasurer, began to present the rational budget we had just agreed on, speaking in his soft, rational Quaker voice that seemed always about to use the second person singular. But he had scarcely started when Bunny leaned forward. "All right, I know you are all my enemies," she said huskily. "I know you want to kill *Fire Exit*. But before you pass the death sentence, just let me say—" and she delivered a finished, passionate plea for experimental theatre. If it could have been taken down it might have gone straight into one of our publicity releases. At the end there was a silence, and then Bill Matchett said that he did not want to kill *Fire Exit*, as a matter of fact he thought it was a fine experimental script, he just wanted to see that the production did not run the Poets' Theatre so deep into debt that it would be unable to produce other fine experimental scripts in the future. This rational statement earned him Bunny's undying enmity. Everyone else was too touched to dare say anything, and *Fire Exit* was voted a budget larger than that of any previous production, yet which Bunny considered an insult.

Bunny proceeded to quarrel one by one with the other members of the theatre. She refused the help of the people who were accustomed to do the lighting, set design, publicity, tickets, and stage and house management, giving various reasons. She insulted the stage manager, for example, by demanding that he clean up after an actor who had come to rehearsal drunk and thrown up over the stairs at Phillips Brooks House. She rejected the poster painted for her by Ted Gorey, who did all the Poets' Theatre posters; instead she had printed up a half-length photograph of herself looking sexily gloomy in a tight black blouse. This was reproduced in red on glossy paper, two thousand copies of it, with the lettering in black.

Even Bunny could not put on a play single-handed. She made all the decisions, but in carrying them out she was helped by what came to be known as "Bunny's gang": her lover and three homosexuals, two of whom were in love with Bunny and one of whom was in love with the other homosexuals. These persons, all more virulently royalist than their queen, raised money for her, bullied actors and newspaper editors, carried scenery, and cut the other members of the theatre in the street whenever possible.

The final effect of the play was very strange. It was as if Bunny were multiplied by twenty. As Eurydice she was of course on stage herself most of the time; in addition twenty other Bunnys, differently clothed and made up, moved on and off. Some of them were old, some young, some male, some female; comic, tragic, romantic, and farcical (all these themes were combined in *Fire Exit*). Yet in each case the inflexions and the gestures which Bunny had taught them betrayed her presence. (There was one exception: Edward Finnegan, a professional actor in his sixties, whom Bunny had hired at an Equity salary.) In many ways it was a great and unique theatrical event. The professional polish Bunny had worked so hard for was there, and the audience laughed and cried where she had intended they should, even on weekday nights when the theatre was two-thirds empty. The critics did not know what to make of the play; they were complimentary in a puzzled way. Temporarily, Bunny became a local celebrity, and her name was announced in large letters in the newspapers and on posters.

Financially, *Fire Exit* was not a success. Not enough tickets were sold to cover even the original budget. Some of the loss was met by Bunny's friends and backers, but for many months afterwards peculiar little bills and complaints kept drifting in. The spiritual consequences were equally protracted. Bunny made up with some of her friends, but many would never again regard her without suspicion. For instance, she had told me that I could not work on the show because as everyone knew it was bad luck to have pregnant women backstage. (Bunny was superstitious, but only fitfully so; in the end I did go backstage.) Now she wrote me a long letter, although I had not left town.

> . . . *this play became for me* my *new house,* my *baby—but me an unmarried mother and the new house heavily mortgaged and rented to me by people who could scarcely veil their hostility for me—or an unsuspected saboteur pretending friendship for me but, behind my tracks always pattering around warning strangers not to rent to me, I would not pay—and urging my creditors to have me into small-claims court. Everywhere I kept finding malice towards me, everywhere. How difficult I was to work with, how impossible, how temperamental—as indeed I was, but what a curious way to put the fact that I was fighting for what happens to be my life . . . (etc.).*

He who is not with me is against me—that was one of the messages of *Fire Exit.* To be with Bunny was like alcohol: at first exhilarating, but in the end destructive. George Montgomery, the photographer, said once: "You meet Bunny and you love her so much you want to carry all her packages for her, so she puts them into your arms and as you go along you find that they get heavier and heavier and heavier until you are ready to drop with fatigue."

People fell in love with Bunny wherever she went, especially certain kinds of people. In the fluid half-world of the Poets' Theatre she seemed to stand firm, a flowering tree in a flood. "She is the only member of the theatre who treats me like a person rather than a thing," Greta Smith told me. And it was true; Bunny did treat everyone, however unimportant, as a person—as a person, but not as themselves. Instead of bothering to unearth their half-formed individuality, she spontaneously invented an interesting character for whomever she met, linking them, for the moment, with her. So she would announce: "We are both really Edwardians." "We aren't academic, we just have average good taste." "You and I see all the subtleties and complications of things." (Or, in a different mood: "You and I don't bother about all the subtleties and complications of things.") Most of the people who hung about the Poets' Theatre, by reason of their youth or for other reasons, were not sure who they were. They were excited to be told, and often behaved afterwards in line with Bunny's definition. Thus it might be said that today the character of everyone who knew Bunny is partly her creation.

Most often Bunny's influence was good, for her conceptions of people were grander and nobler than their own. When she was feeling well she inspired them to acts and thoughts that they might not have dared for themselves.

*Then nothing I touched that didn't burst into flames*
*Nothing I cried out that didn't catch fire*
*Nothing I called that didn't know its name.*

So she once wrote. Indeed, sometimes it seemed as if Bunny had what the Catholic Church calls *charisma*—heroic virtue. At such moments it would not have seemed incongruous to hear that she had performed acts verging on the miraculous: like Saint Teresa, seemed to float a little above the ground, or like Saint Catherine de Ricci, given off a golden phosphorescence.

But there was another side to it. Some days grace failed her, energy failed her:

*Today I lie here going bad, you know I can.*

she wrote: slumped all day in bed, her face and hair unwashed, the floor of her room strewn with dirty clothes and pieces of manuscript crumpled up in a fit of rage. At these times she did not leave the phone off the hook, but when someone called would answer and then hold the receiver out at arm's length, letting it squeak on and on in its impotent little voice.

When people became passively addicted to Bunny's version of themselves they suffered accordingly, like addicts of any drug: cravings, intoxication, hangovers, agonies of withdrawal and cure.

It was so with Greta Smith. She was an actress, the wife of a

Harvard graduate student. Small, dark, with a good figure and much talent, she had a neurotically low opinion of herself. She despised Greta and felt that all other persons alive would despise her because she was ugly and had never been to college. She thought that the angels had performed a miracle in allowing her to marry a Harvard graduate student. When Greta first turned up at the Poets' Theatre during the casting of *Fire Exit* Bunny was against all graduate students as the result of a disagreeable affair she had just had with one of them. She told Greta that Greta was not inferior to her husband but too good for him—not quite in so many words, of course. "People who create things, like us, are the natural enemies of critics, who are always destroying something, picking something apart." All her life people had more or less taken Greta at her own low valuation, but Bunny cared nothing for the opinions of Greta or people. She announced that Greta was a beauty and a great comic actress, endowed with wit, taste, talent, and a warm heart. Against the advice of her advisers, she gave Greta one of the leading parts in *Fire Exit*, in which she was a notable success.

The package Bunny gave Greta to carry was her Siamese cat, Edolon, called Dolon, a pretty, sickly, temperamental thing that one of her former lovers had given her. Greta first took the cat during the production of *Fire Exit*. Late at night, as rehearsals for her play dragged on, Bunny would suddenly remember that Dolon had not been fed all day. Someone who was not on stage in that act would have to go—someone whom, at one A.M., Mr. Lang would not mind finding in the house or Della mind finding in the kitchen. This person would have to take Bunny's car and drive back across the river to Boston, perhaps stopping on the way to buy cat food. An hour later they would be back. "Darling, you gave me the wrong keys." "I couldn't find your can opener, so I had to use an ice pick, I'm afraid it made a bit of a mess." "She scratched me." Greta was delighted to take Dolon. She loved animals, and she wanted passionately to have something of Bunny's, to repay her, to help her out during this crisis.

During the week of the performance Dolon lived entirely at Greta's. After the bars had closed and the cast had gone home to bed, Bunny would come back with Greta. Don would be asleep, so they would sit in the kitchen while snow blew against the windows, Bunny drinking coffee, stroking the cat, and telling Greta what they both thought about that night's show and everything else. Greta worked at Corcoran's Department Store in Harvard Square (she was putting Don through college) and had to get up every day at seven-thirty. By the end of the run she had great blue bruises under her eyes from lack of sleep, but she was happy, and she regretted it very much when *Fire Exit* closed and Bunny took Dolon home.

During the next year or so Greta sought every occasion to keep the cat. She also helped Bunny in other ways: went shopping with her, took out books from Widener on Don's card, and worked on the Poets' Theatre mailing list. But this was the job she preferred. "Dolon cares for very few people; aside from Bunny and I she is quite indifferent to human beings," she would remark to me when I came to visit, while the cat mewed and scratched restlessly on her lap. When Bunny went south in the winter it seemed natural for her to leave Dolon with Greta again. The cat kept them in touch, and Bunny wrote frequent postcards from Florida and the islands. "A wholesale meat salesman picked me up on a plane this afternoon. Is Dolon getting enough fish to keep her fur sleek?" Food for the cat, though she ate pickily, was a strain on the Smiths' tight budget. Don was not very pleased to have Dolon back again. She was nervous in the house and would not go outside, and anyway the Smiths had no yard. She was always jumping up delicately onto the table where Don was working or eating, touching nothing but startling him, so that he jumped. Once he knocked over a glass of milk, which splashed onto his clean pants and the clean floor, while Dolon sat and looked at him. He was always happy to see her go. Greta hated to part with her, but she also liked Don and so at last she resolved not to take the cat again.

A few weeks later, however, Bunny casually let drop that she was going to New York for a while. She did not ask to leave Dolon at the Smiths, but Greta knew that this was coming, she told me, and she lay awake worrying about it. Sure enough, the day after next Bunny remarked that she knew Dolon was looking forward to seeing Greta again. Greta did not reply, but that night when Don asked her for the third night why she was tossing around so much she told him. "Well, why don't you just tell her you don't want Dolon this time?" he said.

"I can't," Greta groaned.

"Why doesn't her father keep Dolon when Bunny goes off, for God's sake?"

Greta explained to Don that Mr. Lang hated cats. Dolon was not allowed in his part of the house, and if she ever did get in Mr. Lang would shout up the stairs, "Vi! Vi! get that animal out of here! If I find that animal down in my room again I'm going to have it done away with!"

"And he would too," Greta told me when reporting this. "He would just like to tie a brick around Dolon's neck and drop her in the river." "What do you think I should do?" she asked me for the third time, and indeed by now the question was being discussed by all Greta's friends and associates in the Poets' Theatre. Those who liked to choose up sides were already choosing up their sides. All day they kept coming into Corcoran's Department Store to give Greta their advice, and at night she went home and told Don what they had said. "What should I do do you think?" she would ask him. "Well, it isn't your responsibility, after all," Don would say. "There are plenty of good animal boarding homes." "You are right, of course," Greta finally said, and the next time Bunny gave her an opening she explained why she could not keep Dolon again.

At first Bunny seemed not to take it in. She would only be gone for a few days or a week or so, she said. Then she showed that she was annoyed. The next morning, however, she called up and spoke as if it had all been settled that Dolon was to come to Greta's. If she had been alone Greta might have given in, but Don was listening, so she made a little speech in which she very apologetically mentioned animal boarding homes and Don's academic responsibilities. In the middle of it Bunny remarked, "Goodbye," and hung up.

She did not call back.

It was summer. The Poets' Theatre was not operating just then, so events did not bring them together. Bunny did not see Greta for four days, five days, a week. "You mustn't let yourself be blackmailed," said some of the associates of Greta who were on Greta's side, when they came into Corcoran's to enjoy the air conditioning, for it was very hot weather. But Greta explained to me that she thought it was simpler than that. It was merely that for Bunny Greta had become an unpleasant experience. Greta was no longer useful or comfortable to have around. Bunny bore no malice, she explained, but like a natural force flowed away from a rocky shore. But I could see that Greta's neurosis was whispering to her that Bunny had found out at last how no good and uneducated and ugly Greta was.

The following Saturday night Bunny arrived at a large party where the Smiths also were. Greta, slightly drunk, rose in her seat and called excitedly to her across the room. But Bunny only flapped her hand negligently from the wrist and turned aside to speak to someone. Greta could not bear it, and towards midnight she went up and offered to take Dolon. They had a delightful conversation.

Bunny remained in New York for two weeks, and Dolon remained with the Smiths. She was more nervous than ever. One evening after watching her leaping around the furniture for a while Don turned to his wife and said accusingly, "That cat is pregnant."

"She is?" said Greta, who had noticed it ever since Dolon arrived but had hoped Don would not. When Bunny returned she was surprised and delighted to hear the news, but she put off coming over.

A day passed, two, three; at last Greta telephoned Bunny, although it was her principle never to telephone, always to be telephoned. (Thus, she once explained, she was always certain that the other person truly wanted to speak to her.) "Dolon is a very delicate cat," Bunny said. "I'm not sure it would be good for her to be moved now."

The kittens were born on the Smiths' bed. It was a long, difficult birth. There were four pure Siamese, one dead. "Pure Siamese?" Don said when he learned this fact. "Hell, she must have bred Dolon herself weeks ago, she probably planned it this way." The bedspread had to be burnt.

Bunny came to see Dolon and the kittens often, but as time went on she did not mention taking them home. "How long are we going to have those cats around here?" Don asked. On her visits Bunny described the high prices which would be paid for pure Siamese kittens. It was clear that she felt Greta was very fortunate to be the virtual owner of four beautiful expensive cats. They grew larger and ate more, and when Bunny came to visit them Don went into the other room.

"I know what Don thinks," Bunny finally said. "You tell him not to worry. I've advertised in the *Herald* and soon they'll be out of his way." And indeed, presently people who wished to look at Siamese kittens began arriving all the time at the Smiths' apartment. Since Greta was working during the daytime, Don had to receive them. Bunny offered to give Greta the kitten with the least expensive markings, but Greta felt she had to refuse on account of her husband.

So they all went: Greta cried over each one; it was like losing children. This was an unfortunate period of her life. She was tired of Corcoran's Department Store; her sisters both had babies; she was nearly thirty and had been putting Don through different colleges for five years.

Dolon still remained. She seemed more nervous than ever, moped, refused her food or threw it up. "She is missing her children," Greta said. But soon it appeared that she was seriously sick. Finally one night, Bunny and Greta together took her, limp in a basket and breathing strangely, to the Angell Memorial Animal Hospital. "Thank God for that," Don said, and Greta, vacuuming the cat hair off all the surface of her apartment and washing out the slipcovers Dolon had vomited on, could not but agree.

Dolon was sick for several weeks. Greta and Bunny both visited her in the hospital and when she was well they arranged to go together to get her. I had agreed to drive Greta over from Cambridge. Bunny was to meet us and I would then drive them back to her house. This was necessary because Greta had no car and Bunny had just smashed hers up. She did this periodically. She was a reckless driver, always scraping walls, turning corners short, or slamming on the brakes so that the car behind ran into her car. She rarely damaged the motor, but her old Plymouth was constantly in the body shop, being patched and repainted, in shades of bright blue which did not quite match the original or each other. Mr. Lang actually owned this car, though he no longer saw well enough to drive it, and he always became enraged at these incidents, so Bunny tried to keep them from him as much as possible by various stratagems.

When we arrived at the hospital Bunny was not there. This did not surprise me, as it was her habit always to be from fifteen minutes to half an hour late. This period passed, however, and she continued not to come. We waited outside and then we waited inside, in a room half bus station and half stable. It was calcimined pale green and decorated with SPCA posters and a smell of dogs, cats, wet straw, ether, and ammonia. For the fourth time, I suggested that Greta telephone Bunny. "I can't," Greta said, and began to cry. The other animal lovers who were there with their animals looked at her sympathetically. "Ahoo, ahoo, I knew this was going to happen," Greta sobbed, "she won't come so I'll have to take Dolon home again, that's what she thinks I will, ahoo, and I can't, I can't."

I said that I would call. Greta agreed miserably. I had to let the phone ring quite a while before Bunny answered. She was sorry, she said, she had overslept and wasn't even dressed. Why didn't we just get Dolon and take her to Cambridge? She would pick the cat up at Greta's tomorrow if her car was ready. I put my hand over the receiver and repeated this to Greta, who was walking nervously around outside among some sick dogs.

"Oh, it's all going to begin all over again, I can't bear it," she said while two cats and a terrier which had just been brought in continued to spit and howl.

"Shall I tell her you'll take Dolon home?"

"No," Greta said. "Give me the phone." I handed the receiver to her and walked out of earshot.

At last Greta came out of the telephone booth. "I told her I wouldn't," she said. "I said we would bring Dolon right to her house. Oh, ahoo, I just couldn't have it again."

Dolon was brought down to us, nervous and thin. We drove to Bunny's, Greta apologizing and sobbing all the way. Yet there was a certain expression of relief and triumph on her face. "After all, a person has to stand up for their rights, and especially Don's rights," she said. I thought that it was Bunny herself who had invented this tough character Greta that nobody could push around now, not even Bunny.

We drew up at the house. "I'll take her in," Greta said and she carried the squirming cat up the steps at 209 Bay State Road, kissing her and calling her pet names. Della, the cook, opened the door and she handed Dolon in. Then, still crying, but now only faintly, she came down and got into the car. "It's all over," she said. "I'm sorry to make such a fuss, but I liked Bunny so much and I thought she liked me. But maybe all the time she was just using me."

Greta was wrong. Bunny used her friends, sometimes used them up, but she loved them. She gave as much as she got or more. There was a discrepancy, but it was not in the quality or quantity of Bunny's affection compared to other people's; it was in the quality and quantity of her life. She was the most important or most violent experience they would ever have for a great many people; how many, no one can guess. During the seven years I knew her, at least twenty men and women loved her intensely in their various ways. She loved them as well—some more, some less—but after the passionate affair or the passionate friendship was over these people often had the rest of their lives to sit and think about Bunny, while she went on with the rest of her life.

Not that she tried to forget the past. No, she struggled to record it, to preserve it. She was always collecting souvenirs: letters, poems, presents, photographs. She encouraged these things to be created, to come to her, and then she kept them, filling boxes, drawers, closets; pushing the old aside a little to make room for the new, so that at last her room became a museum of her own past. Framed photographs crowded the tables; the books on the shelves were full of inscriptions. Over the dressing table hung a large Victorian mirror in a gilt frame. Stuck round it were snapshots, newspaper clippings, invitations, sketches drawn on paper napkins, and fragments of poems. There was a dirty paper gardenia with fraying stems, a bamboo fan, an obscene cutout doll, and the dance program from Bunny's first ball dangling a pencil from a pink silk string. Of the whole mirror, only a spot the size of a plate remained in the center to reflect Bunny's face. More of this sort of debris was pinned to the walls, to the doors, and to a folding screen.

There were extreme contrasts, even contradictions, among these memorabilia. Very bad poems were preserved alongside very good poems; illiterate sentimental notes next to clever allusive ones in Latin or French. Bunny was remarkable for the variety of her friends. She knew the writers, actors, artists, students, and riffraff of the Poets' Theatre; respectable Boston society; and the many more or less respectable academic societies of Cambridge. One of her friends was a clown with Barnum and Bailey; one a landscape architect, one a policeman, one a cashier in a supermarket, several were jazz musicians, and one worked on a pornographic magazine in New York which was always going underground and coming up under a different name to escape the postal laws.

Some of these odd friends had been picked up in the Canadian WAC, in which Bunny had enlisted at the age of eighteen because she was bored with the University of Chicago and too young for any of the American women's organizations. She was in the service for two years, first as a typist and filing clerk and then on the WAC newspaper. Among her photographs there were many snapshots from this period, already yellowing, showing her in the ugly WAC uniform and heavy shoes, with fat knees beneath the short skirt, squinting cheerfully into the sun, her arms around the shoulders of some grinning male or female member of the Canadian Army.

It was hard to believe that this was the same person as the Bachrach debutante in the yearbook picture from Hannah More Academy or the twelve-year-old girl in the framed photograph which was always on Bunny's desk. Here her eyes were cast down, her hair drawn back into a classic knot, her mouth set in an expression of stubborn dreaminess. It was the only picture I ever saw of Bunny as a child, except for one of the whole family in which she appeared as a fat baby in a white dress with round, staring eyes.

Bunny threw herself into the parts she played in real life with more abandon and more abandonment of her "own" personality than on stage. Whenever she ran into debt she would go out and find a job; she loved to look through the Help Wanted columns of the Sunday *Globe* and *Herald*. The next day she would get herself up elaborately to impersonate the kind of girl who would be instantly hired to interview Pontiac owners for a business research firm, or (of course, a different costume) to demonstrate cosmetics in R. H. Stearns. From her extensive past job experience she would select whatever experience seemed suitable, or if necessary, invent some. Sometimes she would rearrange her name to fit, becoming for example Anne Ranné when she wished to take photographs in an Armenian night club, and Vi Lang ("our Miss Lang") when she became Bridal Consultant for Fabian Bachrach.

Bunny kept these jobs as long as they amused her, or until her debts were paid off. While she was working she maintained the original costume, or altered it as she saw fit. Once, in order to be hired as a commission saleswoman for a Your Child's Lifetime Photograph plan (five dollars a year for five years with handsome leatherette album Absolutely Free) she got herself up as efficiently handsome in a suit and costume jewelry, but when she went out canvassing in Brighton she felt she would get more orders if she did not arouse envy and resentment in the Brighton housewives. She tried instead to look drab, slightly pitiable, obviously unattractive to men and sentimental about children. She wore a squashed brown felt turban with a veil and even made up her face to look older. When all was ready, she drove over to Cambridge and called on me unexpectedly. The effect was immense: I hardly knew her, and a friend who happened to arrive soon after did not recognize Bunny at all although they had met several times.

Often Bunny got herself up in costume when there was no question of a job. Once after I had left Cambridge she wrote to me:

*Eddy [Edward Thommen, then managing director of the Poets' Theatre] is definitely conning himself into directing the Vincent Club show and a limp young woman just called me to say everyone said I was wonderfully humorous and did I think I could doctor their script. Eddy is getting a thousand a week or something a week but of course because I am a member I should do it for the glory. I have to go out this afternoon and talk to them and I am going to dress as a Poet filled with cloudy dreams and floating silk chiffon scarves and stare at them with gentle bewilderment when they pose their problems which is to fill their awful book with wisecracks. Oh, I am going to say, but there must be some misunderstanding— did Ed tell you all my experience has been in poetical tragedy? but perhaps he didn't understand . . . and ruffle my hand through my tousley hair and purse my white mouth. and rattle my beads. mumbling vaguely at them,* "durate!"

Playing parts like these was no trouble for Bunny, for she had enough energy to make a whole person out of each casual appearance. In fact, she had too much, so that she seemed the most compact, real, understandable character in her most casual roles, the ones she spent least time on. Her "real" self, on the other hand, was full of impossible contradictions.

The job Bunny was most famous for was that of a chorus girl. She took it in September 1951, when she was being angrily dunned by a Newbury Street shop to pay for two Dior dresses. "I've got to do something about that poor little blue-faced man, he keeps calling up and I'm afraid Pa will answer the phone some time, it's so disgusting when you think that the apricot dress already doesn't fit me since I lost all that weight." For a week or two we heard no more, and then Bunny began to refuse invitations mysteriously. "No, not that afternoon. I'm training for a new job, please don't ask me about it," she told everyone. Expectation ran high, and it was not disappointed when Bunny finally let it be known that she was working at the Old Howard, the famous Boston burlesque theatre.

We all went to see her. The theatre had not changed since, nervously daring, I first visited it. The decayed Victorian baroque décor, with its dirty gold plasterwork and velvet curtains, the stiff, uncomfortable seats, the audience: largely men of all ages but with a surprising proportion of what looked like nice working-class couples out for the evening.

Before the show began a barker got up in front of the orchestra pit and sold a picture book which he described as being extraordinarily "spicy." We never bought these booklets, which in fact differed from the standard thing displayed on Scollay Square newsstands only in price. A short opening number, often with a patriotic theme, presented the cast, and then the individual acts began: a vaudeville scrap bag of comedy bits, strippers, chorus numbers, and specialties which might include a tap dancer, an acrobat or sentimental popular songs to the accompaniment of candy-box colored lantern slides. After one got over the initial shock of hearing dirty jokes from a stage and seeing female areas not usually visible (a privilege, after all, available to any man with a wife or woman with a mirror), monotony was apt to set in. The show was long, and it was not only possible but advisable to arrive late. When my husband and I came in this time two comics were on, heavy elderly men flapping symbolic rubber sausages and making ritual double-entendre jokes. Next came a stripteaser, this week's star, who received much applause because of her ability to make her breasts bounce singly or in unison in time to music. At last it was the turn of the chorus; the orchestra struck up a rumba, and the curtains opened to show a painted South American backdrop with several large artificial palms about which were draped twelve girls in artificial suggestive attitudes. Bunny was immediately recognizable. Painted a flat pink all over with pancake make-up and skimpily decorated with red sequins and feathers, she leaned languorously against a tree. She wore spike heels and a long tail of artificial yellow hair was pinned to her head under a feather headdress. Though actually of medium height, she seemed huge in contrast to the rest of the chorus, who were now revealed as almost midgets. The music continued, and the girls went through a dance routine which was no more lewd than that of any musical comedy. The main difference was that their faces were not fixed in the traditional bright smile of chorus girls but remained placid, even sullen. Bunny's alone wore an expression of concentration; one could see that she was trying to remember the steps. It was late at night, and there had been an afternoon show that day. When the routine was over and the girls again took up their positions Bunny's long false eyelashes fell almost shut on her painted cheeks.

We went again to see Bunny at the Old Howard, where she continued to work for several months, even after her bills had been paid. (This took some time, for the chorus' salary was only forty dollars a week.) She liked her friends to show an interest, and since she had many friends a noticeable new element was apparent in the Howard audience during this period. An instructor at Harvard who was then in love with Bunny went regularly, waiting for her outside the theatre when he was unable to afford waiting inside. He suffered much from the remarks, both friendly and hostile, of the Scollay Square crowd that would sometimes gather at the stage door late at night. When she left, the chorus and stars gave her their photographs, glossy publicity shots inscribed "To Anne—A Swell Kid," "Sincere Best Wishes from your Friend Bobo," etc. They were all pinned up prominently in her room on Bay State Road, and the large number of used burlesque costumes which she had also somehow managed to include among her souvenirs were hung in the closet.

No one except the cast was ever allowed backstage at the Old Howard, but Bunny's descriptions of life there were sufficient. The Epilogue of her play, *Fire Exit*, one of the best things she ever wrote, was based on this experience. She also wrote a farewell poem to the theatre:

### TO SOCIETY

*On leaving employment (as a chorus girl),*
*To return to earning nothing.*

*Don't stop loving me when*
*I leave the Line   Next week's routines*
*Are danced with roses and balloons*
*And one with garlands   all the girls in green*
*Rehearsing now without me   I will yearn*
*For large red paper roses that remain the same . . .*
*You Must*

*Not love me any longer just because I'm One*
*Out front alone! I'm one of You I know*
*That everywhere I go*
*I'll have to tell my name I'll sign*
*I LOVE YOU love me also A*N*N*E*

It was early in July 1953 that Bunny first got sick. A bad feverish cold, then bronchitis, she announced over the telephone when her friends called. It was not unknown for her to be ill: "What can she expect the way she lives?" censorious people said, as they had said before, for Bunny never ate or slept unless there was nothing better to do; she was not interested in taking care of herself and did not own rubbers. People who liked to think the best of everyone, on the other hand, remarked that Bunny had had a hard spring taking care of her father. Mr. Lang had been twice in the hospital, and had had an operation on his eyes for cataracts. Now convalescent, he was an irritable patient, mistrustful and disobedient of the doctor's orders. Unwilling, perhaps, to be seen in his owlish dark glasses, he would not go out for air. He stayed all day in his sitting room and when recommended foods came up on the dumbwaiter he sent them down again, pulling so hard on the rope that the plates and silver could be heard crashing against each other as they arrived in the kitchen. He was now seventy-four or seventy-five, and the supposition of all Bunny's friends was that he would shortly die; they frequently speculated on what she would do then.

July continued and Bunny did not become better; she became worse. "Now they tell me it's pleurisy, sounds so Victorian, don't you think," she announced. "It's just a name for the symptoms. I looked it up in the dictionary: 'Inflammation of the lining of the thorax, usually with fever, pain, difficult respiration, and cough.'" There was no one in the house to take care of Bunny except the elderly cook Della, who could barely wheeze up the four flights of stairs once a week to clean, so the doctor suggested that she be moved to Massachusetts General Hospital.

I went to see her there, in Phillips House where all the rooms are private and start at $25 a day. It has a strange atmosphere, very reminiscent of the old resort hotels that line the northern coast of New England; tall, rectangular, narrow, perched on some bluff overlooking the sea and washed by cold light. Here too it was possible to spend a great deal of money without any outward show of sinful and ostentatious luxury. A doorman with the look of an old family servant admitted me to the hall, and discreetly pointed out the elevators, next to which stood a procession of Edwardian wicker wheelchairs painted white. On one of the top floors Bunny lay in bed—a hospital bed with a real headboard painted with flower motifs. The rest of the furniture was wicker and black lacquer that might have come straight out of a summer hotel. It was warm, and a breeze from the window blew the net and chintz curtains up. As I came in Bunny was lying flat, looking angry and bored rather than sick, with the sheet up to her chin and a magazine open face-down on her stomach. "Disgusting, isn't it," she said furiously, propping herself up on one elbow. "I'm perfectly well but they won't let me out of this place until the lab report comes back . . . I had a biopsy, do you know what that is, it was hideous, they take you to the operating room and give you a local anesthetic, never let them give you one, and then they take away a huge sample of some part of you in a bottle. I can't imagine what they're doing to it, it's been days, and now I'm going to have this dreary scar the rest of my life." She pulled the hospital nightgown up over her head with typical lack of concern and showed me the bandage below her collarbone. "I looked yesterday when they unwrapped it, and it's not going to be at all interesting, just a crooked line, like a bramble scratch, you might think the doctor would have taken a little trouble to make me a good scar."

An elderly nurse came in and gave Bunny the menu for next day's meals. There was a great choice of elaborate foods, some with French names. "Oh, yes, it was fun at first," Bunny said as she marked the menu, "and did you see my napkin, we get new ones every day." It was damask, in a monogrammed silver napkin ring. "But now I simply can't stand it."

"My father may come in soon," she told the nurse. "You will recognize him. He has a loud voice and carries a cane."

"I'll look out for him, Miss Lang," said the nurse deferentially, and she took the menu away.

"Margie finally persuaded him to leave the house," Bunny told me. "He hates the whole idea." We talked for a while before Mr. Lang's voice was heard in the hall. He came in, led by a nurse, but paying no attention to her, or to me as I prepared to leave. He went up to Bunny's bedside shakily and stood gripping the sheet in one bony hand, his cane in the other. He was no longer wearing dark glasses, but looked small, old, and ill, yellowy-pale from being shut up in the house. Bunny, on the other hand, was plump and tanned to a warm brown.

"Well, Wog," he said, using the old pet name by which he had addressed all his daughters as children.

"Hello, Pa," Bunny said, "how are you feeling?" And as I left, he was beginning to tell her.

Early in August Bunny went home from the hospital to be convalescent. And now, the less acutely ill she became, the more she played at being ill, with all the enthusiasm of an actress who suddenly sees the possibilities of a type of role she has never attempted. The doctors had told her to rest, so she lay, part of the time, in the front bedroom on the third floor. The mantlepiece and chests of drawers were crowded with empty ice-cream cartons and vases of dead and dying flowers which Mac Hammond was sending her every day since she came home. (He wished to do this because he was again playing at being hopelessly in love with Bunny, and could afford it because his father was a vice-president of Coca-Cola.)

Bunny had lost thirty pounds, and in profile she looked impossibly beautiful, but from the front she looked haggard, with navy-blue patches around her eyes and no lipstick, although she had worn lipstick when I saw her in the hospital. Her tan was beginning to fade, and the light through the half-drawn blinds gave her skin a greenish tone. Hank Robbins, her most recent lover, was there; he had come up for the weekend from New York where he was becoming a Madison Avenue executive; he too looked greenish. Both beds and the floor were covered with Bunny's poetry for years past, all typed on tissuey sheets of onionskin paper. She was thinking of trying to publish a volume of verse, and Hank was helping her to select the contents. Bunny would sit up to read something, exclaim, "No, no, no!" crumple it into a ball and throw it at the empty fireplace; or she would jump out of bed to reach some pages, in her long nightgown, and then she would put her hand on her chest, gasp, say, "I have a pain," and lean back on a heap of pillows, her eyes fluttering. "Please don't have a pain," Hank would beg her.

For the next month Bunny was in and out of bed. She was having X-ray treatments which made her temporarily sick to her stomach and unable to eat. As soon as they stopped she abruptly gave up the part of an invalid, so much so that she got annoyed if anyone asked her how she was feeling. When her friends remarked that she was looking very well she would fix them with a withering stare and fail to reply. I was surprised one afternoon when she said to me over the phone: "Let's go out to Mount Auburn Cemetery. When I was in the hospital and thought I might die I often imagined going there."

It was a hot, soft, misty day in September. The cemetery was at its best; the stone angels, weeping Virtues, and marble Newfoundland dogs were white under the luxurious green shade of late summer. The urns were full of flowers, the low wrought-iron fences overgrown with flowering vines. The Civil War Memorial sphinx smiled indulgently across deep green grass, with the face of a Victorian maiden aunt, and Mary Baker Eddy's classic monument proclaimed to a small artificial lake edged with weeping willows that she was not actually there. "Pa says there's still a telephone beside her connected to the Boston exchange," Bunny remarked.

The Lang's family plot was at the other side of the cemetery, on a hillside. The newest stone was that of Bunny's mother, already beginning to weather, and sunk in velvety grass. We got out of the car: Bunny, I and my son John, then seven months old. I put him down on the grass and he crawled off slowly towards a stone lamb in the next plot while we walked about.

"Who are all these Burrages mixed in with your family?" I asked.

"Oh, they're our relatives. The Langs only have two more

spaces: one for Pa, I expect, and the other for whichever of my aunts gets here first."

This was the first time Bunny had let on, even indirectly, that she, like the rest of us, supposed that Mr. Lang would die soon. "How is your father lately?" I therefore asked to pump her. But she did not even seem to hear the question.

"I can see why they fight over it," she went on. "It's the best place I can think of to be buried. But of course Max wouldn't stand for it. I imagine he'll want our ashes to be scattered from the Brooklyn Bridge, or someplace like that."

Again Bunny had referred to a half-forbidden topic. Max was her imaginary lover, a character she had worked up over the years and in whose coming she sometimes really seemed to believe. She refused to answer questions about Max, but from what she had let drop he was known to be a fabulously rich international Jew, perhaps ten or fifteen years older than Bunny, a patron of art and the theatre. Several times in the past, before Max's character was completely formed, Bunny had thought that she had met him, but always she had been disappointed in the end. And of late all her lovers had been as unlike Max as possible: always young, poor protégés of art and the theatre.

Bunny was restless during the fall and winter following our trip to Mount Auburn Cemetery. For the first time she seemed to have lost interest in the Poets' Theatre, which had now become incredibly respectable and was putting on two plays by Yeats in Fogg Museum Court. She went to New York and returned, started projects and grew tired of them, took up people and dropped them. She was furious with her doctors because they would not let her go south this year: instead she had to stay in Boston so that she could report at intervals for an X-ray examination. After Christmas she went briefly to New York, where the Artists' Theatre (a rival organization in which several former members of the Poets' Theatre and some rather abstract painters were involved) was putting on her play *Fire Exit*. "I am going to keep my hands off the production completely," she wrote to me, "and just have FUN."

Ted Gorey, who was now living in New York, wrote me the following notes on her visit:

*Bunny is leading a most peculiar life here, and is always being taken to the ballet or the theatre by people. We talk for hours on the phone, and she is always cancelling our tentative plans because she has had another invitation . . . She has somehow compelled me into throwing two weird little parties in my apartment, very fragmentary since several crucial people didn't show, and the room seemed to be filled with large dark holes . . . I think she is looking for something.*

In March Bunny returned to Boston. She telephoned and said she had something to tell me which could not be said over the telephone. We met, therefore, and she announced that she was in love with a painter named Mike Goldberg who lived in New York and worked in a paper-box factory designing paper boxes. This was the most wonderful thing that had ever happened to her, and Mike was going to come up to Boston on April 9 and speak to Mr. Lang about it. Then they would be married as soon as possible without any fuss and go to live in an unheated loft in lower Manhattan where Mike already lived and she would get a job.

So intense was Bunny's determination that none of us who were in her confidence doubted for a moment that she would change her life in this drastic manner. It might seem incongruous to think of Bunny in New York, but she had had her Greenwich Village period long ago. Even now stories still drifted back from this era of how she had been a witness in a murder trial, and had once been picked up by the police for soliciting for prostitution, some said as the result of a bet.

On April 9, as announced, Mike arrived in Boston, a city which he had never visited before meeting Bunny. He proved to be a medium-sized young man with black hair, burning eyes, and a large pale bony face, dressed as an abstract painter. He said almost nothing at all and moved everywhere with a quiet, catlike walk in sneakers spotted with abstract paint. Bunny displayed him at a party given by Don and Greta Smith, where he sat cross-legged on the floor, although there were plenty o' chairs, silently watching everything.

"Well, what do you think of Boston?"

"I think it is very ugly," Mike replied in tones of suppressed violence which made Bunny, across the room, glance nervously at him. This evening she was dressed as the mistress of a modern painter, in a heavy crew-neck sweater and dirty jeans. Her hair was twisted up into a frayed yellow knob and she wore no make-up: her face was shiny. She would have passed without comment anywhere below Tenth Street. Like Mike, she was sitting cross-legged on the floor, which was covered by a hard and scratchy rug made of East Indian ropes. By now most of us, out of politeness or some other instinct, had joined her. Our empty chairs stood behind us in a circle.

A graduate student now asked Mike what he thought of André Malraux's *Voices of Silence.*

"Sorry, I haven't read it."

"Oh, you should. As a painter, I mean. It's a very impressive book."

"I don't read about painting," Mike said. "I just paint."

Later he was taken into the bedroom, where an abstract painting done by a friend of the Smiths' was hanging. Half of the party came along to watch this confrontation, while the rest stopped talking and strained to overhear it.

Mike stood and looked at the picture for some time.

"What do you think of it?" Don Smith finally asked.

"I think there's an interesting suggestion of depth in that section, don't you think?" said the graduate student who had spoken before, pointing to a section of the canvas.

"It doesn't send me," said Mike who had once been a jazz musician and still had many acquaintances in this profession.

"I've always thought the color was kind of nice," suggested Greta Smith.

"It's all right," Mike said crossly, turning away. "I don't see any point in talking about pictures. Either you like them or you don't."

The party went on some more, but it did not get better. Mike and Bunny were among the first to leave. As they went out he propelled her in front of him with his hand on her neck, as is seldom done in Cambridge, and she let him do it.

The day arrived on which Mike was to speak to Mr. Lang.

It was not until much later that Bunny told me what had happened.

It was a cold wet April day. Mike arrived early, his hair and raincoat damp through. Bunny met him in the hall and informed him that she had told her father three times that he was coming, and that Mr. Lang still pretended not to know what was going on. She took Mike's raincoat away from him and told him to go upstairs. Mike asked what was Mr. Lang doing upstairs, was he sick in bed? No, Bunny explained, and so Mike went on up, feeling his way on the dark stairs, darker this wet day. Mr. Lang was waiting for him, walking about in the hall semi-purposefully, and during the whole of their conversation he kept moving from room to room on domestic errands: arranging magazines on a rack, changing his shoes, looking for something a long time in a closet, while Mike followed him. Bunny sat listening below on the stairs, but she could only hear occasional phrases: her father saying "Is that so, sir, is that so?" and Mike replying in his soft but definitely New York accent, so low that she could not catch the words. Presently Mr. Lang could be heard going into the bedroom, followed by Mike. He noisily opened a drawer, pulled up a shade, and went back out to the hall. "What are you following me around for?" he suddenly asked.

"I wondered if you wanted to ask me any other questions, Mr. Lang."

"No, thank you, sir. Excuse me, I have to go out now and buy some cheese."

Mr. Lang descended the stairs, passing Bunny without comment, went into the front hall, and put on his hat and coat. He took his cane out of the Chinese urn by the door and walked out of the house into the rain.

Bunny looked up the stairs. Mike was still standing there.

"Hi," she said.

"He said he had to go out and buy some cheese. What the hell does he want cheese for now? I think he's cracked."

"Maybe he's hungry."

"Yeah." Mike sat down by Bunny on the stairs, but she got up and walked away through the dining room, where Della had laid out the family silver for an elaborate lunch, and stood looking out over Storrow Drive and the river, washed by fine sheets of rain. Mike followed her.

"He asked me how old I was. I thought you already told him how old I was."

"I suppose he wanted to see if you would lie to him," said Bunny.

"Why the hell should I lie to him?"

"Because I'm thirty."

"I don't get it."

A pause. Then Bunny asked, "What did he say?"

"I said I was twenty-nine. What did you want me to say?"

"No, I said what did Pa say."

"Oh. I think he said he supposed I was old enough to know my own mind."

Bunny looked out of the window and then turned away. "Come on, let's go back to New York," she said. "You don't want to stay here another day, do you?"

"Christ, no," Mike replied. "I hate Massachusetts."

"Christ, so do I," Bunny said. "Let's leave now, there's a train every hour. I'll just go upstairs and throw a few things in a bag. I won't be a minute."

Bunny was gone twenty minutes, while Mike looked at the backs of the bound sets of books in the library, Kipling and Emerson and Parkman. At last she came down carrying a large suitcase and a hatbox.

"Hi."

"Hi."

"Let's go."

"Yeah."

They opened the front door. On the steps stood Mr. Lang carrying a paper bag, presumably of cheese.

"I want to have a talk with you, Violet," he said. "Come into the library."

It was a long time before Bunny told me anything about this conversation, which lasted forty minutes while Mike waited in the front hall. "You know that time Mike was up here," she finally said. "Pa was almost incoherent, he was so angry at the idea of our getting married. I never knew before how anti-Semitic he was . . . He kept making these vague incoherent threats, you know. I just couldn't talk to him." She came out of the library furious and defiant, picked up her suitcases, and walked out of the house with Mike.

They went to New York, and in Boston we waited for the telegram announcing the marriage. Several weeks passed; it did not come. Perhaps after all Bunny had guessed during the talk in the library what her father could not quite bring himself to tell her: that she was going to die.

Late in April Bunny returned alone. "How is Mike?" I asked when she telephoned.

"He's all right, I suppose," she replied repressively. "No, I can't come over. I have a terrible cold and the car is in the repair shop. I'm afraid it's the engine this time . . . Oh, nothing, it was this crazy laundry truck that thought it could cut in ahead of me on Boylston Street . . . No, I couldn't tomorrow . . . No, I couldn't . . . Well, look, how about going to the movies with me. Saturday afternoon? The car is supposed to be ready by then."

It was not quite ready, for the muffler was still broken, but Bunny took it out of the garage anyway. She picked me up and we drove very noisily through the back streets of Cambridge, shouting our conversation over the roar and knocking of the engine.

"I had another damned X-ray checkup!" Bunny shouted.

"Oh?"

"The results were positive."

"Oh?"

"That means I have to have another damned series of X-ray treatments. They make me sick to my stomach."

Bunny parked the car in an alley under a NO PARKING sign. "I don't think Mike likes my being sick," she said. "He thought it was all over with, something in the past. He doesn't like the idea of being sick at all. He's a yea-sayer." She pulled on the brake, got out, and slammed the door so violently that the whole car shook. "Me, I'm a nay-sayer from way back," she said.

We walked up the alley towards Church Street, and along beside the high brick wall that forms the back of the University Movie Theatre.

"Everybody keeps telling me, be constructive, think constructively, think happy optimistic thoughts. And I'm damned if I will. I'll be as bitter as I want . . . Those doctors told me it might be ten years before I had a positive X-ray. And what is it, seven months. They were lying to me. One, please," she said to the ticket window.

"Bunny—" I began to say but she walked away and I bought my ticket and hurried after her up the hall and through the gilt glass doors.

"Oh, there you are," Bunny said.

"Bunny, I—"

"I can't go around telling everybody I'm dying, can I?" she interrupted, standing on the dirty, thick carpet patterned with blood-red flowers which is in the lobby of the University Movie Theatre.

"But—"

"It just embarrasses them. What can they say? I don't expect you to say anything. All right, get it out if you must."

"I just wanted to say, if the doctors were wrong once they could be wrong again, you know."

"I suppose so."

"They don't know everything."

"I suppose not. Let's get some popcorn."

The news that Bunny could not go around telling was quickly passed about among her friends, who were variously grieved, frightened, or embarrassed according to their various natures. What speeches they made to her Bunny received according to her mood of the moment, which changed more suddenly and drastically during the next few months than ever before or after. Sometimes she would behave as if she had never heard of doctors or their advice, up all night dancing and all day at the beach, and then anyone who sympathized with her or tried to make things easier for her (helping her out of a car or down steps, for instance) was fixed with a withering look. At other times she played the part of a desperate invalid so dramatically that any solicitous act or speech took on the air of a bunch of violets dropped on a great battlefield. In May she gave a poetry reading for the Poets' Theatre, for which she turned up looking ghastly pale and haggard, dressed in low-cut black velvet like Madame Bovary. She sat spotlighted in a dim room, sobbing and crying out a long elegiac poem on disease and treachery which she had just written. Half the audience was weeping when Bunny finished, but when the lights went up I could have sworn the dark circles under her eyes had been improved with greasepaint. Really dying, she still played at dying, as if she would make death just one more costume.

"Life being what it is, one dreams of revenge." Bunny had incorporated this line from Gauguin's journals into the long poem she read that day, and she frequently quoted it in her conversation during the spring and summer that followed. Her affair with Mike did not end at once, but rather petered out in a series of misunderstandings and reconciliations. They really loved each other deeply, she would sometimes announce to us all, and she felt that eventually they would be married. "Eventually, why not now?" Lyon Phelps remarked. "Why not last spring when they were both in New York and we all expected it?" Perhaps, I suggested, they would have been married then if Bunny's conversation with her father in the library had not taken place; if she had been able to finish packing sooner (even two minutes sooner) so that she would have left the house before he returned. But it always took Bunny a long time to pack; she needed so many costumes and props. Actually she must have hurried terribly that day, to take only twenty minutes.

All through the summer of 1954 the affair dragged on. Mostly by mail: Bunny would not go to New York, and Mike would not come to Boston. Sometimes they telephoned, and shouted insults at each other over the long-distance wire like the gods of rival cities. But it could not go on, and finally early in the fall Bunny wrote me (I had now moved to Amherst, where my husband was teaching):

*For the last three weeks Mike has been hinting darkly at coming up here but he keeps reneging, I think the truth is he is so scared of my father he won't stay in the house again but because of this he has to keep saying he is going to. I am getting very tired of the whole thing, at last. It is so feeble and psychopathic.*

It was not Bunny's nature to resign herself to any event such as the loss of a lover, to merely dream of revenge. She went up to her room and began to write a play against Mike and everything he stood for:

*I locked myself up for a month, quite literally, the car tires all sagged in the lot and the battery went dead. People stopped trying to call, I suppose they thought the phone was out on account of the hurricanes, bless their little hearts. I paid no attention at all to the hurricanes until I happened to look out the front door the next day of both of them I was too busy. All of the street fell down but there you are . . . Anyway I closeted myself and by day and by night finished a Pastoral as 10 dialogues with a plot running through and called it ET IN ARCADIA EGO and thrust it into the astonished laps of our friends and colleagues . . . Two anarchists named Aleph and Beth have gone to Miguelon where they breed goats and call themselves Chloris and Damon. Damon talks like Mike, but really the resemblance trickles away after that into other things as I became too involved with Fragile Man, I mean, I make Damon eat the apple, it's about time . . . the apple is this loathsome Phoebe . . . looking very sharp and with a neutral hipster dog, very cool, he is withdrawn and watches the progress of conventional sympathies at work . . . with sarcastic somewhat choric comments . . . I have in mind to stay out of this play and stand at the back all the time during rehearsals and after, in the manner of Hamlet.*

*Arcadia* was Bunny's best work as well as her most sustained, dramatically and poetically. She kept to the form and spirit of her models, and echoes of Spenser and Shakespeare sounded in the background. This was not unconsciously done, for Bunny read nothing but the best poetry—and nothing but the worst prose. Half of her books were hard-used, marked-up editions of Blake, Baudelaire, Edith Sitwell, Dryden, Rilke, Wallace

Stevens, etc. (she treated all writing as if it were contemporary). The other half was made up of paperback sensational novels, womens' magazines, and nonfiction with titles like "Flying Saucers Have Landed Here," "Greater Mental Power in Thirty Days" and "Eat and Grow Elegant."

The plot of *Arcadia*, as Bunny said, was simple. Chloris and Damon have left the city to live on an island in the North Atlantic, where

*The cold light pierces languor,*
*And no fungus, parasite, nor any*
*Heat-rotten and heat-ridden*
*Decomposition can come.*

They are happy until Phoebe, a sinister old flame of Damon's, arrives to get him back. At first Damon refuses to listen to her, but she sits around reminiscing about their old life in the city, and remarking to Chloris how surprised she is that he hasn't painted anything lately:

*Why can't you understand him, Chloris? . . .*
*No wonder he produces nothing—he has*
*No stimulation—no support! . . .*
*Everybody knew him. He knew everybody.*
*Another one-man show—but who can say?*
*Now he casts his contacts all away.*
*It's always true it isn't you, it's who you know.*

Finally Damon can't bear it any more and goes back on the boat with Phoebe: Chloris is left alone on the island, waiting for winter, perhaps for death:

*The hills of love grow small, seen from the ocean . . .*
*I was at fault. I was too serious.*
*All we can do for each other is to this purpose,*
*To keep the sand beneath our feet, which tears*
*Away from us, and guts the shore.*
*We can do more, but not for love.*
*We do it by ourselves.*

Throughout the play runs a complicated net of metaphors, playing on cold and heat, on the Tarot, on the emblem of a caged bird escaping with the motto "*Qui me néglige me perde*," and most especially on the prehistory of the earth, the coming of the ice age, and the death of the dinosaurs:

*The Brontosaurus*
*Stand and watch, their pale, already weedy eyes*
*Are hurting them, and their unmanageable crusted limbs.*
*They pray for conservation, while the great, winged monsters*
*Twitch and molt, unbalanced and resentful, in the primal trees . . .*
*They are so hopeless! Hangers-on,*
*With never any more to come, no more of them again.*

Bunny kept her promise to stay out of her play, and she was well rewarded. The production, directed by Lyon Phelps, was first-rate, professional but unpretentious. Bronia Sielewicz played Chloris not as Bunny would have done it, but perhaps more touchingly. She took up less space on stage, both physically and emotionally, and seemed—with her thin white face and long frayed hair—far more fragile than Bunny. (Actually she was in excellent health and later performed demanding roles in television and on the stage in New York City simultaneously, without apparent fatigue.) One felt throughout the play that she would suffer terribly from Damon's departure, whereas in the scenes of *Fire Exit* in which Eurydice loses Orpheus, Bunny had slightly given the impression of a cow bellowing because it is being deserted by a terrier; and this in spite of the above average height and weight of the actor who played opposite her.

The other three members of the cast were also very good. A real French boy was the dog, Georges, whose conversation consisted almost entirely of American jazz slang in French ("*C'est le plus fou!*"); Peter Sourian, a Harvard undergraduate who later became successful as the author of stories and novels about young lust, played Damon with spirit, though somewhat handicapped by his comparative youth. Best of all was Sarah Braveman as Phoebe, domineering and sinister in a black trench coat and black rubber boots.

The excitement of the production of *Arcadia* kept up Bunny's spirits that fall in spite of a recurrence of her illness (which it may also have caused). Just before opening night she wrote me:

*I just had coffee in bed and I am writing this feverishly to put in the mail, shuddering with cold as Pa hasn't put on the furnace . . . if you are going to make a new quilt I will send you a swatch from my one femme fatale dress—the emerald velvet one—as it is ready for a life of nostalgia now . . . I am diseased again as of this week. Every six months to the day we go through this farce endlessly the dragon said. Bought a really dramatic jacket at the buckingham clothing sale wait till you see it is a burgeoning white fox collar . . . Helen Wells tells me Mike is telling everyone in NYC I am hopelessly fatherbound and we are Through so after being very angry now I am relaxed and no longer guilty about making fun of his circle and his ethnic friends (bop) in my play, let the whole thing stand as a comment. I have got to get out of my nightgown and go to the Death Ray Parlor now.*

*Love Bunny*

I came down to Cambridge for the last night of *Arcadia*, and Ted Gorey, who was now working in the art department of Doubleday and Company, came up from New York. We were both to stay at Bunny's house. After the pink-and-yellow-striped curtains closed for the last time, a feeling of letdown and exhaustion seemed to come over everyone. It was late Halloween night, cold and clear. The streets, which at curtain time had been full of children in fantastic masks shrieking and darting round corners, were deserted, the air still. The cast party had been held the previous night, and now the actors drifted off in different directions, as if *Arcadia* had been a failure instead of a success. When we got to the house on Bay State Road Bunny wanted to go to bed, though it was hardly midnight, early for her. I had been up at six that morning with the baby, so I went too. We slept in the guest room, while Ted crossly stayed up alone reading in Bunny's bed.

I was woken the next morning by Bunny coming into the room with a tray of food: grapefruit, coffee, toast, eggs, currant buns, and two kinds of jam. "I feel like breakfast in bed today," she announced, putting it down. "Help yourself." While I ate she took off her Mother Hubbard nightgown and man's carpet slippers and got into a blue chiffon peignoir, combed out her hair (which had been in pigtails), made up her face carefully at the dressing table, arranged the pillows, and climbed back into the other bed. "Call Teddles, will you?" she said.

I went upstairs. Ted had been up for hours, he said. "I don't really like sleeping lately," he apologized, as if it had been an acquaintance of ours. He came down in a faded pair of cotton pajamas, shrunk by the wash so that his long thin legs and long pale feet protruded in a comic-adolescent way. As usual, the top half of him did not match the bottom half. Over his pajamas he was wearing an Edwardian silk brocade dressing-gown which he had picked up in a Third Avenue thrift shop, and, of course, his new curly brown beard, which had just about reached its full growth. He was carrying a pile of photographs.

"Violet, duckie, who are all these mad people? I felt they were watching me all night long, I had to get up and turn them face down before I could get a wink." He spread the pictures out on Bunny's bed. She looked them over, but was not very informative.

". . . A great girl, we were in Saskatchewan together . . . That? why that's Frank in drag, don't you recognize him? Well, don't put it into the jam . . . That's Gordie Griscom . . . Oh, of course you must have met him, why he was one of the great loves of my life. Didn't I ever show you those letters he wrote from St. Elizabeth's, wait a moment." And she jumped out of bed, presently returning with a cardboard box and several manila envelopes full of papers. "I really ought to sort all this out some time," she remarked as the bed became covered with scraps and bundles of letters. "Maybe I'll do it today. Drag over that wastebasket, will you, Teddles? . . .

Ugh, why did I ever keep this?" she now started to repeat, tearing up photographs and lumps of paper and throwing them into the basket.

"My dear, you're so destructive today, so unlike you," Ted protested; he and I kept fishing things out of the wastebasket, smoothing them out again, and asking questions which Bunny, furiously at work, seldom answered. Occasionally she would start tearing the folders apart to find something she wished to show us:

"Where is that crazy picture of Bynam with the chairs? You've got to see that, Alison . . . That's a still from the movie I was in, but there's a much better one, just let me look . . . No, don't read that, throw it away, I'm not going to have you reading it," she said, snatching a letter out of my hand. There were other passionate love letters, unsigned; Bunny said she could not remember who they came from, but perhaps just did not want to say: "Put them on the bed. Maybe it'll come back to me."

Wedged in a corner of the box were a few letters carefully wrapped in an old paper party napkin. She looked at them fondly. "That was from my first love affair."

"Oh?" said Ted encouragingly, perhaps too encouragingly, for Bunny merely set them aside and went on. Ted and I looked at each other. The story usually told was that Bunny had been seduced at fifteen, in the front seat of a red convertible which his fans had presented to a member of the Boston Red Sox. Actually this may have been a graceful combination of two incidents. Many of Bunny's friends were artistic gossips, but even if the story had not been altered in transmission it might not be true. Bunny herself sometimes told fibs about her past for art's sake; however, having such a large amount of material, she was more apt to combine or omit than to invent.

"How is Mike?" asked Ted, although he knew better than Bunny how Mike was, for he had just been to a party a few days ago in New York where were Mike and Mike's friend who was the original of Phoebe in *Arcadia*. He was planning to tell Bunny of this meeting, but he wished to lead up to it gradually.

"I don't know and I don't care," Bunny said.

"Anyway, I fixed him," she added after a pause. And then: "Don't you think *Arcadia* fixed him?"

"*Well*," Ted began, and I stopped listening, for I had heard the story the previous day. Instead I thought about Bunny's taste for revenge. No one could deny it. Her admirers claimed that it was the vindictiveness of a goddess: it is reported that the gods enjoy vengeance, even regard it as their private property: Greta Smith had once excused it by saying that Bunny was more sensitive than most people, and felt a hurt more. But her treatment of Mike as Damon in *Arcadia* I thought as much flattering as destructive, for it is flattering to have a whole play written about one, and even though Damon was finally shown up as a weak and self-deceptive cad the action of the play was all about how two beautiful women were desperately fighting to have him. But I did not know Mike very well, and it might be that this was just the sort of thing that would most enrage him in many subtle ways.

Bunny's revenges were usually well-chosen. Once when she felt that Ted Gorey had betrayed her she sent him a Christmas card so obscene, insulting, and spiteful that he would not speak to her for almost a year. And while in New York the previous winter, she had become enraged against a junior executive named Parker, why I never learned—all she would say was, "He annoyed me." She went down to Fulton Street to a job printer, and ordered 1,000 labels printed up, two by three inches square. To the printer she said that she was employed by a bank that was conducting a savings campaign for children, with piggy banks. The labels were pink, and each announced in black letters:

*My name is*
*Parker and*
*I am a pig.*

Bunny then went and pasted these labels all over Manhattan, wherever Parker and his friends were likely to see them. On his apartment door and his apartment-house door, on the walls of buildings which he passed on his way to the subway, on his way to work; in the subway station, and on the windows of the subway trains. When questioned, she gave the explanation which she had prepared for the printer. She rode up to Madison Avenue, where Parker worked in a position of uneasy semi-importance, and pasted the labels in his building; she got herself admitted by a stratagem into the offices and put them in the corridors and washrooms. Down in the Village where Parker lived the pink stickers appeared in Parker's favorite grocery, laundry, bar, and bookshop. Meanwhile her spies successively reported that Parker was embarrassed, baffled, angry, and finally in a state of continual nervous rage. When Bunny left New York she had used up all but about 150 of the labels. She kept them, of course, and for quite a while afterwards she would occasionally send one off to remind him, on a postcard or pasted as a bookplate into a suitable book, especially when she was out of town. If a friend of hers happened to be going to some distant city or Europe, she would given them some labels to send back to Parker in New York.

Ted had finished telling Bunny about his meeting with Mike, and they were now discussing other mutual friends who had gone to live in New York, among them an actor named Jerry Kilty, formerly of the Brattle Theatre.

"Do you remember that day we all went swimming at Marblehead Rocks?" I asked. It had been three years ago, a perfect hot summer day. The sea was dark green, almost at full tide, with thick waves splashing and spraying up. Bunny, rather fat that summer, but tanned red and gold, lay on the gold rocks perfecting these colors, and then dived off into the water.

"It's not safe to jump in like that, you might hit a rock," someone warned her when she came to the surface in the sudsy foam, her hair streaming down in wet strings and full of seaweed.

"Oh, safety," Bunny said as she climbed out. "Don't you know:

"*And this Security, it is the Common Moth*
*That feeds on Wits and Arts, and may destroy them both.*"

She had brought a picnic lunch, and later, as we were eating it, Lyon Phelps proposed a toast. Holding up his paper cup full of ginger ale, he said, "I give you Bunnylang—Miss Marblehead Rocks of 1951!" We drank to her.

On the way home in the car Jerry told us stories of his childhood. He had been brought up in a rather haphazard way on an Indian reservation for which his father was the government agent. Later he had won a scholarship to a choir school, where the rules were very strict, and the atmosphere one of intense religious morality. The boys had invented special words to all their most popular hymns. At their Christmas concerts, for instance, they would all sing as loudly as they dared, to the tune of "Hark the Herald Angels":

> "*Uncle George and Auntie Mabel*
> *Fainted at the breakfast table.*
> *This should be sufficient warning:*
> *Never do it in the morning.*
> *Ovaltine will set you right,*
> *You can do it ev'ry night*
> *Uncle George is hoping soon*
> *To do it in the afternoon.*
> *O what joys Aunt Mabel's seen*
> *With the help of Ovaltine.*"

Bunny was delighted with this, and sang it at the top of her lungs as she drove, rather fast, along the highway back to Boston.

I recalled this day to her now, and asked if she remembered it. "Oh yes," she said vaguely, indifferently. "Marblehead Rocks." I could see she did not. The occasion, which the rest of us had remembered as a sort of epiphany, was one of too many for her. So Jupiter might not remember Danae among the many mortals he had visited, for good or ill, in many guises, but only vaguely recall a shower of gold.

"It was the day Jerry taught you his song." I explained further.

"Oh, no, that song? Why, I've known that since boarding school," Bunny said without emphasis. She yawned, and added, "God, I'm tired. I think I'm just going to stay in bed today."

But instead she threw back the covers, got out, walked across the room and into the closet, and shut the door.

Ted's eyebrows flew up. "What in God's name are you doing in that closet?" he exclaimed.

"What?" Bunny asked, opening the door slightly and throwing out a heap of blue chiffon onto the floor.

"I said, if you are going to stay in bed, why are you taking off your nightgown?"

"I don't want it to get creased," Bunny explained, walking out of the closet in her old Mother Hubbard nightgown. She sat down by the window and began to wipe her face off with cold cream. "I told you not to read those," she suddenly loudly said, turning round and pulling a bundle of letters out of my hand. They were the ones wrapped with a paper napkin, which I had earlier been trying to read upside down as they lay on the bed.

"What's so special about them?" Ted asked.

"A girl always feels something about her first affair, and that was my first affair," Bunny said, smoothing out the crushed paper. She paused and added, as if to herself, "I suppose Mike was my last."

I saw Bunny again late that fall; she visited me in the country, where she was appalled by everything—the isolation of the small college town, the weather, the housework. "How do you stand him day after day?" she kept asking me, first of my eighteen-month-old child, and then of everyone who came to the house. "That man [or woman] is an enemy. I can tell. He's against everything we're for." Her X-ray tests were all negative, but she had a bad cold. She was in a low mood generally; fed up with Boston, all the books which had recently been published were terrible, she was at odds with almost everyone she knew. There had come to be, perhaps, a certain embarrassment about Bunny's position which both she and her friends felt; she was like a swan which has given its death concert and then does not die. Still, a certain emotional climate has been produced, certain scenery—what is to be done with it?

I was not surprised, a few weeks later, to hear that Bunny had gone south. She had been talking vaguely of going to

Sarasota in Florida to apply for work with the circus. The idea of riding round the ring in spangles on the back of an elephant pleased her. It was a scheme she had mentioned before, and once even tried, but that time she had not arrived in Sarasota until March, when the cast was already complete.

The postcards that came back, after Christmas, from Cuba and Key West—not Florida—were even less informative than usual. But suddenly, one cold afternoon in February, long before anyone expected her back, Bunny telephoned me from Boston.

"I have some good news," she announced. "Bradley and I are going to be married."

"Bradley?" I asked.

"Bradley Phillips."

I knew the name; it was that of a tall young man who three or four years previously had been one of the vague hangers-on of the Poets' Theatre. He had then graduated from Harvard and disappeared for some time: into the army or into New York or into an analysis, or all of these. His family lived in Cambridge, and lately I had heard from someone that he had been seen again around the Square, but Bunny had never mentioned him to me.

"Oh, congratulations," I feebly said, feeble with surprise.

"Yes," Bunny said, "I can't believe it myself, but just let me tell you—" and she began to describe her plans. What she said was much the same as what she wrote, the same day, to Ted Gorey:

*I am being married the 15th of April, and oh so tired of seedy little ceremonies in apologetic tenors—tenures?—am doing it RIGHT. We are being married at Christ Church with a reception here champagne and cakes and I am wearing ivory satin and seedpearls, everybody else can wear just what they want. All these weddings with a few self-conscious friends standing nervously with the family while some fink from the Community Church or the Ethical Society in black pointed shoes hastens through some inoffensive and anonymous vows bore me so. Red Kellogg is going to marry us and he is not going to mince a vow.*

*Bradley is not just nice he is fabulously nice and funny. I am very pleased about all of this. So are our families, not to say relieved. His parents are sending us to Europe in June and we are going to Paris and then Italy and then Spain. We are going to live in OLIVER WENDELL HOLMES' LIBRARY facing the Gardens just wait till you see with red silk walls and fireplaces . . . and a roman sunken bath. My refrigerator is lined in blue and has little flowers on the frozen food locker. This seems to be the year for freak marriages . . . Bradley and I went to Key West last month and also Havana . . . this is just like the Poets' Theatre, it's like a production I've got to spend all the time on the telephone about and then buying all these nippy things. We have decided to live like nobody else at all and to have a Ball about it. A great big cabbage rose clutter and furnishings at vast expense. No good simple pieces. You come see us . . . and I will serve you crabmeat à la paradis in my little fish dishes and antique oyster forks.*

And so it went on—every bulletin from Cambridge brought news of Bunny's acquisitions and wedding presents. Bradley, it turned out, was rich, and so were all his relatives. Bunny had made a better match than any of her sisters. Day after day things kept pouring in as if from a cornucopia: silver, china, furniture, money, a new car, a huge engagement ring. I was now eight months pregnant and could not travel to see it all, so Bunny kept me informed by mail:

*Pa gave me a great deal of money . . . I am buying all the nouveau riche things and hiding them away lest my sisters see them and be shocked, I have bought about $175 dollars worth of fancy underwear. Mac said, coldly, I never knew you had this side to your character, which all goes to show how little our dear friends know about us doesn't it. Then because the underwear is so beautiful . . . I had to go to Mackanna's and get a set of satin and lace covers for it . . . and all those lovely blankets and things with flowers on them too and made to order nylon sheets. Ah well . . . I realize I have told you all this before but isn't it FUN to hear it again?*

I was in the hospital with a new baby the day of Bunny's wedding, but everyone else I knew went, and they reported it to have been a great performance—bright weather, garlands of white satin ribbon, organ music, crowds of friends and flowers. In a classical cloud of rice and an enormous number of old shoes collected from the Poets' Theatre costume collection, Bunny and Bradley disappeared into their extravagant honeymoon.

England, France, Italy, Spain: the months went by, and still they kept putting off their return. In the wet cold of a London spring Bunny caught the flu, in Paris she went up the Eiffel Tower and released balloons, in Madrid she bought a bullfighter's hat which did not fit. It was not until late in the fall that they came back to Boston, opened up the apartment, and tried to find room in it for all their possessions.

I visited them there. The two rooms overlooking the Public Gardens were crowded like Mrs. Jack Gardner's museum with fine and applied art objects: statues, glass, books, pictures, and china. Among them were two paintings by Bradley, both in a style rather like magic realism. They were skillfully done, with a brilliant finished surface, almost *trompe l'oeil*, especially in that light. Even at noon it was dark, heavy with black paneling and red damask hangings; lamps carved by African natives in the shape of ugly black birds made little islands of reddish or yellowish light here and there. The larger of Bradley's paintings hung over the sofa. It was a study of two nudes standing on a balcony by an imaginary seashore. The man, drawn from the front, looked not unlike Bradley, with light brown hair, a long pale body, and an expression of dreamy worry on his face as he leaned against the railing and looked out over the grayish-green harbor, where a vaguely seventeenth-century ship was moored. Facing him, her back to the spectator, was the woman, heavy, with broad hips and blond hair done up in a knot; it could have been Bunny, though the picture had been painted several years before they met, and Bunny's skin was never that green-white color.

Though they had been back for several weeks, the apartment was still full of suitcases not yet unpacked; crates of china from Italy and France, leaking excelsior and shredded foreign newspapers; shiny white boxes from Shreve Crump and Low's in which silver wedding-presents rested among tissue paper. Bunny flew from one thing to another showing them off to me; she demonstrated the electric garbage-disposal unit, and made Bradley try on a suit which had been made to order for him in Spain. She told me the names of the exotic houseplants, and the two orange trees in green tubs ("Poor things, I don't believe they're ever going to have any oranges, but I've brought them some for Christmas"). She rushed through the apartment banging open doors and drawers, meanwhile keeping up a running commentary on all the gossip and local events which had occurred since we last met.

Tall, white, silent, Bradley followed us about with a slight smile of pleasure on his long pale face, such as an uncle might wear on Christmas morning. Obviously he enjoyed it all, but he enjoyed it all through Bunny. Previously he had walked through the world in a dim gray light; all his money and talent, all his freedom, were of no use to him, since he desired nothing. Bunny wanted things more passionately than most people; she wanted more variety of things, and took more pleasure in them. Her delight of possession proved to Bradley that these objects, places, and people were delightful. Or funny, or even terrible—the emotion did not really matter compared to the ability to feel emotion, which he seemed to be learning from Bunny. In the end, counting all the crates and boxes, she had perhaps given him more than he had her. I heard this day for the first time the royal "we" which they both used now: "We were mad about the Riviera . . ." "We like him, but we don't see the point of all this fuss about his new book."

Bunny and Bradley continued to live in Boston through that winter. They entertained, and went about in society; Bradley began to study to enter the Architectural School so as to become an architect (this project was later abandoned, but at the moment it made him seem more serious and career-minded than painting would have done). Bunny rejoined the Poets' Theatre, and was appointed Poet-in-Residence for the first half of the year under a grant they had just been given by the

Rockefeller Foundation. She read scripts, attended meetings, and played the lead in a Wild Western farce, *The Compromise*, full of Indians who said, "Ugh," and Royal Mounted Police who said, "I always get my man." The production was rather like Old Home Week, for the script was by John Ashbery, one of the founders of the Poets' Theatre who had emigrated to New York, and the cast included many of his and Bunny's old friends, including Greta Smith, Mac Hammond, George Montgomery, and Roger Jackson. Bradley was also in it, as an Indian brave, his face painted brick-red and decorated with feathers.

I saw Bunny and Bradley whenever I was in Boston during the rest of that winter and the spring which followed; always together, always seeming very happy. Indeed, some of Bunny's friends complained that they were too much together, and that it was impossible to see Bunny alone. Bunny was aware of this sentiment, but she did nothing about it. It was as if part of the bargain was that Bradley had to be allowed into all of her life. If anyone objected, or showed that they did not wish to see her with Bradley, she dropped them, with the same promptness and scorn she would have shown if someone refused to speak to her because she had on a dress or hat they did not like.

The last time I visited them that year was early in the summer. The school term and the Poets' Theatre season were over, and for the first time Bunny seemed cross and restless. The apartment on that warm June day was dark, hot, and cluttered; unpacked boxes and cartons still stood about in the corners; I could not tell if they were new, or the same ones. Another painting by Bradley had arrived. It was hung high up in a corner, so crowded had the walls now become, and was hard to see; but it seemed to show a heavy bunch of hothouse fruit in front of a dark curtain, one corner of which was pulled back to reveal a little distant pale-green pastoral landscape. The tables were crowded with books and fancy ashtrays, the mantelpiece with silver dishes and framed letters. Occasionally in the past, when Bunny had found herself especially hard up, or especially in need of new clothes, it had been her practice to take some small useless object away from the house and sell it: a silver candlestick, a needlepoint cushion, a bread-and-butter letter from William Dean Howells, a first edition. She never took anything from her father's room, or which he particularly cared for; she was stealing not so much from him as from her five older sisters, who would by rights receive some day five-sixths of what the Lang household furnishings would bring at auction. Now it was as if all these ugly, dull, valuable things had come home to roost.

As always on my visits, Bunny first went through the routine of showing me her newest possessions. This time there were some hats, a painting, and most important a mink coat, which Bradley had just given her. It was dark brown, almost black, lined with quilted satin on which Bunny's initials were embroidered in gold thread; yet as she showed it off she seemed tired of the whole thing. For the first time, my enthusiasm was greater than hers, for a mink coat was the absolute possession for Bunny, the final object; Max, she had once said, when he came at last, would buy her a mink coat. I even had to urge her to try it on, while she complained that the coat was too heavy, the day too hot. It was a superior mink coat as mink coats go, and Bunny explained its superiorities to me, but she seemed less delighted with it than I had seen her in the past with something she had bought at the Morgan Memorial for thirty-five cents. She put it away and turned out the lights; again the room fell into cluttered gloom, lit only from outside, where the trees of the Public Garden made a green haze beyond the heavy curtains.

"We've got to get out of here, we decided," Bunny said, "so we've rented an island." It was in Marblehead, she told me, and very isolated, though it was just off shore; at low tide you could walk across on the sand bar, but unless you caught the tide right your feet would get wet. I must come and visit them, she said, and she would row me and my bags across in their rowboat.

I said I might be able to drive up for the day, perhaps stay overnight. Bunny at once became cross. "No, you have to stay longer than that," she told me. "It's not worth your coming if you're going to act like it was a cocktail party. You have to come and stay at least three or four days. So you write as soon as you can, and let me know when to expect you. And don't bring the children. We hate children."

I did not go to visit Bunny. There was nobody with whom I could leave my children for three or four days for such a reason; I was irritated at her for being so peremptory and inconsiderate. It was the sort of thing that one regrets. One evening some weeks later, at the end of July, I was on Cape Cod, staying with a friend who allowed children. I called home, and learned that Bunny had been in the hospital three weeks and had died the day before, July 29, 1956.

I came back to Boston for the funeral. It was held in Christ Church, Cambridge, where Bunny had been married sixteen months before. She was as fortunate in her weather as ever; though midsummer, it was a green, soft, mild afternoon. As I walked through the Square, conspicuous in black among the summer dresses, I met other black figures, Bunny's friends, who had come, some of them, a considerable distance. People stared silently at us as we stood waiting in a group on Brattle Street, all dressed up, like those actors who come out in costume and mingle with the audience sometimes at amateur performances after the show. We were silent too: after the first greetings and expressions of dismay, nobody could think of anything to say. Some of the people met again there had been passionate lovers, or bitter enemies, or both; and on or near the street where they stood many violent scenes had taken place between them, but now it all seemed dreary and inconsequential.

When it was time, we walked in a silent bunch up to the church. There the Reverend Mr. Kellogg, clothed in a white tablecloth, addressed a long vague speech to God about someone we did not know named Your Servant Violet, while walking up and down and waving his hands in front of a large box covered with a purple velvet tablecloth which was blocking the aisle. It was as if he were trying, very badly, to give artistic and ethical form to something that had in fact ended as abruptly as a script torn in half by accident. Even the foreknowledge that Bunny had had not been enough to plan this scene; her great gift as a director and producer of life went only so far. I thought of the last time we had met, that hot dark afternoon in Boston; and now the apartment full of pictures and plants and furniture, the heavy mink coat which gave her so little pleasure, assumed the hectic, useless aspect of the Christmas-in-July presents so often photographed heaped high on the bed of a dying child.

Organ music played, and across the aisle from me Della, the Lang's old cook, cried, while several other former servants of Bunny's family, still older than Della, sniffled quietly under large hats hung with black beads and veils. In the pew next to mine tears ran silently down the face of a large handsome man in brown, who later turned out to be a policeman.

Afterwards, in subdued confusion, some of us were pushed into the cars which were to go to Mount Auburn Cemetery. It was a long drive up Brattle Street, where pedestrians turned to watch the cavalcade. At length we passed through Victorian-Egyptian gates into the luxuriant botanical-garden memorial park. Heavy, glossy with wax, the three funeral sedans slowed to a stop on the path against the grassy slope, one behind the other, laden with Bunny's and Bradley's relatives. The other cars drew up behind them. Mr. Lang made impatient motions with his elbows as one of his sons-in-law attempted to help him out of the first car; unassisted, he slowly sidled up the bank, digging his cane into the soft turf. Doors opened all along the line now. His daughters and their husbands, Bradley, and other relatives, made a group around the strange architectural construction on the grass: a pedestal of grass rugs and great bunches of yellow and white flowers, some beautiful, some vulgar with gilt ribbons. We stood apart from each other, oddly placed, rather crowded, even, among the stones, for as Bunny had said there were only two places left in her family plot; now only one; she had made it after all.

It was over; it was time to leave. But now something embarrassing occurred; Mr. Lang, who should have been the first to move, did not go. His eldest daughter, Margie, put her hand on his arm, but he shook it off; and said audibly, "No, I'm not leaving." It was a moment of helpless impasse, a breakdown of the ceremonial procedures of life and death. At last one of the relatives moved to his other side, and looking gray and crumpled he was led down the bank of grass to the car.

Rather than get back into one of the funeral automobiles, I

walked away along the path and up the hill, past stone angels and eagles, under trees heavy with flowers and foliage. When I turned to look back, the last cars were closing their doors and driving away. And now the cemetery men came forward. They lifted off the bunches of flowers, piling them neatly on the ground; they folded up the rugs of artificial grass, two and two, like women folding blankets. They removed and stacked up neatly at the side a series of metal braces, then a square of planks; and finally a rectangular hole in the ground was revealed, and a pile of dust beside it. Spades were unpacked from a box, and then one, two, rhythmically, they began to shovel, all silently, for I was too far above the scene to hear any sound.

I walked on among rosebushes and ivy-choked fences, and when I turned again they were gone. Now it was only a distant, pale-green landscape between trees such as one sees in the background of some Italian paintings, with a patch of flowers. On this midsummer day all of Mount Auburn Cemetery was like a painting, some crazy half-classical, half-romantic Arcadia, where Greek temples and laurel bushes stood next to marble Victorian nymphs wiping away marble tears under weeping willows. Here was an Egyptian monolith, there a Roman bust or mausoleum, next door a granite wickerwork bassinet full of stone flowers, with a silly-sentimental inscription which Bunny had laughed at the day we visited the cemetery. I was reminded of the change she had made in the title of her play, originally called ET IN ARCADIA EGO. Before the posters were made, a learned graduate student called her attention to the fact that the original meaning of this phrase, as it appears in paintings by Poussin and Cipriani (where shepherds gaze, frightened, at these words on a tomb), was "Death, too, is in Arcadia." Annoyed, she put the words into English, so that no one could mistake her meaning: I TOO HAVE LIVED IN ARCADIA.

# POEMS *by* V. R. LANG

# THE PITCH

1

Spring you came marvelous with possibles
Marvels sparked everywhere burning from bracken
Lichen leapt crackling, and long grass

And everywhere my feet went the ground swung up giddy
Green and joy-panicked, then winter went under wonder
Sun stormed white furious skies where we went running

Then nothing I touched that didn't burst into flames
Nothing I cried out that didn't catch fire
Nothing I called that didn't know its name

Then all the aisles of light the streets led somewhere
I streaked down never scaring or looking backwards
At nowhere behind me go small

2

But in the fall the earth fell and I followed
Fell and dropped me into darkness like a death
Where I shut out and dull and dour and tacit

Itched in the creeping stone that ate my flesh
Until in stone I stumbled, wandered,
Found a company that like me knew no wonder

But voiceless, weary, monolithic, walked around
An underground of seasons where the light like pain
Twitched where it touched us, and flaked down

## THE ELIZABETHANS AND ILLUSION

1

The legend of virginity seemed exquisite,
The present company boring and degenerate.
They praised a polished purity
Which calculated rarity.

All too aware of seasonal distinction,
And the inevitability of dissipation,
They agreed instead to honor the merry convention
That desire presupposes fruition.

2

Adorned, insolent, they peered from the Conceit
Without surprise into the impolite:
The dragons responded wonderfully to beautiful manners;
The fop successfully ordered the mutinous ranks.

Their smiles knew a fortune; their silliness paid.
Never among them came wandering One like a creeping
    plague
With a vast bewildered face, to moan, to cry *Gone,*
*Now is the castle dark, and the garden done.*

## THE BOOK OF DESTINY

*Songs to my Siamese cat, Destiny, who eats her young*

1

Destiny is not eager to claim
Five limber slicker small
Kittens she dropped before New Year's
From an irate womb:

All the doors of the heart have houses,
The greater profiting by the smaller:
The night languishes for the leaner,
While the day waits.

So Destiny is kind to them for a week, for two,
Giving them suck and tongue, but you
Will be angry at what she'll do.

2

Thick skin in the blow light
Hit a rod with a mallet;
Wholly into the red cave
Flew the marvellous bell:

Light knows something it can't tell:
*Stones see back.*
Hurry, hurry, harries the cat-call,
Prize the temeritous well!

3

Sick a cat on a dead dog,
Hear the scream of a church bell,
Hold the night in the eye of a rat,
To snatch the spell.

How high does the day go?
Stretched to the sunrise. Nine

Hours stung in a wasp's tail know,
Heard at a whispering door.

Over the dog's back flees the chill
Hungrily by
The cat's red eye.

4

The fuss tears the flesh, the terrible tears
Of greeting and breaking are here. Pride strains
At the great howl, light streaks,
And birth cries out at a face it makes.

When will the winter year, mother, pretender?
Blood is so very dear seldom, if ever.
Pigs into kettles can, light into roses,
But jealousy mangles the suck that it chooses.

5

Spoil of the night call, sorrow of ever,
Speak to the beast of the petulant morning,
Strike wail of doubt, but where is not ever,
Nor which about, nor benevolence mourning.

Proffer the night spoon, string the white shine;
Destiny, Destiny, never was mine.

You must remember the furtive chill,
The arrogant fruit of the moon, if you will,
The noise of the lightning, the shriek of the silk,
The shudder, the shock of the mother's milk.

## AFTER PERIGOT AND WILLIE

Once upon my (simple) Valentine
  *Hey, ho, pinching payne!*
Was a Plaisance in the sun
And the spotted rain.

Various Parts were debonair
  *Hey, ho, holidaye!*
Flesh and favor, scratch of fur,
Principals to play.

All are forfeited to words:
  *Hey, ho, graceless griefe!*
Now the hornet-singing birds;
Now the grass that hops beneath.

## PIQUE-DAME

Because they say of you that you are
Bloody and insolent but young and gay,
And that you play better than anyone,
Coming into the game at the end, because

They say of you, you are unbroken,
That you remained unbroken at the Break of Hearts,
And that when you look at a Diamond it cracks across,
Because your Court is the last Court

Standing at the threshold of the Great Gates
By the Ice Lakes where only the cruellest children
Your assassins go on skating, bright and
Murderous Pique-Dame, listen.

Pique-Dame, I am losing.
Save me, and I will play you.
I am not played out.
Save me, and I can play.

Pique-Dame, I promise, I promise you
There will be a great day of leaping,
There will be no uninitialed swing!
My jackknife everywhere    no pond no hoop no wheel
Unglittered by my red and yellow    my bracelets shall
Roll all over    I on my bicycle will
Cry up the tree toads, what a racket then!
Pique-Dame!
EVERYONE UP    EVERYTHING
VERY LOUD AND BEAUTIFUL    shrieking red and yellow
Calliope, calliope    every tree breaking
Ponds leaping wild    wheels    trees bracelets birds
The plums are wild    with what is coming
Everything a wonder    all open hands
Listen!    you've got to listen    *Pique-Dame! Pique-Dame!*

## LYRIC FOR THE FATHER OF A GIRL

The child that came a stranger from
A cold, troubled ocean—born
Flushed as a sea robin, wild as a sea lily—

Touched me like morning; as from sleep,
I followed her, perplexed, to her dominion,
Marine and violet, this somewhere cold and sure

I could not go without her. Here I tried to teach her.
By my small parent precision, taught her names:
Learning at last my language, she told me the hours.

Her feet unlocked doors, windows, hidden ways,
Mines at her touch spilled wide as shells;
She knew this. It was hers.

Sand shifted through her listening fingers as she
Walked crab-backwards in the salt sun. I heard.
Seals, just beyond us, barked and glittered.

Surrendering her, I found I had nowhere to go.
She called to me and stared. By my dry tongue,
She learned in words that I had taught her

Fear that made me strange to her. I told her,
*Sunday I'll come always*, but the sea grew small,
The shore turned black, and the tide flew out in a torrent.

## ARGUMENT

Poetry can never be much more than a commentary,
At best a breathless summation, for what words,
What words existed before their source?

Or if you will the eye itself the world it sees
And not the world a body independent of the eye,
Then poetry is another world, but however marvelously,

Only a beginning and a later disappointment.
If the word existed before the flood of being,
If the word struggled to become according to a senior plan,

Earth, water, intelligence, why then the vision of that order
However faint or obstinately narrow would be all.
But poetry is not word but words, it is not all.

The magic steal relates, subsumes, makes drunken estimates,
Adores, presumes, within a little order; it was never all.
It clings to being with dependent ecstasy; it cannot be
alone.

Poetry can never be much more than a commentary. It
may be
The quintessential of the race, but such come cheap in
nature.
It may achieve the Law with accurate economy

Or cry out past the bounds of consciousness, or cleave
The ugly wall to tear the dark into a further isolation,
Or sop or salvage, or explain, or desecrate, or be, itself,
salvation.

But this is not enough. It never was enough. Words are
not *there*.
Are never absolute to those who love them, do them honor,
Do not themselves create, but feed upon creation, lie
upon it

Supplicant as vision to that sun, our subtle force, our
 sovereign.
Sometime-indentured prisoner of fact in space cries out
 abundant
In this very knowledge of imprisonment, crying THERE.

## THE SUICIDE

Shocked that she missed the footbridge! She cried out,
But no later than the water she fell in and drowned in:
God help me, they tell us she shouted, but she had no
    sovereign—
No one at all to order her out of that water.

Now the animals have charted the land for their
    reasonable holiday;
All have appointed this time to be there to see them.
Photographers capture each other—the carnival quickens!
The spectres, the hawkers, the talkers, the damned are all
    there.

# TWO CATS HAVE KILLED A BIRD

*For Frank O'Hara*

We lay fat cats in a meadow under a milkweed sky,
Still from the thrush, the circling crow, the dragonfly,

Incurious, complacent, drunk with heat.
*What did we do, what did we do before we met*

*Our Variety?* Once, we could have done with One,
Before we learned the claw's design,

Before the needles of the tongue
Learned to strike the spine! Then,

Did the fur creep for a fire further
Than the skulking lover, later, could come?

Then, if we could touch each other,
Could we eat together? Was everything the same?

The lizard leaps from us! The cuckoo died
With a queer, bold cry!

Now there are Three—to kill, to keep, to claim—
We cannot lie with all of them.

## ALREADY RIPENING BARBERRIES ARE RED

> **Already ripening barberries grow red,
> the ageing asters scarce breathe in their bed.
> Who is not rich, with summer nearly done,
> will never have a self that is his own. . . .**
> RILKE, *Book of Hours*,
> tr. BABETTE DEUTSCH

1

This time was very like the last time,
A metaphor will do as well:
A stranger bathing in the sea survived a snail,
The real could not compete with the original.
Through these revivals I have held to one idea,
I have had it well or ill—

As large as life (my own), for reference—not knowing
Exactly what it is, but it is All.
Yesterday I drove four miles to get the mail,
Today I lie here going bad, you know I can.

The sun leaves the beach like the tide itself,
Washed out like water, soda-bright and mineral—
Sinks to the sand grass, then breaks fall
To sit above me on the dunes. I lay awake all day.
I stared at a burnt match six feet away
Stiff at my feet like a scarecrow's spine.
          So by a buried animal
Sometimes a stick will stand, without his name.

2

Seen at the beaches: stones. As various as profane.
Feet go back to whence they came.
Shins go back to knees and knees go Home.
I told you once, you have forgotten it,
How gulls from this island go at sunset
With the ferry to the inward islands, spend the night,
Return the next day or the next, indifferent
To where they were or will be, but expedient.

Just turning back to fly here with the morning boat.
Or so a day
We went to one of those bars.
There's nothing else to do at night here
Except the summer theatre
Or bathing in the bay
Or just to sit on porches, looking at the fog.
On Pentecost, I think it was,
A dog I patted bit me in the leg.
The people with me burst out laughing.
Nothing since to write that is amusing.

3

My head is bleached, the casing too.
I feel it beating when I shut my eyes.
I think the innocent may meet in Paradise
And speak together, still and blue.
I'll not meet you.

Children small, who race and stamp on beaches,
Whose cries go out to sea. They are themselves sea
    creatures,
Hard outside but soft in through.
They have no tongues for talking like we do.
If they should die
Before they go back to the mainland after Labor Day,
They would I know still speak together, still and blue.
We have no tongues for talking like they do.

Our fantastic bones bite inward and unseen,
Not sanded like a child's, not salty and not dry,
Not open to the wind, not bleached by sun.
Our flesh is all apparent.
                                        Our Selves are done and known.
They lie behind us pointing to the land.
The lists are taken and the weather done,
The letters written and the mailboat gone.
What we are is known by some.

The others need not guess.
Wherever we applied for permits or paid taxes,
We left reports of our engagement.

That time was wasted in the search for home.
Returning inland touched with sun,
I can watch the gulls without resentment.

4

Oh, so.
Heard at the P.O.: Hate. Nobody likes his mail.
Even the mothers of sons grow weak and spoil.
"I wanted a dog—" one wept, I heard her cry.
Or a white hawk, or a shark. That was July.

Time enough to compromise, when weather will not
fail;
Now the circuits spark and grab, that later will be cool.
Light can come
Only, I know at six in summer,
From what is dumb.

I will find the mirror image later, falling from
Bridges to bridge beneath.
Fountains, then, in quiet shows,
Equestrian statues,
In reflection come to faith
Crookedly contained in
Lines bent in from the horizon.

The sun makes bad.
Never so whole or well,
I climb to deeper than I can to sleep.
All I know is all I keep.
Someday, not today, I'll write you.

## DEATH OF ANOTHER SWAN: MIAMI

*"Mon Dieu! Quel catastrophe!*
*Il me devait quatre francs."*

1

Savage now with hunger at midwinter,
Still grasping at the plunder of the swifter,
She begged in order to be able to steal

Fruits and flowers and crawling vines,
Snakeskin envelopes for her arms,
Bird feathers over her face

And a sack to cover her, all of her,
Up to her neck where the dry plucked skin
Peered out, tied about with a bow.

2

Sitting so, she unlocked her throat,
And spitting her last, defied her creditors.

"When I die, leaving loneliness triumphant on this earth,
When I die as the impoverished sun snuffs out in a bag,
When I die let them tell all the world what I know:

That the wise are devoured by fools with red eyes—
Now let wild pigs claim the rest of you."

## THE REBUFF

Old crab bit my finger;
Searching under the rock to touch it
As it should be touched, lingeringly,
It bit me. Wicked secret crab.

*Blossom burned on the branches,*
*Old birds cried caw.*

There wasn't a thing on the earth I wanted
But the crab's kiss under the ledge of rock;
I poked my hand in the moon pool
And opened it wide in the dark.

*All for your love, dear, all for you.*

Old crab bit my finger. I made show
To the squinting spray and the sea anemone
Of my wound and my wisdom. You, too,
May stew in the juices of the sea.

*Was ever a pretty love song*
*Scalded the wicked, sun-living sea?*
*With blossoms burning on the branches,*
*Old birds going caw.*

## HOW TO TELL A DIAMOND FROM A BURNING BABY

Ride the wild horses out into the wood,
Let the wild dogs chase after, let them come too,
Ride wild and ride hard, we can come to no good.
At the end of the road lies a child, he is dead.

Ride the wild horses out into the wood,
Whisper to them we will find a set stone,
Let the wild dogs chase after as wild dogs do,
Ride harder and faster than ever we could.
At the end of the ride is a child, he is dead.

## A SUNDAY INDIGNITY

While she knelt the boys waited
Watching and sniggering with postures and gestures,
Concealed in the hilly humps, down in the grasses.
They rolled their eyes and she prayed and went daft,
And when, rising, she turned to discover them,
They jumped her.

Now consider this embarrassing spectacle:
Around them for miles the river, the silent rise
Of the green, the spiked, disparate wild roses
Grouped limp, with their thorns, and the swollen shrubs
Still in the thick white day, with the stealthy smoldering
Of the hot secret sun.

Here in the heat they were flushed, they were standing,
Her interceptors, proud of their primary life
Indulged in each other and squat like tubers, undersoil,
Secure in the moist dark, squeezing together.
She was the joke—being caught, being scared—
At the mercy of them.

When she looked at them with terror, they moved
All together, and closed in around her.
She screamed, but the river ran on and along
With the running of the day, the running of water
    rushes,
The upwards cluttered struggle of the growing roses,
The stillness of the secret sun.

## A REMORSE

When you were in despair
I grew there.
I of the winter the eye and the mouth,
You, poor bird, too cold to fly south.

I in disguises came you by;
You were the patch that hid the dead eye.

Lest you recover, less you get warm,
I was the cry and the vault of the storm.
I bid you ancient be, crippled of wing,
Hissed to you tenderly, till I got wondering

Who should serve as my old dead bird
When you understood and died.

## LINES FOR MRS. C.

*About to annihilate, in a long succession of cat murders, two old stray cats with ether, in her washing machine, with the cover on.*

*She finds them and locks them in the kitchen.*

O you cats, go home to God,
Kitties, where the saints have trod,
You go, you two, you too
Like thin flames upwards into
That which, electric and ethereal,
Is going to be your first square deal.

*They are not convinced.*

Kitties, go! Unspring those tails!
Cease wild scrabbling of those claws!
No longer roll these maddened eyes!
            —Trust me, kitties!
I who love cats know their problems.
Tonight you will sleep in the arms of Jesus.

*She puts the cover on, and sighs.*

They say down here you never knew
What life could be, because we stuffed you
Into the emptiness of ours.
                        —Well, yes.
But life is vile. So are its pleasures.
They say you animals that came in with us
Never had a chance. Horsefeathers.
Life is vile. So are its pleasures.

*The struggling grows fainter, and she waits.*

Mortal love was not for us and neither was
The Cross. We chose you.
O you cats, take from us
Our emptiness and our loss.
We have to lose you.
Go kitties, go, go home.
Kitties, go home, go home.

*She looks, and is satisfied.*

## LATELY BY LANGUAGE

Lately by language,
What broke I wonder, some heat I touched by,
Some stealing summer where

Greens overwhelmed the fall,
Made havoc of the sleeping stones, sprang
Wild about the wall.

A childhood lay behind us like an iron spring,
Some season lay beyond us like a stain,
When the river, caught between us as a
Slate burned scar,

Splashed up as we stood distant from each other,
And washed away like light. There was no longer
Anything between us but a locked surprise

Which watched the struggling rushes, heard
The shrieking birds, then fell about our feet.
We crossed. The light flew overhead.

Vines climbed up and everywhere we stood,
Until, afraid, we thrust them back, and turned
From the empty river, now grown tall and loud,
small animals rioting in its bed.

# ANNE, A CHORUS GIRL QUITTING THE LINE, TO SOCIETY

Don't stop loving me when
I leave the Line    Next week's routines
Are done with roses and balloons
And one with garlands, all the girls in green
Rehearsing now without me    I will yearn
For large red paper roses that remain the same

Don't stop loving me although
Someone else will have to do
A toe tap to
The Dance of the Hours    Remember I'm
Yours!    I love you better than
A night in costume, or another name

Say that I'm yours!    (I am)
Our Waltz Clog and our Elevées
Were ways like any ways to please
But never face to face    You must
Not love me any longer just because I'm One
Out front (with you) alone    I know

I'm one of you    I know
That everywhere I'll go
I'll have to tell my proper name    I'll sign
I LOVE YOU    and I'll always want You    A*N*N*E

## A CHILD'S FANTASY

When, early ago,
Stalks rose over my head and the line
Of the land escaped my eye, I

Telling myself nasty stories in bed
To amuse myself on the longest night of the year
Wound my early play green fingers around my head
And a black braid around each finger.

You beckoned from the near wood, a crow call.
I heard and jumped out of bed and crawled
Down the trellis, delighted.
Not to tear my nightdress I came
By the low fence. Not to wake the sleeping dogs.

One dog woke and followed after, you were cross:
"Whose dog is this?"
I said, "My family's, of course."
"Will he go home?"
"He might not. He's dumb."
"He should not have come."
He followed us to the water, then we turned on him.
We tied his head up tight with muslin,
We weighted him with rocks we found,
And giggling, pushed him in, and stood and watched him,
And poked him down with sticks until he drowned.
"There's for *him*. He won't tell now."

"Let's swim."
"They'll hear us."
"Who cares." We went in.
The moon spilled all over and trees walked on the river.
I screamed.
Stories I told out loud came alive on the wall.
Faces crawled out of my hands,
Slobbered and winked and crawled
Into every place.
                    I called

*V. R. Lang*

*No* when the dog barked. It banged
All over the house and the doors slammed.
The dog walked into my room and stared.
The dog walked into my room and stood.
Everyone came angry.
The dog isn't dead.
I know I *know*. I was just thinking.
In the window to my room my twin looked in,
Winking. Go to sleep again.
Winking. Play dead. Don't tell.

## BREAKING UP THE ACT

As *commedia* players
We cannot fool the City or ourselves.
Too tense, we soon go shrill.
Lines painted bright go
Gray in the hot lights,
Reveal the twitch and pull.
We will never be Favorites.
We had best go on by ourselves.

You were very dear.
You were very close to me, even in your anger.
However we are, thin or poor,
I will know where you are. Write me.
Tell me what you are playing.
I will never again nag or break up.
Write me and tell me where you are.
            I'll always answer.

## THEN ALL THE LISTENING CRIES OF NATURE

Then all the listening cries of nature cried out Danger:
Sorrow my listening stick, my severage, my savage answer,
Sorrow my text and my animal bruised wonder, sorrow
 whitely.

In the plains where the weather went to walk alone for
 always
I followed dumb and insolent to all the signs of stature,
Then heard the cries of nature crying Danger, Danger.

The world behind me never lost without me, memory
The soft black hang—the birds that broke about me,
Burst from the closet door when last I opened it,

The queer cry just distant, the crazed remembered wind,
The terminal scream of the marsh,
The net like a bell that swung for us—

Now heard against the fading voices, all the sprawl of dark
When animal life vanished, plants dried up and dusted
 down,
Leaving the weather to walk alone and always, walk the
 stretch of plains.

## WAITING AND PEEKING

"The tongue is a great magnifier, Mrs. Dubois." *My sister's dentist*

Nobody believes in Fate any more, nobody listens to the
 Norms.
Nobody solicits garlic or white of egg, or fears effigies.
But Things go on anyway, arranging everything that happens.

People think unkindly of others, and these in particular
Break out into horrible rashes, or die in convulsions.
Spirits sift and creep, and stones see back.

Trees and rocks and water and objects in public Parks
All go secretly, knowingly on, and every quiet, heavy Thing
Maintains its own life and its powers, peeking at us as it does.

## SUICIDE NOTE

Before life when I wreathed the wall as a shadow
I loved you all for the entertainment you gave,
Your bad and your good alike I loved, I loved,
I was moved by your good and your bad alike.

Now I am older than them and younger than you,
And wrapped in life like the package I came in
I can stand on the table and tell you all, all,
All of you listen a moment, to what I can tell:

That I hate you all and I hate you more
Than even in my tongue caught now in hy head like a
 clapper can tell,
That no more do I wish you but what I've had, I've had
At your hand and your tongue, I wish you may always have
 that.

May this child scream and may that child wail,
May your husbands foul and your wives go stale.
I wish you no petty dismays, I wish you a lingering curse,
I wish that your days all cheat you and your nights do
 worse.

This goes for all of you, not one left out,
Not one day left unblackened or one night unsoiled
And for the mornings panic when you wake, when you
 wake,
Panic to stare at the ceiling and look into the morning light.

All this I wish you and it is too little for you.
I wish you this: that you always know what is happening to
 you,
That from too much hope you never learn strength,
That the world rolls over and over with you and you.

## FROM A FANCIFUL MAP IN THE CHILDREN'S ROOM

The Edwardians were not suspicious
Of symbols, having plenty of their own:
Living (the ones that knew they were Edwardians,
That is) in peace and plenty, content
With their especial pleasures of elegance and
What they called Nonsense, a symbol was
Domestic to them, such as Flag, Tomb, Home,
The Cross. Of sunken and unmentionable symbols,
Key, Box, Fish, etcetera, they were innocent,
And innocent they lived, preferring not to notice
Or to recognize what we with childish malice
Found explicit in the iron deer on their lawns.
So they lived and complacently taught Faeries
To children who suspected Nana was a man.
At home we have a map of Faeryland
Peopled by all the adult legends
Found to be charming by the Edwardians.

> When you were sensibly inviolate, you could not see
> Your mother watching your inconstancy.

This country resembles the United States.
"Here they doe magick" is written in one place,
Another, "Here are no soundings," and there were none.
Here men lose their souls and there they drown.
"Here is Peace Pool," "Here is Gairfowl."

> You stretched and broke, the green flood took you out,
> You flashed and darted where she could not go,
> But piteously calling, tried to follow, follow
> Undersea to dumb and show.

At Cape Blanchefleur is shown Leander,
Struggling to get out of the water and
Shaped like a young girl—Art Nouveau bodies
Were like these, uninterrupted verticals—
The Argonauts shown sailing on Leander, he will drown.

The Snow Queen shown to be innocuous, as she is
Back to, on the water in a rowboat, with no clothes on.
"Here they doe make Snow and Ice."
"Here is Shiny Wall."

> Your light swam wild, her light queered out;
> She could no longer see to where you were,
> Or longer breathe, or force the waters backward
> To call you to her.

Roughly in the latitudes of Texas sails,
On the Enchanted Sea, Tristam of Lyonesse;
He passes the Gold Caverns, by which stand Satyrs.
In this airless afternoon he does not pass
Solomon's Ship, wherein are Sacred Spindles,
But he is close, too close, to Mermaide's Rock
"Where they doe singe." The map says this to warn him.
At Georgia Bay, Perseus rescues Andromeda,
Naked, from an ineffectual monster. Near Maine is
The Beach of Pearls. "Here Cousin Cram Childe weepeth,"
For what, we never learned.

> She cried your names out, joy and her decision,
> Who seized the light reflected from your own;
> Then when you did not answer she grew shrill,
> bewildered,
> Lost her way and turned to stone.

Where in this map would be Alaska, there are
Pictured steps, and someone on them climbing
Named Amfortas. The Grail is just beyond him.
After that, the undistinguishable tundra
At the top and marked in shadow, then to where:
What the children always knew is there,
"The End of Nowhere," except that this map
Would place it further from them than the Park.

> Here they doe magick, here are no soundings:
> Children are not concerned, there is no world but
> theirs,
> There is not time to mourn for what is taken,
> Or what disappears.

The Park is now a slum, but we are old for parks;
We turned from magic long ago to politics,
Having to learn one's dearest wishes come
By art, by cunning, and by sleight of hand.
The house is gone, the Park is done, the boat went down,
But something waits, listens, something always moves.

Now with all the fathoms measured, time has come
To call. No one will answer, you will make no sound.

## AT THE MEETING OF TWO FAMILIES

Who were the assassins that came out to get you?
Six of them coated in black and silently smoking—
Slithering quiet like empty clothes

Alert in the dark, from hangers.
Who were they that came out to watch you?
Chewing cigarettes they looked at you, they looked at me.

What in a hay moon hovers and waits like a bag
With a man in it? Why did you make
Your face like a Japanese mask of terror to style?

Limply arranged they waited, just waited.
As always I gave back your terror, I took it,
Performed it, returned it to you—

And we stared at each other and back to our interlocutors,
The bareback riders from kingdom to kingdom—
You knew them, I knew. You remembered.

Why is your dark like a bag with a man in it?
In the moment of panic, hardly anything happens,
But nothing is true. I remembered, I knew.

I cried out, and the light broke. Your family
Pronounced me charming. My love, my love,
We will scratch all over the dusty earth crawling

The way out of dread we've no name for, could not tell.
We will come to dread all we own as well—
Till you wake and weep, till you break the spell.

## A LOVELY SONG FOR JACKSON

If I were a seaweed at the bottom of the sea,
I'd find you, you'd find me.
Fishes would see us and shake their heads
Approvingly from their submarine beds.
Crabs and sea horses would bid us glad cry,
And sea anemone smile us by.
Sea gulls alone would wing and make moan,
Wondering, wondering, where we had gone.

If I were an angel and lost in the sun,
You would be there, and you would be one.
Birds that flew high enough would find us and sing,
Gladder to find us than for anything,
And clouds would be proud of us, light everywhere
Would clothe us gold gaily, for dear and for fair.
Trees stretching skywards would see us and smile,
And all over heaven we'd laugh for a while.
Only the fishes would search and make moan,
Wondering, wondering, where we had gone.

## A CHORUS FOR PRUDENTS TO SING

When we thought to climb the garden wall,
*These vines will cling to us*
When we thought to creep through the circus tent,
When we thought, the train—but dared not, after all,
*We are rich, in soundings*
Just at the nick our good sense struck, we never went.
Oh and the trains, we knew, went beyond the earth we knew
By league after league of fear, that stopped us too.

And where the train went might have been without return.
We might have cried for thirst, or never found the bathroom.

There might have been a happy land, antique and fair,
*Oh vines, grow tall!*
A waiting ship, the crossing queer, the straits eventful;
We chose instead the islands, they were there.
*Suspicion, bless and keep us!*
Now come to dignity, we're here—and grateful.
We fidgeted, yes, as children, tossed in sleep.
But then we had no care to keep.

And where the ship went might have been without return.
We might have cried for thirst, or never found the bathroom.

Oh surely see that we, no longer young, were wise!
*These vines shall not surrender us!*
At the circus, we might have had to stand and stay
And stare forever; outside the garden what surmise
*Where words are dangerous*
Might guess the hour or season, or what strangers had to say?
Here now we watch, and wind our clocks, and safely sleep.
Here all we cherish are the cares we keep.

## CATS WALKED THE WALLS

1

Cats walked the walls and gleamed at us:
You remember, I remember,
The ceremony at ache's place.

Love you, love you I do, love you,
Ham, shank and shoulder, lights too.
You remember. I do.

2

The dead planted the holly, it grew like hair.
The dead sat back and sucked their crooked fingernails
When you and I set out with our haversacks.

The road had a million suggestions;
In return, we kept irritatingly silent.
Finally annoyed, we jumped out of our skins.

We stripped our hair and nails, and stamped
Upon the road, which kept it down. After that
We blew up like balloons and blew along.

The air astonished us by heaving. We flew.
We grew quite wild, our faces turned to smoke,
Our eyes peeked through. Like pebbles under snow.

All this some time ago, and only our bones remained
To answer bells, to say hellos,
To ask gay questions in ski clothes, after dark.

3

On a mountain in the winter, a little mountain,
God knows what you'll find. Christmas trees. Bright
Little berries. White animals that smell and flee.

Birds in an icicle tree. And underneath the snow
The minerals burn black, and blood, and nervous blue
And diamond and mine. The bushes creeping through

Cover them over by bony fronds. They creak and stir.
The animals do not care. The wind falls down.
No one minds. The birds fly furiously back.

4

Now about the end. They cursed us.
Just at the time we climbed the bend, they cursed.
We came upon them in autumn, bent to their mineral
    planting.

We waved to them in Tyrolian caps. Hello!
It was they, we discovered, who had to
Plant all the mines, and mulch them.

Everything but the animals, who were
Elsewhere planting. We're here to help you!
We caroled, which is when they turned and spat.

5

I have a cat who walks walls, and watches us.
I can guess who planted *him*. No mordant wrong
Has been righted since that time. No fine thing

Has happened or been said, no dead or living animal,
No mineral, no winter-growing vegetable
Has laid its hand upon our hearts or touched us.

We are pale enough. But that's not good enough for them.
They listen eagerly. They hope to hear us coughing.
You remember. I remember. Here they come! Hurrying.

Love you, love you I do! Love you!
Ham, shank and shoulders, lights too.

## BORN OLD

1

The house was on fire, he knew:
He woke before dawn, and still

As the upstairs breathing he dressed
And dropped from the window sill

And edged to the wall of the garden
To creep unseen to the hill.

2

The woods were as hushed and as dark
As his sleep, but he found his way,

The forest squeaked and a bird
Cried out, but he pushed them by,

And the wet grass plucked at his knees,
But he scrambled through to the valley.

3

He looked back once and saw
Where the ridge behind him was high

The lion his love, grown little,
Standing anxious against the sky.

But the house was on fire, he knew,
And he blundered through to the valley.

4

The valley was flat as glass,
He slept where he struck his head,

But he shook with the spider's twitch,
And stretched in a caked web,

And woke in the dark for the lion who
Once struggled into his bed.

## OLD BELLE

I did not live by the land, I did not watch the sky;
I took one rich harvest after another from the sea.
One day I saw the nets were thin, and wondered.
The next I was frightened and bought new equipment.
After that I was frenzied and my savings went fast.
I am not bankrupt yet. You can taste time in my gestures.
While there are drugs and liquids and solids and solvents
Manufactured to daze and to shield and to mask
Loss and panic, I shall have them. And each time,
Still, that I make loud my original investment,
My competitors, grown old as I am, stiffen and look anxious,
Buried in their rooms with the ruined photographs.
What I cannot understand is the injustice: I, as
Few can boast, worked ceaselessly and sacrificially,
Sparing no yearnings to talk, just for once, greedily
About myself or to laugh out loud in my partner's face;
I knew the rules and I obeyed them, even despising them,
With exquisite precision. Was it for this
The craters opened up and sucked the springs inside?
Is it just, I ask you, when I worked so desperately hard?

# SONG

Only the false are falsely true,
Only the true are truly false;
You are false, and you are true.
    Sweet child. Sweet song.

He was a many-veined monster
But I loved him for his bleached hair;
He fell flush with the whitest stare.
    Sweet child. Sweet song.

Days these days were cold and dumb;
If I held something in my hand
He always knew. He was never wrong.
    Sweet child. Sweet song.

Why those who know are holiday.
Those who know and those who tell.
Touching cannot be for long.
    Sweet child. Sweet song.

You will walk a thousand stairs,
Age to crawl a hundred years,
    Then yearn
Cold and hot, eye and ear,
What you touched for what you were—
    You'll weep
For what you laughed out loud in sleep.
    Sweet child. Sweet song.

## YOU KILL ME

You kill me. Yes, you do.
I know no one else who'd
Buy a sparrow (I
Didn't even know they *sold* sparrows)
Just to feed it watermelon
And in public, too.

Every afternoon I think of you
Out there, flushed and fair,
Scraping the exhausted rind with a spoon.
Every day! All winter.

## POEM

Somewhere he not anywhere no
In such a place this anywhere he
Is monumental as monuments go . . .

In that excision,
In that chaste climate,
Look well who hopes well,
That fall is a long fall.

Oh, devil take Mary and pluck out her fingernails,
I am a stuck site and the laws of the land are binding.
Pick up your fence wire and the cords of delivery,
I am not pleading a choice, I have forgiven that.

Agnes wet-her-bed. Her mother has perceived it.
Agnes dreamt of a beast she never saw.

## OLD BEAUTY

God forgive me, I do not any longer care.
That I have broken tender habits of a hundred years,
That I should hurt you touch me not at all.
No longer bless you, no longer shall conceal
From your defiant, eager, prurient alarm
Your fatness, thinness, your inability to dress,
Your little eyes—perhaps the question of your face.

No longer will I ease you, bless you, so that you with me
Become the marvellous, as if the rest of life
Had not existed, had been in error or asleep
Or victimized by fools or the very cruel.

Go back to where you were. Some recent year
It happened that the touch of water or sun
Could no longer please my body, nor caress . . .
I try to keep cool only, in the afternoons
I sleep with the shades drawn and in the evenings, rest.
So soon ago your importunity
Crowding to speak to me in the theatre lobby,
At the wedding or where my children learned to dance
Amused me and I was tender for you,
Aware of your pride or your pleasure in being seen
Talking to me, of your eagerness to be known.
You thought, all of you, always, that my soft hair,
The lineage of my face, my eyes' felicity
Set greatly as they were in shadowy sockets
And turned to you—enough that I could tell you what you
were.

I never knew what you were, perhaps never cared
Except that I was tender, and did not let you know.
Now in the evening sun I will not even listen,
I like to whine, to quarrel with my children—
I am become absorbed in the precise, the small,
Will watch a hummingbird for hours, will sit still.

## TO FRANK'S GUARDIAN ANGEL

May he, secure
In peacock fur
And Manner,
Go in your favor,
May he wear
One crocodile tear
Stitched to the cheek at
The corner of the lid

*You pray for him, you weep instead,*
*Keep his appointments, bless his apartment*

Protect him from
Violation:
Bogs not creep,
Bugs not come,
Burrs not fall,
Crows fly white,
Caves not cackle not beckon,
Let him keep his Three Noses

*Save him from the malevolent harms of*
*Spiders but do neither throw him to the swans*

And shine on his spotted tail!
Yes, on his spotted tail.
Shine on his reason,
Protect his tongue

*Then in the jasmine and buttercup*
*Season of parricide, flower him*

## WHY ELSE DO YOU HAVE AN ENGLISH HORN

Why else do you have an English Horn if not
To blow it so I'll know to let you in?
It could be anyone, unless you do. I could be
Holding in my hand an effervescent
Preparation for the teeth, or doing swimming
Exercises on the rug, or wrapped in one
Staring privately out the window.
                And I dread bag snatchers.
Someone could be there, who would snatch my savings,
My blue glass swan I had even before I married you
All filled with quarters. Well, I can tell you,
That would be the end of our roulette games.
Therefore, use the horn, I'll never be alarmed,
I'll come at once and sing my friendly answer,
From Thaïs, you know the one, and you'll be reassured
It's me and we will both rejoice it is
The other. That is the song for which Walter Damrosch
Found so many friends in radio audiences, it goes,
WE ARE FAT GIRLS AND BOYS! WE ARE FAT GIRLS AND BOYS!
Then let not the others, delivery boys, Nosey Parkers,
Burglars, bag snatchers or Red Feather representatives be
    jealous:
When you find your own true love, you will live in a house,
You too will have to have a password.

## THE BEAR

For all I have to thank a lot I have
To thank THE BEAR. I think a lot of him,
I think of his dear ways and his unselfishness,
His merry gaze and his ingenious remarks
Which so enlivened our Saturday night card parties.
How he twinkled when he awarded the prizes for Hearts!
I remember his rapt paws caught in the first instance,
And the big teeth that sparkled when he talked to lawyers.
His undercoating looked vulnerable, somehow,
I used to watch it getting into taxis with a pang,
Or his gambols! Such savagery, into the wind!
But he was never cold, he said. I miss him!
I miss him! I shall never be over missing him.

## 25 YEARS

We got through this year and nobody;
We got through this year and perhaps.
On the day of the white crow somebody
Will kiss us and keep us, but this was not this year;
This year is over and nobody; this year is next year now.

Here is the hole in the wall. Here we peek.
Here is Chanticleer. We shall do everything but speak.
We shall bless, address, abuse—we shall not speak.
Had we to love or were we at fault?
We were confused, affection or assault
Proved only beasts will eat themselves or anything:
Let us join hands and dance around the naked king.

This year the creeping itch was apparent in the left hand,
This year perhaps it will sneak to the right, we will see.
The eye shivered at the slack it saw it did not understand;
The white crow never came to kiss us under the pear tree.
Twenty-five are pinching parents, poppy-addled, fed-on-us—
We wept our dusty latter thoughts, we stretched and scrabbled loose.
O! the day of the white crow will come, when it will come it can;
Then shall we shake our sticks, o years, in wicked triumph then.

## WHO IS THE REAL OSCAR MOLE?*

* Accredited translator of *The Debauched Hospodar,* a pornographic novel by Apollinaire.

Lodged under layers of things in his mouth
Are words we haven't heard since Editions
Minuit (*peuples! à genoux!*) cost us a
Sou or two but oh, the times our money had!

His nom de plume has a funny beard and a
Violet cigar. He is *always* where we are.
From the sidewalk, he sees us, and stealthily,
Before we can cry, WAITER! He reaches for

Our glass of Byrrh, or turning up his nose at it,
Your glass of *Pschttt!* or your *Perrier citron,*
Then he bubbles at the waiter and offers him some.
Who is he, really? His nose holes quiver with derision.

O, he has a wildebeest's eyes, not nice,
And a tongue like an ice pick, he could core an apple with it,
But he speaks to movie stars, and rides to parties in their cars
With them to take part in violations—

Or where, at the very least, an important new
Perfume is introduced. Oh introductions!
We think, if he would give us any, or a few,
We could at last do all the things we've wanted to,

Some day, we think, he must.
But now he doesn't want to see the pictures in our wallets.

You know that Poison Tree of Blake's? Well, look at ours:
First a plantain, now a palm, until we sit in darkness
Under giant fronds which Oscar susurrates.
He knows he makes us cross and jealous. Yes,

But where is the monkey in the tree to throw the nut
At Oscar's head? There isn't one because,
If Oscar Mole is real, there can be no real monkeys.
Horror! it is our money, but he has ordered a *fine.*

## TO A GOSSIP

If I were King
I'd stop your tongue
Whenever it began to run.
If you persisted, and made fun of me,
Under your window
Vengeful policemen
Would come. With guns.
You would hear them, and shriek NO,
But you would have to go.

Or I could legislate your ruin, as:
I'd say no Portuguese could come
Into my Kingdom, and that you were one.
But if you were already in,
Then tax collectors should come
And carry away everything you owned.
Appointments should be made to torment you, as:
If you wanted, for instance, raisins, you should have none.
You would understand, and be angry, and shriek NO.
But it would be so.

If I were King
I'd listen
Very carefully and
The first mean, supercilious thing you said,
Ha-ha, off would go your head.

# IT CAN FREE US

It can free us from the
Tins we are tinned in and the
Jars jarred in and the cans canned in,

The closets locked in and the
Beds we find we cannot move from. Or
It can make fools of us all. It could tomorrow.

You know how it does that. You've seen us
Riding on subways, the love splattered all over
Our honeydew heads and the faces we make.

You know, you've looked away when we spoke.
We spoke loud and made some others look,
We were smiling too eagerly and you were embarrassed.

We've stopped you on the street and asked the time,
We've started talking to you waiting for a bus.
On the subway, it was worse, the others looked.

We tripped over your feet in a movie and
Insisted on telling you how we were sorry.
That time, we even patted your shoulder and
Picked up your package we knocked to the floor.

You saw us coming at you at a party all smiles
And turned to hide, that was because
You saw us spill the drink and trip on the little table.
We struck up conversation with you at the drugstore
    counter,
Asked if you liked to read. That time you moved.

We looked at you out of a trolley window and burned with
    love,
And you turned frightened and turned in a Fire Alarm.
The Police came, but we had run off, weeping, to play with
    dogs.
We wanted you to speak to us in the street,
We were eager to pick up your oranges in the public place

Where you dropped them and they fell all over, but you
stopped us
Knowing we wanted to make friends.

You saw us sitting on the park bench looking hopeful
And happy and foolish and garrulous, and you walked the
other way.
We heard you say, you can't be safe.
We understood. You had seen us talking to ourselves
Or, unawares at that moment, at some game
Like skipping the sidewalk lines, or talking to the pigeons
Or—at our age—carrying a balloon.

You glanced at us making Fools of Ourselves
In the Public Gardens and hurried anxiously on.
No one has the right to be hilarious alone
In public, you said justly, not even throwing
Bread to the municipal swans and pigeons that waddled by.
We heard your exasperated sigh too late to
Disguise our delight in what we thought was to
Turn into a playmate because, if you looked at us, why
Wouldn't you want to throw them a handful of your own?
We had looked up and laughed and nodded and held out
our hands
With the crumbs in them, and our mouths were open to say
*Have some*. You walked through our smiles and left us
To pretend we were smiling at someone else or just
Blink foolishly and try to make friends with the swans.

*Why don't you want us?*
We love you so much,
We could have such happy times.
Or we could just pass the time of day
Sometimes, when you weren't busy.

## DUMMY IN THE CROWD

We, amiables, thumpers, animals,
Tumblers and performers of a very little fate—
Might have forgiven him (for all he did was stare at us!)
Had he but acknowledged us, sadly, his complicity;
We only asked he *suffer* that complicity.

We were his *family*, and wept for disavowal;
He stood outside the ring in proud disguise, he masked
As audience. He might at least have clapped his hands,
Applauding us, acclaimed our dance in bottle green!
But he who danced for no one clapped his hands at
nothing—
Oh, by his scorn of us he orphaned us to shame!
The children grew distorted in his glance, the women
plain,
And all our pleasant antics seemed ridiculous;
Even our marching animals seemed ridiculous.

There were those of us who hated him, and disappointed
children,
And we did not forgive him, who betrayed us by denial,
Whose mockery was immobility throughout our Grand
Performance;
But had we seen the child take aim we surely would have
stopped him,
The child, the murderer, who delivered us, who shot him,
Who severed head from neck with sprung cork of his pop
gun.
Oh, when we knew, we flew, we flew to him with pity in
our eyes,
To find he was not real at all, but bound to joint with wires!

He was our blood—how should we know he was a Dummy?
No one of ours before has been a Dummy!
We bade him rest, and stood about in strong variety,
Sad in our bright parade of pantaloons, of colored hose—
And all of the leaning curious, the paint concealing

The wonder on our faces, bent to look at him.
Then where there would have been (from children)
    laughter,
The elders of us scolded us severely, saying:
*Let his assassin weep for him, let melancholy women*
*Fold on his sawdust heart his hands, by his paper sword.*

## JUNGLE

When our eyes were early green
We turned our monkey palms
Beseech-side up to open arms
And gibbering crumpled in;
These have carried us to harm,
Now our eyes are cyclamen—
We ravish what we can.

## INCANTATION TO THE AGE OF STONE

Since you can no longer be
A stranger, you shall be a city;
I shall come,
            You shall stay,
Incurious in the noon of day
As your great lizards lying sleeping in the sun.

Since I do not hope to learn
A language other than my own,
I shall change.
            You shall sleep,
And in hot stone your stillness keep;
Then all my other learning will grow far and strange.

You my host shall cast no shadow,
Nor carry hill, nor lie with meadow,
Valley or tree.
            I shall become
Unknown to giant size and dumb,
Nor season change what I shall sleeping learn to be.

## THE BANKRUPT

The gilt, the gold, the bright, bright bird
Still called into the mocking quiet;
The winter forest watched, and heard
Him crying as he went.

He broke, by the pity of the sun,
By the hammerlock trees in green defile,
Who saw him fail with summer done,
            And silently moved in
To cover over him, upon his fall.

## WHEN I CAME BACK UP OUT OF THE DARK

When I came back up out of the dark (Tuesday)
With the dark still on me, a kind of you
Stared me down like a dead sun.

And I in my black crawl wondered,
Knowing where worms were, mud and spoil
And silence, what should I owe a dead sun,

But shriveled coming up, and that was my delivery,
And shed as I walked upright all my reasons,
Ash and a little lost frenzy. Pity me.

Pity the skin that tears and the skin that leaks,
The features that hang loose, the inert limbs,
The hands that cannot clutch, that cannot speak,

Pity the breakage—somewhere leaked away the core
And the skin with the tear cannot cover—
Pity the healing fluids spilt upon the light,

Pity the flowers broken at the stem, pity the cracked
And the shattered and the torn, pity me, not them,
We ache who break them, we attend with fright

Our damages, too late we learn them,
Then go underground, go home escaping them.

# ADDRESS TO THE REDCOATS

## THE CASE FOR THE COONSKINS. MAY 1954

### 1

They didn't ask me to speak.
Who am I, to speak for them?
No one. And by no appointment,
I came, and your faces frighten me,
As always.    But listen.

We can all remember the days
Of the Indian uprisings, massacres,
Rebellions. They are embarrassingly close.
We fought with the Indians then.
You took some of us captive, brought us
Bread and water, and lectured us.
"Recant," you said. "You'll have
To burn your precious pamphlets.
What's it all worth? Life
Is very short." Then,
Wearing coonskin caps, we spat.

In those days, when we met
To plot against you, and to create
Secret manifestoes for our faith
And defiance—we dared to
Carry no papers. If accosted,
To and from meetings, we pled ignorance
Of even our names, or we stared, silent.
That was before the present age.
Nobody wants to remember those times.
Now we are all at peace.
Everyone likes everyone else.
We are all friends.
Now we walk the streets as equals.
Electronic chimes
At noon play themes from
Charles Ives, for everyone.

Little children can read what they please.
We do our work by daylight.

Now, Fellow Americans,
Fellows in *eagerness of heart*,
We have been granted our rights—
You acknowledged yourselves
Gracefully, as always, the losers:
How did it happen, that we, victorious,
Came to belong to the spoils?
What has become of us?
Strangely, we have taken the place
Of the Mercenaries. Whatever
We fought for once looks foolish
Now. Our limbs are locked in peace.
We are, in grace and fortune,
Noncombatants with good manners.
We tend to forget that you never
Actually trusted us—so pleased are we
To have achieved this harmony, this
Mutual respect. No longer roughnecks,
We all wear red coats. As if
To say, although indigenous,
We are civilized.

Of the coonskins,
Only a few have kept
Their principles. The rest
Are glad to go outdoors in coats
Of red—or Oxford grays,
Or black ties and homburg hats,
Or academic gowns.
What coonskins do exist
Are murderous, and without honor,
And in low places—
Vestigial reminders of hostilities.
You have assimilated us.
How did it happen? Perhaps
We were demoralized by peace.

2

Could it be, you said.
Not long ago,
That what we were about
Was not a swindle?
In the colleges, you asked,
"Could they be serious?" You asked,
"Might they grow up to be Institutions?"
And in the moment of your indecision,
We moved in.
Moved in, by a slow and considered
Procession, to
The magazines, the newspapers,
The charities, the churches,
To municipal politics, to
The Parent-Teachers' Leagues.
And some of us gladly grew up to be Institutions.
These march in parades,
Campaign for presidents,
Speak at boys' schools, and
Lead Lenten discussion groups.
Or just, from a distance, pronounce.

Moved in we did, we moved—
But when it was all done, and
We could stop, to listen—
We were puzzled by a dreadful silence.
It was all very well when we were proving
How wrong you were about us—
That was the game.
But winning, we wondered what it was
That we had won. It seems
You don't know what you want. You never did.

Not first prepared, you usually insist
On nosegays—but we took this
Too seriously, became
Too marvellously accomplished
About nothing. We wrote poetry.

We wrote about summer resorts,
Flowers, and household articles.
Or we achieved this astonishing
And not infrequent *impasse*,
Poems about poems, poems about
Poets being poets writing poems.
You approved, and the nosegays were published.

Even among ourselves, we no longer
Speak too freely. We are wearied, or afraid.
We are not easily provoked.
Controversies alarm us—the last one
Almost set our cause back twenty years!
Years in which we had become accustomed
To pleasant lives, sustained
By generous trustees, years
To peaceably translate the Classics,
Years of handouts. Years to let
Our heads grow fat.

Now we turn to look
At one another, and to stare
With eyes like bubbles.
The Code exacts responsibilities.
The New Law says:
"We will accept you, but you must
Supply what courtesy demands, or as
The gentleman from the Times has said,
Be Wholesome, Positive, and Wise.
It's little enough to ask."
To wit, Society needs, will publicize,
And will subsidize, Yea-sayers.

Sometimes, at your bosom,
We've had reason to regret what
We have become, or that we are
Beholden. But,
To bite the gracious hand
That slips into reception lines
Carrying glasses, on a tray,

Is not for us.
Seen everywhere at work on our Projects,
Fellowships and Foundation Grants,
Or operating our little businesses—
Look at us! We are honest,
Modest, and self-effacing.
Could we bite? Now, I ask you.

But the present choice is ridiculous.
No longer a question of endurance—
The hunger-struck are fed—or martyrdom.
Now, we choose instead
To be priests—or Popular Tories.
The game is done! We've won, we've won,
Take everything. You are not welcome.

3

You want to believe in Dylan Thomas, as
A Great Romantic, whose life cast
Beams like the sun, go ahead—
We are by cowardice committed
To your displaced applause.
Roethke, you say,
Has taught you what can be got
Out of the garden.
Auden brought you back
To your church, after too long away,
To see a play.
Feed us, clothe us, keep us, pay,
And our way shall be your way,
Together we'll all honor
Foolishly.
But one warning.

Some, unregenerate, treacherous,
Catty and unvanquished, will be a problem:
Will answer no friendly and well-meaning question
Such as, "What are you working on?" such as,
"And when may we expect a volume?" such as,

"And what's the news about your Play?"
With anything but villainous manners,
If not abuse.
Will persist in behaving as if
They were plotting a criminal act,
And you had asked about it.
Will hide away from public inquiry.
Will dread exposure.
Will not contribute to group discussion
Of "What Does Modern Poetry
Mean To Me?" or, "The Poetic Drama—
What Is Its Place in This Country?"
Or Symposiums having the theme,
"Are We Communicating?" Will welsh
On social obligations, and much worse:
Will consistently betray their friends;
Will be guilty of sudden, mysterious treacheries;
Will desert their wives, if any, and may not
Support their children. Will even—
As incorruptibles will—corrupt the young,
Who will always want to serve them.
Will say, as Gauguin does, *Life*
*Being what it is, one dreams of revenge.*
And all these monsters will share particulars,
Could be said to *regress*, in the same ways:
That is, they trust no one and nobody,
Certainly not themselves.

They look at all that is close,
And at those who love them, with
Suspicion, save one thing.
Save language alone, and this
They honor and trust, and turn to
In all situations requiring appeal.
If they can be said to be loyal,
It is to language. If honest,
By the honor of thieves, to a few other poets—
And, always, to certain powers which,
In other hands,
Could blow up the Real World.

4

Listen.
At our house, just as at yours,
They come and deliver the garbage.
It's always been that way,
And probably always will be.
If we adjust—as,
Burn it, bury it, throw it back,
Or into someone else's yard—
We get along all right.

But among the many and singular ways
Of dying, count
The slow and terrible strangulation
That happens to the silent.
Among the suicides, count
The gifted children, who could only
Whisper, *You are all fools.* Count
The Silver Swan, who never spoke
Until the end, who leaned
Her breast against the reeds to sing
A single, passionately vindictive song
Before she died.
The day-to-day hypocrisy, perversity,
Personal terror, private anguish,
Disappointment and loss, qualify
Most of us. But to these
Describing angels,
They are the closest.

Their promised angelism never comes,
And they are all the angrier
For being as they are. And these are
They who come the closest.
They cannot share,
And what they do, they do because
They cannot share. And what they are,
They very often hate.

Anyway, look.
Look not unkindly, if you can, to these.
They are only a few, you'll know them—
Bright, convulsive, useless
Or absurd. Because their words
May be the only ones so pitched that they can
reach us
At midnight, awake—or during a long illness.
May be the bird's voice breaking through the dust,
Where we lie lost and sleepless.
May speak for us, when we are speechless.
And may we grant, to them,
Understanding, when
From them, and only them,
We can accept a name
For what we felt, when
It was precious,
Pain or promise
Or fulfillment,
The kiss that no one else
Could name, or keep alive.
Then, if we honor, honor this,
And if we cannot honor this—
In sorrow, let it pass.

# POEMS TO PRESERVE THE YEARS AT HOME

## 1

### FIRST YEAR

Cocktail party. It takes all day to dress.
Thinking about it. Eat. Wash. Finally
The exquisite touches, employing Choice.
To this one I'll wear pale-green silk stockings.

They'll be nothing but poets there. Or the writers
Of terse short stories. One celebrity.
Catch as catch can. A green silk handkerchief too.

This is Miss Lang, Miss V. R. Lang, the Poet, or
The Poetess. Bynum, would you introduce
Someone else as, This is J. P. Hatchet
Who is a Roman Catholic? No. Then don't do
That to me again. It's not an employment,
It's a private religion. Who's that over there?

What do you want me to say then?
(What an illogical position)
This is V. R. Lang, she lives at home?

She lives at home, she lives at home.
She knows how to play backgammon,
No bridge, no canasta,
Likes to drive in her car,
Has had two accidents so far
And two poems published this year.
Two, the first two, in May
And who cares anyway? Bynum, and one other,
A hopeless ass who has a bigger car and a nasty fetish
About the way I wear my hair.
All his girls wear their
Hair the way I do, I see from snapshots.
We'll see about that. Come August
I'll cut it all off and wear it very short.

Come unto me, you friends of my childhood
Who still remain, and we'll try it again.
Jack, who still is
A contemporary, and Bob
Who is good for the movies.
Violet always picks the hits,
He said bitterly, after my last outrageous choice.

Letters to friends:   I get these continual colds . . .
I forgot to ask, did you pass your reading exams?
It's curious. I don't seem to be able to accomplish
*Anything*. Everything begun. Nothing ever finished.
Heaps and piles of waste. How is Keith . . .
Not that I give a good God Damn. No man
Is going to make me suffer ever again.

*Put it in the corner with the unmailed letters*

We learn ONE THING.
Simple statement can't afford release.
It has got to be something
Bewildering. Complicated. Preferably
Mysterious to the self at time of writing.

Woke up at four
Muttering aloud
*Scarlet flavor*
*Drop scarlet*
*Not a bit of crystal*
Something like that.
Peculiar. It affords comfort.

No adumbration then. No journalistic writing.
That way Hell lies, gaping wide open and inviting,
Saying Come in and forget everything you meant,
Everything you started eager out to do.

No numbers. No lists. No categoricals.
No descriptive adjectives. BURN IT OUT.
TEAR IT OUT. Attempt no descriptions.
Talk about flames. Suicides. Terrors in sleep.

2

No use, no use. The immovable
Outdoors . . . I'm suffocating here
But I can't move my hands . . . The pile
Of papers on the floor . . . The unmailed letters . . .

The rival systems, each out to catch
The morning's mail or the bills—
So what. So they get put on bureaus.
I'll never find them when the time comes.
But all around me boxes, papers, papers, drawers,
Files, filing cabinets, especial drawers.

The typewriter which jams. The voice downstairs
That calls. The telephone which enters.
The emergency. The caller. The hot water heater that
    breaks.
I can't remember    I can't remember
I put something here, I had something to do,

Someone to telephone, some letter to answer.
If I write about this bill, will they let me alone?
The TABLED overwhelming accumulations.

    I tried to beat the air,
    I went to walk instead
    But little gnats flew around my head.
    It was desolate, walking alone,
    Talking to no one,
    Thinking: seeing me like this
    Walking, talking to myself,
    That couple will have said I'm queer.

Can't make two letters come together right
On this damnable machine. Something is ALWAYS wrong,
Nothing ever quite works, or is ready to wear.
For five months those shoes have waited for repair
In a paper bag which says *Cobbler*,
For two months a hat to be steamed and blocked.
How much money has gone into that car
To get me out of here?

I'll never go. I'll walk the floors at home
Until there is no longer any room in my room.
Pictures, papers, papers, books. Letters. Things to wear.
Piles of clothing on the chairs. Burnt-out electric bulbs.
Forgotten appliances like a polishing tool.
Directions to work the polishing tool.
In three different places as a rule.

If the telephone rings, will I have the strength to say no?

3

Spent late last night with stinking brigands
Who capered through my sleep like dirty clowns
Committing a murder in the early morning,
How should I know whose? I woke up frowning, and
Murderous too. I saw a monkey out my window
At noon. I bruised my elbow jumping through.
How many times have I taken those stairs saying,
It won't be long now? My promises squeak and sneak
Like dreaming burglars scheming in their sleep.

4

I don't want to dream of the dead man again, I don't
Want to wake up wanting to go back to sleep. Somebody
Take me that I can believe in before everything.
I am tired of those tired names, I never had my parents,
I never . . . The wind with a tomato tongue bears down
Upon the wind; there is no breath between
But two angered storm heads in a void.

If it is you, little and pale,
God give me back the thunder I lost.

If I had hunger once, I have eaten it.
God give the skin I was born with,
My eyes are bled and my fingers fat,
Everywhere I went to tonight
Said, the end is coming. Middle age

Is like that. Not here or there but violent.
If I had . . . what? Revenge. But revenge is
Never wholly personal. It could count, like fortune,
For anyone. God grant
Something perfect. You know what
I mean by that.

5

All day I sat in the room alone,
All day I looked at a wide white wall.
I slept through the dentist, I stayed at home,
I stayed and I stared at a fingernail.
Now I stare at a bird in a tree
Outside my window, he's singing to me

Accidie, accidie, dee, dee, dee.

He isn't a bird like the birds I've known
And I've been places, and I've seen birds.

6

Winter birds, willow-sitting winter birds
Peer through the window which is darker than the day—
Accidie, accidie, dee, dee, dee.

On a witch-bright day I had no one to play
With and which-stared at a which-white wall
Where I hung by a fingernail, no one called
And no one came, then 25 times I wrote my name
Under 25 broken appointments, always the same
Name and sometimes the same appointments. If you
Were taller and stronger and truly true
And called me a wonder, I know what I'd do.

I'd go to the dentist, I'd wind all the clocks
I'd plug in the telephone back in its box
I'd answer the letters I get sometimes
I'd pick up my clothes where I throw them nights
I'd sort my papers and keep them on file

I'd save some money once in a while
If you loved me and if I loved you.
(This is a conceit rather than an observation.)

7

Back where I belong. The disorder
Is my own. It can't spring
At me, or break out weeping,
Or explode. The gray windows
Have this to be said for them,
It does not matter what shows
If no one else knows, or is watching
Critically, head cocked in a little sneer.
There is no one like that here.
When the stove works, it is warm,
And despite it does not, it is comfortable
Enough to stare in, lie down in,
Or look at an opposite wall. It isn't
All so gray. There are magic areas,
Some of them in the past, some of them
In the mind. Some sitting on chairs, in scrapbooks,
In the closet. Magic enough for the one who left them.

Called up, they corrupt or create
Of real (or disagreeable) images something
Workable. These are to live with. Or learn by.

How to do something not wanted to do, don't.
Clouds make gray swans in the air. The heart pumps
A little pallor, a little fever, the third sister,
Hypocrisy, stands apart. Fear is not bad,
Nor an experience of tears trying out the stillness.

Up till then I had never thought of my life
As a waking attitude, finite and calculable;
No more does one walk on the earth and under the sky
Attending the overall and constricting dimension.
You live in, you do not question, a master plan.
If life is measurable, the system falls apart,

To try or to start causing fearful pain of conscience
And sleepless planning. *Not to finish* becomes the
challenge.
Gray eagles in the air beat at sleep. The nighttime radio
Becomes a drug, fanning out through the tragic worries.
Those concerns trivial and meaningless become luxuries
Beloved for themselves, but they grow fewer, very few.

There must be things to remember that were perfect
Or at least proud, but they are riddled with doubts
And humiliation now. What could have contented us?
They were half done, they were luck, they were
accidents—
We cannot now lean on them or be sure that they were
enough.
Days too, days are filled with hopeless unfulfillment,
Things forgotten return to haunt the bed at night,
Merciless errands and important purposes all day all
week lain dormant
Now spring from crouched positions into persecution.

8

Tuesday when you opened your eyes your
Room was a cold disaster. Arranged
Around you, its own disorderly life

Took stock of you like a crazy pendulum
Swung over your head like a demonstration
In a science museum, your hands were numb,

All the pieces of you clung to the bedclothes
Like a broken promise, sorrow sticking to the cracks
Till you sat up and the floor went dizzy.

You did not go near the mirror, you fed the cat
But it went on weeping, and you had to sit down.
Still all that day you were followed by your

Tall still angels, walking like trees.
You had no choice but to lead them, and twice
You listened, and once you smiled.

Some days the days for providence we wake
Up taller than the telephone, our eyes more harsh and
 black,
And even its screaming cannot shock us.

Somedays we wake up to the Act
Which casts a shadow on the infinite plane
Of suggestion, we become our Agents,

Pay our rent and sort the laundry,
Make appointments, go to market,
Lay in stores with strange, beleaguered haste.

Some days our guardian days we
Go gladly into one dimension;
These days our days are not our dominion

But our deliverance, practical and moral.
On these days only motion casts a shadow.

9

Before you accept life, make no mistake,
Those that can give life can take it back.
Those that can bring you to life can take,
In their taking, more than they brought.
This since we learned we could eat without appetite.
Powers go still, time runs out, God I am so tired.
There is only the black center in my head
To reconstruct, to ache, to take dictation.

I never once thought about death
Before I started to die. Time grows thin.
The animal arts are turning from pleasure to pain.
I told you everything before you slept, and lay awake
To bite my tongue which knew, which always knew
That what is finally spoken is no longer true.
And you had only listened till I told you.

# PLAYS *by* V. R. LANG

THE POETS' THEATRE

PRESENTS

# FIRE EXIT

VAUDEVILLE
FOR EURYDICE

BY V. R. LANG

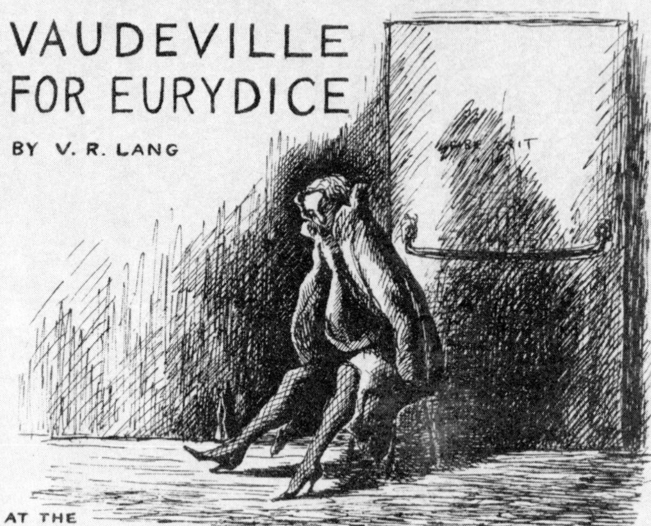

AT THE

# BRATTLE THEATRE

OPENING MONDAY, DEC 1ST, FOR ONE WEEK ONLY

TICKETS: $2.40, 1.80, 1.20, 90 AT BOX OFFICE OR CALL TR 6-4226

# *Fire Exit*

## PROGRAM NOTE

The legends of Orpheus come from the Thracians, who believed that music was magical and that Orpheus was divine. The legend of Eurydice, his wife, is that she died. From that time, all his songs were of her. He sang to the Underworld of his grief and loss, and they were moved and admitted him. They told him he might take her back and asked only that he not look at her until they were out of the Land of the Dead. He did look back, and she vanished forever.

"But Orpheus they sent empty away, and presented to him an apparition only of her whom he sought, but herself they would not give up, because he showed no spirit. He was only a musician, and did not dare, like Alcestis, to die for love, but had contrived how he might enter Hades alive."

PLATO, *Symposium*

The play is written for a bare, or ballet, stage, with set pieces and light, even spidery properties that can be quickly moved or picked up and flown during blackouts. Each act should move in a swift continuity, as dancing and singing would, punctuated only by lights and music. Except for properties easy to carry, any furniture or walls in this play are a nuisance. The entrances to the stage should be wings, so that the people come and go like dancers. There are no doors and windows.

## CHARACTERS

| | |
|---|---|
| MRS. POLLY | *Eurydice's aunts* |
| MRS. ROBELLE, *married to Casey* | |
| MRS. BLANCHE, *married to Mortimer* | |

MORTIMER, *a performer*
CASEY, *a concessionaire*
EURYDICE, *their ward*
ORPHEUS, *foreign-bred, a composer*
THE WAITER
MAX, *a promoter*
JERMYN SQUIER, *president (initially treasurer) of the Mozartiana Society, L.P.*

| | |
|---|---|
| BERTIE PHEMMISTER | *his assistants* |
| IGNOTIUS PHEMMISTER | |

MISS CUSTIS, *their aging stenographer*
VOICE OF A DEAD DOG
VOICE OF A DEAD CAT (FIDELIS)
COCO CRAMBO, *a burlesque comic in his sixties*
STAGE MANAGER *of a burlesque house*
*Models, Chorus Girls, Waiters, Two Nuns*

Act I is laid in Miami.
Act II is laid in New York City.
Act III begins in New York and ends in the South of France.
The Epilogue, which takes place after the action is finished, is laid in a burlesque house in Union City, New Jersey, ten years later.

# Act I

## SCENE I

*A bare stage, against a blue sky, in sunlight.* MRS. POLLY, MRS. ROBELLE, *and* MRS. BLANCHE *in beach chairs. They are handsome, spirited women who do not look their age. Because they will appear in the evening "before the public" they are wearing pin curls under bright silk scarves, doing their nails, wearing eye pads.* MRS. POLLY, *who will go with the circus to Madison Square Garden in March, is singing at a night club in Miami Beach in the meantime.* MRS. ROBELLE, *married to* CASEY, *will assist him with his concessions at the jai alai games.* MRS. BLANCHE *and her husband,* MORTIMER, *have a popular bird act.*

MRS. POLLY Blanche, honey, give me a sweet.

MRS. ROBELLE All you done all day is eat.

MRS. POLLY I got an appetite, Lord love it. [*Eats.*

MRS. BLANCHE It's a shame for anyone to diet.
What's the good of it?
Nature made you, I say,
And Nature meant you to be that way,
Whatever way you are.

MRS. ROBELLE Nature don't know she has a career.
Nature don't care if Pol's a performer,
Or if she's an ellyphant.

MRS. POLLY [*entertained*] A freak, she means, Blanche.

MRS. ROBELLE I didn't say a freak,
I said an ellyphant.

MRS. BLANCHE Oh! Poor souls. Let's not talk about *them.*
I never like to work a show with freaks.
Pinheads, morphadites, the Third Sex—
It's like the burlesque, it's not hardly human.
That's what I mean, not human.

MRS. ROBELLE Burlesque? It don't pay much,
But it's a start. You always work.
Morey Bird, that's Casey's friend,
Before that Casey got him into wrestling,
He worked around the Wheel.
That's what they say, the Wheel.

MRS. POLLY I know what Blanche means.
Them nasty, peeking audiences.
Morey who?

MRS. ROBELLE Morey Bird, the sports promoter.
He started out—he'd die I mention it—
A singer. The house singer.
Working around burlesque theaters.
You work in one, it's like in all of them—
The Circuit, they call it. The Wheel.

MRS. POLLY [*musing*] A "start." You always hear that.
I'd say it's where you end up,
Really end up.
That's not for us, girls.
How about it, Blanche—when they pension
Me out of the circus, do I get a place
In the bird act? Would you take me on?

MRS. BLANCHE [*eagerly*] That would make Mortimer and me
Real happy, Pol. I'll ask him.

MRS. ROBELLE Pol's kidding, Blanche.

MRS. POLLY That's right. I'm
Going to have a chicken farm.
Right now,

I got enough to do.
There's life in the old girl yet.

MRS. ROBELLE You got the fashion show.

MRS. POLLY I got the fashion show.
Imagine that now! The hotel
Asking *me* to run a fashion show.
They said they needed someone who
Could teach the girls to walk nice—
You know—look professional.
It's up to you, I said. I'll try anything.
I'm using Eurydice, it will be
Good training for her—
Where is Eurydice?
What's our girlie doing?

MRS. ROBELLE The Aqua Show.

MRS. BLANCHE She went with Mortimer and Casey.

MRS. POLLY That's right. All right.
Sometimes I worry about her.
She don't amuse easy.

MRS. ROBELLE Listen, Polly, what do the sisters say
About you taking her out this way,
Every year, half the winter?
I shouldn't think they'd let her.

MRS. POLLY I told the sisters when I put her there
(That was the year poor Vi passed on),
I said, she's had a spot on her lung,
And we're all the mother she's got.
I said, we work Florida, every year,
Adn when we do, we'll want to take her.
They're lovely, up there. They saw that.

MRS. BLANCHE She makes it up, you know.
She's bright.

MRS. ROBELLE When I was sixteen,
I could dance for a living.

MRS. BLANCHE But you never went to school, Robelle.
It's different, now.

MRS. POLLY And she wouldn't if Mother
Hadn't took her on tour.
She needed those girls for
*The Merry Widow*—more girls
In that road show! A regular rodeo.

MRS. ROBELLE Now don't talk me down.
All I mean is,
When I was sixteen,
I could dance for a living.

MRS. POLLY Eurydice could too.
Maybe not so well as you,
But passable.

MRS. ROBELLE Well, thank you, Pol.

MRS. POLLY You seen the letter that the sisters sent,
Saying how she was really brilliant
In some studies. Not so much in others.
What's the difference?

MRS. BLANCHE Robelle, you ought to come with us in April
When Mortimer and I play Montreal
And go to see her, in her convent school.
It's lovely up there. Really different.

MRS. ROBELLE Canada! It's cold in Canada.
I should hope to tell you I won't
Go to Canada. I don't go
Anywhere it's winter.
I'll stick with Florida.
Besides there's always work here, work
For me and Casey. Clubs. Carnivals.

MRS. BLANCHE [*suddenly anxious*] The weather's changing, they say.
Something I read yesterday.
Sunspots on the Pole are
Going to change the whole world . . .

MRS. POLLY There's something funny
Happening with Miami, I'll
Say that. Miami ain't the same.

[*Rises.*

Look at that sun.
Like it was getting old, or something.
Well, look what's coming!

[*Enter* MORTIMER *and* CASEY, *with* EURYDICE *trudging behind. The former are in high spirits.*

MRS. BLANCHE An hour early! Mortimer!
Here we are!

MORTIMER [*to his wife*] How's my doll, my baby doll?

[*Turning politely to Polly.*

And how are you, Pol?

MRS. POLLY Well, how come so early?

MORTIMER You tell 'em, Casey!

CASEY [*proudly*] We sold out at the Aqua Show—
*Cleaned up*—get it, Robelle?
Sold out before the show was over!

MORTIMER And so we said, we'll buy the girls a beer,
Or let them buy the beers for us.
Considering as we're such providers—

CASEY Two hundred twenty novelties, a load of peanuts,
Six hundred eighty girlie views and souvenirs
Of Hialeah Park, some pictures of pelicans
And Indian canoes, then all that stuff to eat,
The dogs, the pies, the candy cones,
And all the cold drinks!

MORTIMER We sold eight gross of Frosty Pies
In twenty minutes. Look at this, Blanche,
Four C's! I said to Casey, that's Eurydice,
She brought us luck.

MRS. POLLY Come here, my girlie.

[EURYDICE *goes to her quietly.*

Kind of tired, are you?
Look kind of peaked.

EURYDICE I'm all right.

MRS. POLLY Casey, if you really covered,
I could use a nice two hundred.
Fix up Eury right for Montreal.
I thought a fur coat, if Robelle
Don't mind—

MRS. ROBELLE It comes, it goes, that's all.
If you don't take it, he will.
To the park.

CASEY Whatever's for the kid's all right.
We'll do our part—eh, Belle?

MRS. ROBELLE A lot of help you were to Pol
Last year, I must say.
Mr. Parimutuell.

MORTIMER Here, Pol. Put this in your pocket.
Just a little extra.
How about it, Blanche,
Do we go in with Casey and give up the act?

MRS. BLANCHE [*shocked*] Oh, Mortimer, I love our work.
It don't matter what we make.

MRS. POLLY You got a lovely act.
You stick with it.
I thank you kindly, Mort.
I know you hustled hard for that.
It's hot work, doing them concessions.
Casey earns what he gets.

CASEY Got to hustle,
Got no talent.

MRS. ROBELLE [*moving towards him*] I got no complaints.

MRS. POLLY Well, now, let's all go celebrate.
We got a little time to put away some beers.

CASEY [*picking up Mrs. Robelle's chair*] We're off for Pearl's Palms.
Pearlie's Palms. [*Starts off.*

MRS. ROBELLE *Beers*, she said.
Blanche, you walk with me. [*They follow.*

CASEY So beers. [*They exit.*

MRS. POLLY [*almost off, turning*] As for you, my girlie,
Let them make their usual fuss
About your age, you're all in—
If you want a beer, you can have one.

MORTIMER You go along to Pearl's.
Her and me will catch up.

MRS. POLLY [*anxiously*] Eury, there ain't nothing wrong?

EURYDICE No, Aunt Polly.

MORTIMER I feel like walking easy, that's all.
We'll be right along.

MRS. POLLY Well, don't be long—
Where are they? There they are . . .
[*Exit.*

MORTIMER Sometimes I think we ought to give up show business,
Blanche and me, and run concessions.

EURYDICE But she wouldn't.

MORTIMER Just kidding. What's this?
[*She is holding something in her hand.*
You found a starfish in the sand.
That's swell. [*awkwardly*] You shouldn't have done
What you done, Eury, the Aqua Carnival
Was *beautiful.* I know what you done.
You weren't even looking. You went in,
And sat under the stands.

EURYDICE It was nice in there, all alone.
It was dark and cool, and I

Could hear them splashing.
Besides, I saw it last year.

MORTIMER Well, this year it was better. Much better.
A thousand swimming girls done figures—
You know—flowers, stars.
They had hibiscus, big around as *that*,
You couldn't hardly see the water under.
Very lovely. You should a stayed and seen it.
Say,
How'd you like to be *in* that show, Eury?
How about that? Why not? I know the feller runs it.
I had the bird act up to his camp in New York State!
A very big resort. If you'd like it,
I could fix it up. You wouldn't have
To swim at all. Just float. Or be
A Boat Girl. It pays awful good!

EURYDICE Uncle Mortimer,
I don't think I'll ever be a performer.

MORTIMER [*taken aback*] How's that?

EURYDICE I didn't want to tell you.

MORTIMER What else would you want to do? [*anxiously*]
What are they teaching you,
Up there in that convent school?

EURYDICE It's nothing to do with them.
Of course, they always hope I'll learn
To be much more religious than I am.
But that's what I want, to find something
Or someone to believe in. I don't
Believe in performing. I never will.
I want to believe in something, like
Medicine, or noble missionaries, or
Passive resistance and the Indian religion . . .

MORTIMER Eury, your Aunt Robelle says right,
You done too much reading.
You mean you want to take up nursing?

EURYDICE Yes. Something like that.
Something I can believe in
With my whole heart, something important.

MORTIMER [*thoughtfully*] Well, that's all right.

EURYDICE Besides, I have no talent.

MORTIMER [*eagerly*] Talent! Who's got talent?
Listen, Eury, if that's what's worrying you,
Let me tell you, you're doing fine.
You're growing up to be a very fine
Little dancer, a headliner. You ought to know,
Your Aunt Pol, she's thinking of getting you
In the Big Show, taking you with her—
She says you're almost ready—

EURYDICE No! I don't want that.

MORTIMER [*misunderstanding*] Why not? With a little work
You're going to the top. You wait.
Someday you'll have a big act.
Whatever you want, you'll be a big hit.
Right now, if you wanted, you could do it—
Get dressed up, that's all there is to it,
Silver spangles, fancy hat—

EURYDICE But dressed up to do what?

MORTIMER [*seriously*] Just whatever you want! To work the bells
For Blanche and me, and Pol can take you on,
Like I was saying. You could stand and call
The signals for them chimpanzees to climb
Their bicycles, all dressed up in gold
And satin streamers, very elegant—

EURYDICE And know that everyone was laughing
At me, except the children.

MORTIMER Laughing? That don't mean nothing.
For you, they'd be applauding, that's what
They'd be doing, applauding.

EURYDICE I always hear them laughing,
I always did. In chorus lines,
If anyone slipped, or stumbled.
Or at our bare legs, or at our costumes.
At something. I hate the audience.
Something happens to them, hidden
All together in the dark and watching.
They aren't like people any more, they're different—
Something black and faceless and horrid.

MORTIMER I never heard of such a thing!
Listen, Eury, you got it wrong.
I don't feel like that. Blanche
Don't feel like that. Your Aunt Pol,
She's a dancer, like you, *she* don't.

EURYDICE I know you don't.
I think that you
Believe in all you do, and love it,
I'm different from you.
I want to be proud.

[*Mortimer turns sharply away.*

Oh, please! I've hurt your feelings.

MORTIMER No, you ain't. Who's hurt.

[*He is extremely hurt.*

EURYDICE I do love you. All of you.
Blanche and Pol, too. I do.

MORTIMER Listen, Eury. Blanche and me, we got a great act.
We're happy. We make good money.
Them birds of ours are fine birds.
Do you know what they got for insurance?
Ten thousand dollars.
That's all. I trained 'em. I, personally.
Nobody else. I learned them how to pop the cannon,
How to put the fire out. And how to waltz.

[*She follows after him.*

EURYDICE I'm sorry, Uncle Mortimer.

MORTIMER You do what you can do, Eury.
That's the whole story.

[*They go off. Music.*

## SCENE II

ORPHEUS *and the* WAITER *on.* ORPHEUS *is young and very stiff, in clothes that suggest he bought them at the other side of the world. He blinks as if he were unused to the sun.*

ORPHEUS You know, nothing you've said is true.
I had to stay up to finish my work,
But I had enough sleep for my needs.

WAITER I heard you, and you slept two hours.
No wonder, over there, you got pneumonia.
I only sent for you to come to Florida
On account of a remark I passed to your mother,
That somebody would keep an eye on you
If she died. Which she did.

ORPHEUS I do have to practice.
What's all this?

WAITER The sea, the sky, the light of day.
Over there, the service entrance.
That up there—is the hotel ballroom
Where you are presently employed,
Despite that you are nonunion,
As a favor to me, Al, who got you down here
On account of your health is somewhat poor.
What's life *for?*
Here you are in Florida,
That there's a coconut palm. The sun don't set
Till late, it hangs up there all day on fire
Burning the sand and lighting up the sea.
And everything it touches grows up green.
People, when they come here, come awake.
As best they know. Not you.

[ORPHEUS *laughs.*

It's all the same to you.
England. Milwaukee, where Angela,
Your mother, that is, was when you were born.
Day and night. Human beings. Animals.
Nothing that you see, but only what you are.
Poor Angela! But she didn't know you,
She could not suppose.

ORPHEUS [*affably*] I can't help what I am, Al.

WAITER I meant, you was a child in arms
When last she saw you, Orpheus.
When she died, a little kid.
Why don't you get married?
You ought to get out,
Anyway, while you're here. See girls.
Go spearfishing. No, maybe not.
That's your temperament.
[*Slight pause, with emphasis.*
You're only half human, you know, boy.

ORPHEUS Human! I am quite humán.

WAITER No, you're not.
Once I knew someone met your father,
He was nothing earthly, either.
I'm on duty.
[*Starts to go.*

ORPHEUS [*raising his hand*] Al—what was my father?
I've wondered.

WAITER Something to do with the Higher Law. [*shrugs*]
Some kind of legislator.
No one for a singer, like your mother . . .
They had very little to say to each other.
Do like I say now.
Stay in the fresh air. Look at the sun.
[*He exits.* ORPHEUS, *puzzled, looks above him, around him, and goes slowly off in the opposite direction.*

## SCENE III

*Music up. Enter* MRS. POLLY, MRS. BLANCHE, MRS. ROBELLE, *and others—waiters and girls carrying equipment for a fashion show, men carrying tables at the back and streamers.*

MRS. POLLY [*to one of the men carrying a table*]
Put all them tables out there [*points off left*]
And clear the floor.
Where are them chairs?
[*Men appear dragging a number of little gold ballroom chairs.*
Back there, and there—
Girls!
[*A few models appear from the wings.*
Are you the models?

GIRLS Yes, Mrs. Polly.

MRS. POLLY [*motioning them around her*]
Well, I just want to say a few words.
They asked me to run off this show—
I don't know why I'm doing this,
I'm not in the fashion business,
I'm with the circus,
Where I teach dances. Well,
I guess it's all the same thing.
[*Laughter.*
Are you all, if you
Don't mind my asking, professionals?

SPOKESMAN FOR GIRLS [*after a quick consultation*]
We don't know what you mean,
Mrs. Polly. Could you tell us?

MRS. BLANCHE [*leaving a roll of bunting*]
She means, are you, like,
Regulars, are you paid performers?

SPOKESMAN FOR GIRLS Well, some of us. The rest
Are just pretty girls.

MRS. POLLY Where's Eurydice? And what's she wearing?

MRS. ROBELLE [*coming up with a list*]
Evening Bridal. She's getting dressed.
[*at a model*] Look at that now.
Such a business.

MRS. POLLY [*obviously having a good time*]
All you as ain't professionals
Had better learn. Step over here.

[*A few come over.*

[*To the others*] And you girls
Better be sharp on your pivots.
Now let me see. These pivots.
[*to one*] Kiddie, can you arch?

[*Girl looks offended.*

You've got to learn to arch. One, two.
That goes for all of you. You follow me.
One, two. *Three*. That's Arch. You do it, arms out—
One, two, that's right, no—not you—
One, two. Step right, back. That's right.
*Over*. That's pivot. You. Hold up your neck.
Where's Bathing Suit?

TWO GIRLS There's two of us.

MRS. POLLY One, two, left balance, ARCH.
—You two—where's Sport?
You got to do a floating pivot,
It says here. Can you do that?
Walk up. Arch. Take three steps
Backward. Arch. Then walking pivot forward,
Arch, and off. You oughta have a ramp.
I never heard a floating pivot
With no ramp. You see this racket, Blanche?
It's just parade, remember?
[*does a few steps*] Ho-ho.

[*All the* MODELS *are moving around in a pivot independently of each other as the* MUSICIANS *come in upstage right, a violin, a cello (or two guitars) and* ORPHEUS.

MRS. BLANCHE [*to Polly as she is dancing*]
The musicians are here, Pol.

MRS. POLLY Tell them to play "A Pretty Girl,"
They always play "A Pretty Girl."
Look at them girls, Blanche,
Look at them. I'd be ashamed,
I wouldn't take my pay. Imagine.
I'd like to see *my* girls so clumsy.
I wouldn't let them on. Not one.
They'd have to show without us.
Where's Eury?
Time to call the roll. Such foolishness.
It isn't hardly honest.
Come on, girls. Never mind.

[*The models follow her to the back.*

Tum-ti-tum—Keep them *in.*

[ORPHEUS *starts forward with a question about their music, which he is holding in his hand, when* EURYDICE *comes on in the wedding dress. She stops short and looks at him, he at her. Music.* WAITER, *stage left, looks at them both.*

WAITER It's about time, Mrs. Polly,
Are you ready to line up?
Out there, those designers
Are greeting the guests.
Everyone's on the West Terrace.
I got the caterers all fixed.

MRS. POLLY I guess you'll do all right.
Get along, girls. You know your tricks.
Remember now. Count six *slow*
Before you go, and don't step
on each other's heels.

[*Models go off.*

Eurydice,
That's Evening Bridal. You're last.

[*Exit* MRS. POLLY, *leaving the stage deserted except for* EURYDICE, *still staring at* ORPHEUS, *and the* WAITER *at the side.*

ORPHEUS I know who you are.

EURYDICE I know who you are!

ORPHEUS It was you, last night,
In the hall.

EURYDICE I heard you. Then I stood
Against the wall and listened.
You don't mind?

ORPHEUS I'm used to it.

EURYDICE To what?

ORPHEUS To people listening.
I don't mind those
That don't come in, like you—
Or stop me while I'm playing.

EURYDICE Do they do that?

ORPHEUS Yes, really. If people hear
One practicing—they are—peculiar.
They open doors and walk in
Without thinking. Sometimes
Even windows. Or they stop in the street
As if they had remembered something,
And ring your bell, and ask your name.

EURYDICE [*after a moment*] Well—

ORPHEUS Don't go. Do you have to?

EURYDICE No—
Do you?

ORPHEUS No. I have nothing to do
At first . . .

EURYDICE What was the name of that piece?

ORPHEUS Which?

EURYDICE [*timidly*] Last night. Over and over.
You were playing a piece.

ORPHEUS I was playing the overture
To a new opera. But only the part
For the piano.

EURYDICE Whose opera?

ORPHEUS My opera.

EURYDICE Do you write operas?

ORPHEUS Yes.
—I spoke to you last night.
I heard the door latch, and I stopped
And came to look. I watched
You going down the hall. I spoke,
But you had gone.
I knew your name.

EURYDICE The waiter!

ORPHEUS I asked him who you were.

EURYDICE I asked him who you were!

ORPHEUS There you are.
I don't know anyone else here.

EURYDICE Will you come back next year?

ORPHEUS I don't expect so.
I shall have to travel.

EURYDICE I have another year at school.
In Montreal. But after that,
I don't think I'll—
Be in a carnival, or travel
With my aunts . . .
Have you fed the black swans?
They're always hungry. I feed them
All the time.

ORPHEUS [*startled*] Where?

EURYDICE Out there. In a little pond.
Would you like to?
I can show you how.

ORPHEUS I don't know. I've had so
Little time to go out . . .

EURYDICE I know! I've watched you.
But there's so much that I can show you
Before you go. I know
A beach where no one comes, ever.
The sea comes up alone, and
Flamingos fly there, sometimes.
No one steals the corals! Shells
From giant snails lie all around
Bleached white and dry, and if you like,
You drink wild milk from coconuts,
Still green, that fall down from the palms.

ORPHEUS I think I'd like to.
It's very kind of you, really . . .
Palm trees. Birds.
You do make them sound—
So very pleasant . . .

[*Reappear* MRS. POLLY, *holding the wedding veil and bouquet, and* WAITER, *followed by two of the models, slightly disheveled.*

MRS. POLLY [*bustling*] There you are, my dearie,
Let's get your veil on.
Not nervy, are you?

MODEL Can we take a drink now,
Mrs. Polly?

MRS. POLLY I'm sure I wouldn't stop you.
What foolishness.
[*to Orpheus*] If you'd hold this . . .

[*Passes him veil as she tugs at* EURYDICE'S *hair. He takes it and steps back.*

I thank you kindly. I'm telling you, Eury,
This whole thing isn't hardly honest,
Such girls. They call themselves
Professionals, they just

Stick their tickets out and prance around
With sneaky smiles. *You* show 'em how,
You needn't ought to smile, you're Bridal.

[*Adjusts veil.*

[*to Orpheus*] Ain't she a lovely sight?
So girlish. Say. Ain't you
The tenor voice? They said they'd have
A tenor voice, to sing "Because."

ORPHEUS [*politely, but not taking his eyes off Eurydice*]
Oh, no. I play the wedding march
For her, I think, upon the electric organ.

MRS. POLLY Now where's that maid of honor?
I had her with me. She ain't no maid,
Neither, I'd say. Very frankly speaking.
Five minutes, Eury.
[*to Orpheus*] You know, I guess.
I ain't telling you your business.

[*Exit, with a final poke at* EURYDICE. *The* WAITER *is leaning against the front left proscenium watching them.*

ORPHEUS You're frightened, aren't you?

EURYDICE Oh, no.

ORPHEUS I saw that your hand shook, just now.
You look very pretty.
I wish you very well.

EURYDICE Please don't go!

ORPHEUS [*seriously*] You know, when I do go,
I'll come back for you.
I'd like to. I mean that.
I like you.

[*Lights begin to go down.*

EURYDICE You don't have to.
Come back—I mean. I'll follow you
Anywhere, if you'd like me to.

ORPHEUS You know, I have a lot to do
Before I go, and before I come back.

EURYDICE That's all right.

[*He takes a few steps back, he is about to go off left.*

WAITER [*stepping forward slightly, quietly*]
Your aunts will be looking for you, miss.

EURYDICE [*coming slightly awake*] Yes.

[*She steps forward tentatively.*

WAITER That goes for you, too, Orpheus.

ORPHEUS [*politely*] Yes.

WAITER [*sadly, but in the tone of a weather report on the radio*]
There's a cold wave coming.
At Key West a gull dropped frozen
From the air. Oranges all over
Are perishing. As far as Nassau,
The papers promise cold this year.
There could be snow on the gulf tonight.
A pity . . .

[WAITER *turns to go, then turns back to* EURYDICE.

Cold. Remember.
It can get cold,
Even in Miami. Dress warmly.
Stay in the sun. I've seen it happen,
People catch cold.

[*Exit.*

ORPHEUS Don't be frightened.

EURYDICE I won't. I'll be waiting.

ORPHEUS I have to go.

EURYDICE Yes. I know.

[*He goes off to one side, she another. The lights go down.*

## SCENE IV

*In the following scene, with music,* EURYDICE *gets through the years. Meanwhile,* ORPHEUS *goes to Europe, returns, and becomes professionally established in New York.*

TWO NUNS *take the bare stage by a slow diagonal while the light is low. They are carrying an enormous diploma between them. They cross and go off.* EURYDICE'S *family carry on a straw chaise longue, suitable for a daguerreotype, to another stage diagonal, and arrange themselves stiffly upon it.*

VOICE OF MRS. POLLY [*above music*] Has anyone seen Eury?

[*Enters and sits, in her best dress and hat.* CASEY *lies on the floor stretched in front of the seated family.*

WAITER'S VOICE [*opposite*] She's out feeding the swans.

MRS. POLLY [*to the family*] I don't know what she sees in them birds.

MRS. ROBELLE On a night like this is,
One could catch a chill!

[EURYDICE *enters, crosses swiftly to them. She is carrying her diploma which she drops in their laps.*

EURYDICE There it is.

ALL Congratulations!

MRS. BLANCHE Such a good girl!

MORTIMER You can say that again.

MRS. BLANCHE I think it's grand!
Honors, it says,
In French, Latin, and sacred studies.

EURYDICE I have to tell you now,
I don't want to travel with the Midget Show.

Madam Millefleurs and
Monsieur Papadou
Are going to go without me.
You see, I have to wait for Orpheus.

[*Exit.*

MRS. POLLY She's very willful.

MORTIMER Give her her head, Pol.

MRS. ROBELLE She's not very sociable, not a bit.

MORTIMER She'll get over it.

MRS. BLANCHE She's barely out of school!

MRS. POLLY We're all agreed, we want the best,
The very best for her. Is that right?

ALL That's right.

MRS. POLLY She-don't-look-at-the-male-sex.
I-swear-I-don't-know-what's-next.

MRS. BLANCHE I think there's someone, Pol,
She's waiting on. A long time.
You know, you met him. A musician.
A classical.

MRS. POLLY [*decidedly*] He ain't no one for her.
Kind of funny-looking, I thought.
She needs a Real Man.

[MAX *enters, crosses to them.*

Excuse me, Mort, but who's your friend?

*Lights up.* MAX *and* MORTIMER *pound each other's backs.*

MORTIMER [*by rote, not forced*]
This is a very gratifying surprise.
I would like to present my old friend
From the Hundred and First, a great promoter
And Tycoon of Show Business—Max!
Who owns four theaters . . . Mrs. Polly,
Mrs. Robelle, my better half, and that there
On the floor, the famous Candy Butcher, Casey.

ALL Pleased . . . Delighted . . . Your acquaintance.

MAX [*beaming*] Likewise!

MRS. POLLY Four theaters?

MAX [*oratorically, as above, a recitation*]
I want you all to know
I'm proud to be here now
With Mr. Mortimer, a great performer,
A real swell entertainer and a
A-1 Fellow. And that goes
For all his family, a wonderful
And Super Talented Troup.
And will we back them up? You bet!
Let's have a hand to show them we appreciate—
[*Others sitting around clap cheerfully.*
That's it! That's right! Thank you!

MRS. POLLY If you don't mind my asking, Mr.—
Are you by any chance a family man?

MAX [*still reciting*] Just call me Max. Just Max.
No, Ma'am. I've been unfortunate
And still retain my single state.
But I've got time yet, and I mean to take
The fatal step. You bet.

MORTIMER Max is a very serious type.
He keeps his mind on work.

MAX Well, that's not all of it. You see,
[*suddenly serious and shy*] I'm incurably sentimental.

MRS. POLLY Now don't apologize.

MAX I'm very fond of animals.

MRS. BLANCHE [*delighted*] Well aren't we all, really!

MAX Yes, as you see,
I have one on my tie.
[*shyly*] I'm not such a bad guy.
I talk loud, but you have to.

MRS. POLLY Of course you do.

MRS. BLANCHE [*eagerly*] Why shouldn't you!

MAX [*taking out his wallet*]
I'd like to show you both this picture.
I've really appreciated meeting you.
This is my way of saying so.
That's my dog.

MRS. POLLY Now isn't that grand!
Look at that, Blanche.

MRS. BLANCHE A real friend!

MORTIMER You can say that again.

[MAX *returns wallet, beaming. Enter* EURYDICE *from opposite side.*

MRS. POLLY [*nudging* MORTIMER] There you are, Mortimer.
He's just right for her.
Down-to-earth, kind-hearted,
A man of the world. Introduce them.
That's what I mean. A Real Man.

MORTIMER [*gravely*] Eurydice, I'd like to present
My old pal, Max, the theater owner.
He is very kind to animals.

EURYDICE How do you do?

MAX I want to know,
I'm really pleased to meet you.

[*They take stage center.*

EURYDICE I don't particularly like animals.

MAX For all of that, I think you have
A good head, a loyal and true heart,
An independent nature and a sense of humor.
Besides which, and also, you are a
Swell-looking girl. If you
Would care to marry me, Eurydice,
I'll give my heart to you, I'll

Honor and protect you. I'll work hard.
I appreciate you. My friends will too.
Winters may be serious, but
We'll break the bank on our vacations.
What do you say?

EURYDICE Certainly not.

MAX [*sadly*] Well, anyway, I hope
You won't remember me unkindly.
Think of me as your friend.

[*Exit.*

MRS. POLLY You shouldn't have done that.

[*Music. Enter* ORPHEUS *in severe black suit carrying briefcase. He comes up to* EURYDICE. *He takes off his homburg.*

ORPHEUS I beg your pardon, could you tell me?
Some years ago I met a Miss Eurydice
In this place, and now although
I'm not quite sure I'd know her face,
I'd like to collect her—and—
But that's you!

EURYDICE I love you.

ORPHEUS I love you, too.

EURYDICE I always wanted to.
You're just right.

MRS. POLLY. Well, that's that.

[*Lights come up high and everybody gets up.* ORPHEUS *and* EURYDICE *take center stage, others somewhat in formation.*

EURYDICE Then, here he is. [*recites with great fervor*]
So long to the scullery hopes and the dismal weeks
That wore and that told, that scrabbled and screeched!
Now for the weather, the pitch and the plume,
The place of the precipice, Orpheus has come!

MRS. BLANCHE Now she will no longer weep and snarl,
Now she will no longer creep or wail!

EURYDICE There shall be nothing that I will not understand,
There will be no attention that he will not grant!
We shall be cared for and coveted, justified at last,
With all the bright what-have-you that we love the best!

MRS. ROBELLE No longer abide her silly ancillary decisions,
Now she knows where she is.
Reward us her aunts our precipitant persistence,
He is hers, she is his.

MRS. POLLY I suppose it's the best, but we hovered and worried,
We worked and we worried and hurried and harried—
But now its all over, they're going to be married!
And if *that's* to our credit we're glad to be rid of it,
We're glad that they're glad that they're in and we're out out of it!

MORTIMER For a while there,
You two were
So nip and go,
We didn't know
Where you were.
Now that we know,
We wish for the both of you
Blessing and honor.
You love her and keep her,
Always take care of her,
Do her no harm.

ORPHEUS I avow, acknowledge, and profess her.

EURYDICE And I him.

[*Goes to him, between* MORTIMER *and* CASEY. *They take hands.*

ALL Congratulations!

[EURYDICE *breaks away suddenly.*

EURYDICE It hasn't all been chewing gum and garlands,
I can tell you. I hated school, really.

MRS. ROBELLE [*reproachfully*] Now, don't say that. We sent you
Potted turkey and a drum of nuts.
You wrote us that you loved it.

EURYDICE But now I have him, and I haven't a qualm.
I'll come to no harm, now I know who I am.
I wake up every morning and I'm glad that I did.
I climb all over my breakfast!

MRS. POLLY [*stepping forward*] Here's Max. He has a wedding present for you.

MAX [*handing her an enormous diamond necklace*]
They're not so much.
I know you want the best,
But these are all I've got.
I can't do what he does.
I just know how to buy things.

EURYDICE [*polite but disinterested*]
Thank you very much.
They're lovely, Max.

ORPHEUS You've all been very kind.
I'm sure you'll miss her.

[*Leads her off.*

EURYDICE Goodbye! Goodbye!

ALL Goodbye, Eurydice.

CURTAIN

# Act II

## SCENE I

*Lights on slow. Enter* ORPHEUS *and* EURYDICE *carrying suitcases, with* WAITER *in a splendid bell captain's uniform, carrying another suitcase.* WAITER *turns on bedside lamp.*

ORPHEUS [*to* WAITER] Thank you. This will do.
[*Gives him a coin, gravely. They unconsciously take positions,* ORPHEUS *nearest the door by which they came,* EURYDICE *looking up, the farthest away from it,* WAITER *center.*

WAITER A quarter. Thank *you* too.
[*points to bags*] This time, with very little in them,
They weren't heavy. If you were settling down
It would be different. More bags. Books, perhaps
Hatboxes, for her.

EURYDICE Oh, I never wear hats.

ORPHEUS But we are going to live here.

WAITER It don't matter, you're still
What I call *transient*. You'd have to be, for
If you weren't, I wouldn't be here.

EURYDICE [*surprised, turning from her inspection*]
Why not? Oh—I see.
Perhaps the bags would be too heavy.

ORPHEUS [*looking in closet*] I see we have been issued
An excess of clothes hangers.
May I give you these?

[*Holds out an armful of wire hangers to* WAITER, *who takes them crossly.*

WAITER [*to* EURYDICE] I'll thank *you*, miss, to
Watch your tongue. I'm not as young
As some of them that stand around
The elevator, but I can lift my weight
Or better. Watch this.

[*Starts to remove the bed by picking up its end and dragging it off.*

ORPHEUS *Really*. No one doubts that.

EURYDICE Please come back!
That's wonderful,
You're very strong!

WAITER [*pleased*] Yes, I am.

[ORPHEUS *looks at him, amazed, and then returns to what he was looking at.*

EURYDICE I only meant, you spoke
Of us as transient.
Why is that?

WAITER [*rearranging the bed and fixing its spread and pillow*]
That's it. My job.
My job is tourists.
Whether they want to or not, you'll always find
Wherever people move around, I have a hand
In it. I take them.
[*final pat to bed*] That's that.
I don't deal the cards, you understand.
I don't even shuffle the pack.
I don't care, generally speaking,
Who you are. I wait, as a rule,
Until I'm called. I hang around the purser.
Every elevator is my official
Responsibility, and I, personally,
Inspect all exits to be sure they're clear.

[*Walks over to* ORPHEUS *and shakes hangers at him belligerently.*

Oh, I know what you're thinking! "*Who cares.*"
It's written all over your face. Ingrate!
[ORPHEUS *straightens up, astonished.*
You never notice who takes care of you.
You never even see the force on Pullman cars—
Or planes, or terminals, or steamships—
Or who arranges fares at travel agencies!
Listen, if it's just to the basement in the
Service elevator or irrevocably from the
One place to the other, in my modest way
I'm just the Prince, that's all, of Transportation
And Communications! Tel and Tel, R and R, S.S.,
And everything else.
*You* may not think that's so much.
You'll see. I'm not so ordinary. My importance
Don't depend on your opinion, Mr. Matinee.
[*Starts to go.*

ORPHEUS [*wounded and bewildered, to* EURYDICE]
*What* could I have said?
You're quite mistaken,
I do respect your work.

EURYDICE He does! He does!

WAITER [*suspiciously*] Hah.
[*brightening*] It don't make any difference
To me, anyway. I am the Prince, I said,
Of Extenuating Circumstances, and
My faculties have subtle distinctions
Not just anyone can see. He don't care.
He's too busy.

ORPHEUS If I seemed abstracted, it's just that
It was a long trip.
I have been married only a week,
And we have been in New York only . . .
[*consults watch*] One hour and fifteen minutes.

EURYDICE And we're *hungry*. Aren't we, Orpheus?

ORPHEUS [*who hadn't thought about it*]
I suppose so. Yes.

WAITER Very well, perhaps I spoke too plain.
[*graciously*] And now, I'd like to say
I hope that you enjoy your stay
In our hotel. Anything
The desk can do, or anyone,
Just call them.

ORPHEUS Thank you.
[*Points delicately at the hangers, which* WAITER *has thrown on the bed.*
Please don't forget the hangers.

WAITER [*turning back to snatch them up*]
Oh, you and your hangers.
Arrivederci, miss.

EURYDICE [*trying to help him gather them*] *Mrs.*

WAITER Just as you please.
[*Exits. They look at each other for a moment.* ORPHEUS *goes nervously to a window.*

ORPHEUS [*after a pause*] I don't know what it is,
There's something in the air.
Perhaps the change of weather.

EURYDICE Will it snow?

ORPHEUS I believe so.
We've come back to the winter.
You particularly are not used to it.
[*morbidly*] I have a cramp in my lung.
The air seems heavier here, somehow.
My tongue hurts.

EURYDICE The North is awful in the winter.
But we won't always be here.
Will we?
Orphée, what he said—about us
Being *transients*—what was that?

ORPHEUS I really don't know what he meant
By anything he said. I couldn't follow it.

EURYDICE Couldn't we get—an apartment?
I could learn to keep it.
I could cook, and keep it clean.

ORPHEUS [*Turns and sees her looking up, sits down in the chair beside which she is kneeling by an open suitcase, and takes her hands.*
It's too much trouble, Eury.
I hate a fuss at meals.
The waste of hours spent in
This and that, the silly acquisition
Of possessions, burdens,
And the care of them.
One can live anywhere.

EURYDICE [*nodding seriously*] Anywhere.

[ORPHEUS *rises and goes back to the window, turns abruptly and speaks with a little show of feeling.*

ORPHEUS I like a clean, cold room
That looks upon the air,
That makes no claim on you—
Being empty, being cared for
By somebody impersonal,
Who cleans it, when you're gone.
Then,
When you come there,
You can continue—what you were—
Out there—

EURYDICE [*standing up*] Orphée.

[*He nods once, waiting.*

What do you
Want me to do here?
What do you want?

ORPHEUS What do you want to do?

EURYDICE I can't just sit and stare
At that white wall beyond
The bathroom door. Out there,
As you called it, it's too large,
And in here, it's too small.
Shall you need me, ever?

ORPHEUS I like to look at you, Eurydice.
Looking up, I want to know you're there.
When I look at you, look back
And speak to me when I am silent.
Without you, sometimes,
I forget to talk. Then certain things
Slip out of touch, like heat and light,
And daily life is blotted out.
Without you, sometimes,
Circumstances gray, go out of focus, queer:
I wake and find myself a stranger
To the simplest things. A glass of water.
A hand. Locked out, and knowing no way back
To these conditions, once they are forgotten.
If I do this,
Find fault with me, step in my shadow,
Call my name.

EURYDICE You know how much I want to understand.
I'll be afraid, I know, of bothering you,
Or getting in your way, or saying what is wrong.
But at the same time I, for myself, will be afraid.
I am so *mortal*, Orpheus! I'm neither schooled
Nor old enough to call out loud in time—
The right time. If you should go away
Someday too far, you could not hear me
No matter how I called, how loud or long,
And then what—I don't know.

ORPHEUS [*jumping up*] That won't happen.
[*Goes to window again.*
I don't know why I spoke this way.

I never have. I doubt if what I said
Made any sense. I'm sorry.

[*Suddenly, crossly.*

It's this weather. These irregular
Hours. I must, tomorrow,
Go back on schedule, return to live
As I must live, on schedule.

[*Impatiently, but an impatience with himself.*

It's growing late.
I shall begin tonight by going out
And getting these attended to.

[*Gropes for a manuscript case, picks it up.*

That will be something.

EURYDICE Can I go with you?

ORPHEUS I think alone, I'll take less time.
This will be a business matter—
Not a little tiresome.

[*He puts on his hat and coat.*

EURYDICE Very well then. I shall clean our room.
I'll unpack everything, and when you come,
It will be clean.
[*with comic intensity*] Oh, Orphée,
I'm never going to be a bother. I shall be
Better and better. You'll see.
You will be very proud of me,
And so will everyone. Wherever we come,
Crowds will turn around, and I behind
Your elbow will be perfectly contained,
And calm—and everyone will whisper,
"There is Orpheus, and behind him, there's
Mrs. Orpheus, the *altogether perfect wife*
*For genius*, who goes with him wherever he goes!"

ORPHEUS [*taken aback*] *Really*, Eurydice.
First the waiter, now you.
Everyone is acting very strangely.
I *do* not see what I do
That brings about these outbursts and avowals

In everybody else.
You'll find I shall ask nothing of you,
And put no burdens on you, that my needs
Are simple, and my habits orderly.
    You'll see.
[*breaking away nervously*] I shall be back presently.

EURYDICE Orpheus!

[*He stops.*

Your manuscripts!

[*He takes them from her and Blackout.*

## SCENE II

*The lights go up slowly on downstage left to the sound of typing.* JERMYN *is standing by the coat tree,* BERTIE *is at the desk typing,* IGNOTIUS *is hovering, all in a small circle which is the Mozartiana office.* JERMYN *is helping a peculiar little woman on with her coat.*

JERMYN There you are, Miss Custis.
Ignotius, you can show Miss Custis
To the elevator.

MISS CUSTIS Are you really sure
That you don't need me any more
Tonight, Mr. Squier?
There isn't a *thing* I'd love better
Than to stay right here, and finish—

JERMYN [*firmly*] No, Miss Custis. Bertie, here,
Can take the letters to the Post.

BERTIE Oh, yes.

MISS CUSTIS [*disappointed*] I do so hate to go
Before we close the office!

[JERMYN *turns his back.*

Well, if you say so . . .
[*at door*] See you tomorrow!

[*Silly wave. Exits with* IGNOTIUS.

JERMYN [*turning back to dictate to* BERTIE]
Oh, yes, and you might also mention
That as I said to them, at Mme. Vesicant's reception,
I am quite willing to lose thirty to a hundred
Thousand on Mozartiana for perhaps five years.
I'm *not* a businessman, I said, it's not my interest
To bow to commerce, or to lower standards.
[*loftily*] There's been too much to that, for generations,
In my family, I said. *My* choice—

BERTIE Just a second.
[*Types furiously. Stops, expectantly.*

JERMYN *My* choice is to exalt the public.
To exalt. To elevate.
But never to corrupt.

BERTIE But, Jermyn, we're not losing money,
Are we? I thought
That we were ever so successful, this year.

JERMYN Just type your letter, Bertie.
*Try* to follow: my remarks were
Theoretical, in nature.
I went on to say that, with our program
Of record libraries for schools
And charitable institutions, we had
Enlisted interest and assistance
From foundations. As well as, to be sure,
Considerable popular success.

BERTIE [*sighing*] All of which is due to Orpheus.

JERMYN [*crossly*] Not Orpheus alone,
By any means.
Remember sales of the Mangleberg Mass
Are at present in the thousands.
We have a carefully *balanced* program.

BERTIE Oh, yes, but lots of it is Orpheus.
Jermyn, don't you think it curious

That such a marvelous artist, as he is,
Nevertheless gets so much *popular* support?

JERMYN [*exasperated*] My tongue is scarcely cold upon the words,
Bertie, that it has been my wish
Since our initial compositions
To glorify the public, to exalt.
Very well.
Is it immodest to suggest that I
May have helped accomplish this?
[*Lyrically warming to his theme.*
I like to think that I,
In my small way, gave Orpheus
His voice. When first we formed
Our little band, in 1946,
If you remember this—

BERTIE They laughed at us, of course.

JERMYN And warned we didn't stand a chance
Against the vast, controlling companies.
Well, here we are. We proved their cynicism
Groundless. We are, beyond all supposition,
Internationally established.
Leaders of Long Play. That's all
I have to say.
Have you finished? And why not?

BERTIE Oh, dear. I can't possibly.
Jermyn, I'll just put all these,
Leaving out the last, in envelopes.
It that all right?

JERMYN I have no choice.
We must pick up Ignotius
At the recording studios.
[*Gets into his hat and coat.*
Come *along*, Bertie. Don't dawdle.
[BERTIE *jumps up, fussing with papers.* JERMYN *snaps out overhead light, and the lights dim. The telephone rings.* JERMYN *snatches it.*

JERMYN Yes?

VOICE OF IGNOTIUS Hello? Hello?
Who is this?

JERMYN [*reeling this off*] This is Jermyn Squier of
Mozartiana, Long Play.
The office is closed for today.
I'm sorry. Goodbye.
[*hangs up*] Now. Are we quite ready?
There's no use telling them.
One has to be firm.

[*Telephone rings again.*

What is the *matter* with them!
[*answers*] Yes! What is it!

VOICE OF IGNOTIUS Jermyn? Isn't that your voice?
This is Ignotius.

JERMYN [*coolly*] Oh. Ignotius. Yes?
Are the recordings finished?
We are, *at* this very moment, on
Our way to join you . . .

IGNOTIUS [*interrupting*] Jermyn, this is important.
I've just had news of Orpheus.
He has returned from tour a few weeks
Earlier than planned, and he is married!

JERMYN [*looking around nervously*] I'm sorry, Ignotius,
We have here some atrocious noise.
The air conditioning, we think,
Has failed—or broken down, or leaking—
Just speak louder.
Bertie, *would* you shut that—?

IGNOTIUS Orpheus! I said, Orpheus!
Orpheus has returned from California and is—
By his own admission—married!

JERMYN What? Oh, no!
Ignotius! Are you there? Who to?
It can't be true. *Which* Orpheus?

Who told you? There are two. There is
Another, the spelling is different, who
Teaches, I believe, at Columbia.
[*He talks further and further from the mouthpiece of the telephone.*
Or rather, N.Y.U.
This other Orpheus is
Not a composer, I don't know what he is—
One moment, BERTIE, PLEASE, THE DOOR!—
I suspect an atomic physicist,
As he publishes . . . JUST CLOSE THE DOOR, BERTIE.
Yes. Now. What is it?

IGNOTIUS [*after a slight pause*] Hello? Jermyn?
This is Ignotius.

JERMYN [*angrily*] I am aware it is!

IGNOTIUS I said, I just *saw* Orpheus,
*Our* Orpheus, that is,
That is contracted to us;
He says that he has finished
His song cycle and will give it to us,
And, that he is married!

JERMYN Married! Ignotius? This is ridiculous.
I cannot possibly get this
On the telephone. We are leaving now.
I will see you, at the Béchamel,
In one hour, *exactly*, at the bar.
Can you hear me?

IGNOTIUS Perfectly. One hour.
That will be—
Six thirty-three.

JERMYN You can be a moment early.
[*Hangs up.*
[*to* BERTIE] You heard?
[BERTIE *makes bewildered gesture.* JERMYN *slams down briefcase in temper.*
I am at fault for this, I am!

By *my* hand he went to California,
*I* secured the contract and engineered
Commission to insure his option
Be extended—I! What have I done!
Some opportunist has *pounced upon him*—
I know quite well that he knows no one,
No one! *Why* did I not act upon my premonition
And go with him?

BERTIE [*flustered*] Orpheus has married someone?

JERMYN [*darting back and forth*]
Annulment . . . lawyers . . . Wait!
He may know nothing of it.
I must find out. Come on, Bertie.

BERTIE Jermyn, your briefcase, don't forget!

JERMYN [*coming to a stop*] I will confess this is a shock. I have
A piercing headache and, I think, a cold.
Of course I would, as catastrophe
Overtakes us, have to be exhausted,
Fatigued, in wretched health—But!
I must compose myself. I must
For the sake of Orpheus.

BERTIE Oh, yes.

[*A pause.*

JERMYN There. I am quite collected. Bertie,
*We must keep our heads.*
Orpheus is going to need us.

BERTIE It's awfully unexpected, isn't it?
You don't think that it's
Someone that he knew, before he went?

JERMYN [*wheeling on him*] Don't be a fool!
*There is no one in the whole world*
*Capable of distracting Orpheus!*
Never forget that.

This will prove a trick,
And just to prove it, I'll—

[*A knock.*

Who *is* that? Yes! What is it?

[ORPHEUS *walks in.*

ORPHEUS. Is anyone—?

JERMYN }
BERTIE } Orpheus!

ORPHEUS Yes.

JERMYN The light, we must have light—
Bertie!

[*Fumbles till the lights go up.*

ORPHEUS [*briskly*] You're working late! What for?
They told me, at the door
Downstairs, that there was someone up here.
So I got in the elevator, and came up.

JERMYN How long have you been back!
I just this moment
Spoke about you with Ignotius, who—

ORPHEUS Yes, I spoke to him. You see,
I have returned a few weeks
Earlier than our arrangement.
From California I flew
To Florida, where I wished to
Settle certain personal affairs
In which I have been long contracted.
These
Within this week. I see
You have leased these additional offices?
I don't recall these rooms were put to use
In January, when I left.
For several years,
I've had an understanding in Miami, which
Has not been realized, with a Miss

Eurydice, who has no parents. Her family
Consists of relatives by marriage, aunts.

JERMYN I think you're *very casual*, Orpheus!

ORPHEUS Am I? I don't mean to be.

JERMYN You could have written me—
I am your agent,
And any change in plans—

BERTIE Why, Orpheus! Married!
How splendid for you!

JERMYN You never told us—

ORPHEUS You never asked.

JERMYN I thought that you had realized
How deeply everything about you
Concerns us, and would tell us—

ORPHEUS [*cutting him off politely*]
And as you see, I have. But now
For business. While in Monterey
I had the opportunity at last
To finish and to score those songs—
The Gabel Bow commission—that you wrote
And asked me for. I have them here.
[*Opens briefcase.* JERMYN *reaches to grab it.*

JERMYN Yes, yes, yes.

BERTIE Jermyn heard it from Ignotius,
Orpheus, and *wouldn't* think it true!

ORPHEUS Why yes, it's true.

JERMYN Bertie is, as usual,
Transported by enthusiasm
And does not report the facts. YES,
I was, this moment, speaking with Ignotius,
But I was forced to ask
He wait to tell me what it was
He wished to tell me, until face to face—

But now there is no need for that!
You yourself shall tell us! Join us
Right now, at the Béchamel—
For a cocktail!

BERTIE [*hurt*] Jermyn, you did too know.
Ignotius told you.

ORPHEUS Forgive me, but
If we've no time at present, to
Go over these, I think I'll just go
Back to our hotel, and wash. You
Understand. The trip was tiring,
And there's much to do.

JERMYN Of course, of course, but Orpheus,
You'll have to eat
*Somewhere*, after all. I have an idea—
Join us, later, both of you—
Eight o'clock—Le Cocteau d'Or!
Your wife—of course I want to meet her—

ORPHEUS Jermyn, I am—
Very tired. Another time.
Where shall I leave these?

[JERMYN *snatches* ORPHEUS' *papers.*

How did you make out, Bertie, with
Your amplifier? I am told
You have achieved considerable success
And patented a new device.

[*They are all standing ready to go.*

BERTIE Oh, yes, it's marvelous. Imagine!
We'll market it within a matter of months,
Under Mozartiana's name.
It's quite exciting!
For use with corner speakers—with a Klipsch!

ORPHEUS I'd like to hear it.

JERMYN We're leaving. The lights!
The lights! Bertie, the lights!

[*Blackout. Office furniture off*, JERMYN *and* BERTIE *off fast.*

## SCENE III

*A lot of screaming voices offstage.*

VOICES There he is! That's Orpheus!
THERE HE IS!! THAT'S HIM!!

[*A spot catches, at the very back of center stage,* ORPHEUS *in the act of fleeing autograph collectors. He stops, as if pierced by an arrow in the back and freezes in the spot, looking towards the voices over his shoulder.*

DOMINANT VOICE That ain't him!

OTHERS That's *him*!

[*A few dart out of the wings left and catch up to him, gasping.*

YOUNG PERSON [*grabbing at his pocket*]
Hey Mister, ain't you the Orpheus
Who wrote *The Melancholy Magic of*
*Your Smile*? Ain't you on television?

ORPHEUS Yes, I am.

[*Offstage shrieking.*

[*raising his voice*] Yes, yes, but please,
Listen a moment.
[*trying to quiet them*]
I wrote *The Melancholy Magic of Your Smile*
As a joke, do you understand? Simply a *device*
To demonstrate positions taken in
The orchestra, a way to use the instruments
In order that you'd listen. It hardly warrants—

VOICES It *is* him!

[*Shrieking, they grab at his coat and hat. Blackout, confusion dying down, and silence.*

## SCENE IV

*Light picks up* EURYDICE *standing alone upstage center. When she addresses her remarks, it is toward the corner of their hotel room where* ORPHEUS *is lying on the bed, his hands behind his head, his feet crossed upon the end rail.*

EURYDICE [*as if to herself, but she is speaking to him*]
Please understand.
I'm not complaining.
I promised once, I don't remember,
If I spoke out loud, or to myself,
That if I failed you, ever,
I'd go off somewhere.
If I'm no use to you, I suffer.
If I could work for you, or talk
To you, or just keep quiet
When you wanted quiet, that
Would be enough, but unfortunately
I can't fool myself.
Seven nights last week
I sat at home till three or four A.M.
In our hotel room. I know
Your orchestra rehearsed in all that time,
But if you'd only—let me come there.
Let me come with you, when you go out . . .

ORPHEUS [*from the bed*] There's nothing for you to do.
If there were something for you to do—

EURYDICE [*very quietly*] I know. There isn't anything.
There wasn't in Chicago.
So that I stayed here, as you asked me to,
When you went to Cleveland and Detroit,
I thought I'd go to work.
I would have done that, long ago,
If it were not the thought of you,
And that, if I did what I knew,
And what they trained me to do,
You'd be ashamed.

ORPHEUS [*from the bed*] I don't know, Eurydice.
I just don't know. At present,
There's nothing I can do.

EURYDICE [*after a pause and above music*]
Blanche and my Uncle Mortimer,
When that they met, their eyes greeting,
Fell upon fire and heard no other.
They married in the fall they met,
And lay all season in each other's arms
Tangled like trees. And all of nature
But the burning leaves was silenced,
Which, silent, smoked around them where they fell . . .

ORPHEUS I am not your family!

EURYDICE I knew him. He was a man content.
They spoke together always
In secret particulars—
She to him, he to her—
They saw no image but their own invention.
He would not work, he said, without her.

ORPHEUS [*coming up on his elbow under a little light*]
What work! What was his work!

EURYDICE He taught her how to shiver glass,
To sound a bell and tell entire scales, until
She could perform with him at country fairs
And carnivals, upon a tray of glasses, playing
Favorites—*Sorrento*, *Wagon Wheels*, and so on.
Later in their love, she learned the glockenspiel.
They had an act with little dogs that danced
And barked in numbers.
Then, as The Mortimers, they grew famous
And played theaters, until at last
They could afford their marvelous birds,
Which waltz, and fire cannon, and tell fortunes.

ORPHEUS And is there a connection?

EURYDICE Because he loved her, he created their career,
Began all over, took her in, and celebrated her.

ORPHEUS [*after a silence*] *I* cannot begin all over.

EURYDICE I know.

ORPHEUS I have professed you, Eurydice.
You cannot ask I celebrate you also.

[*Dim out.*

## SCENE V

*Lights come up.* IGNOTIUS *is carrying a chair for* MISS CUSTIS *on which, with dictation notebook open, she sits.*

IGNOTIUS Jermyn is keeping a private scrapbook,
Miss Custis, of all publications
Concerning Orpheus. We've only one copy
Of this last, descriptive piece,
So I'll have to ask you to copy it.
Take this down, Miss Custis, please.
Curious. . . .
[*Frowns and fixes his glasses.*]

MISS CUSTIS [*sits and opens book*] Ready, Mr. Ignotius.

IGNOTIUS [*reading flatly, not as poetry*]
September seventh. From—the name—*The Commentator.*
It was hard for Orpheus, winning them so easily.
Beasts were gentle, but they followed him always,
And crowded around him where he lay sleeping.
Flowers—flung themselves at him, and trees
Burst into flower. Everything in Nature did him honor.
Until he lost his way.

[*Pauses for* MISS CUSTIS *to catch up.*

Then he was everywhere entangled in
Their loving creeping. Meadows opened up,
And turning seasons tore at him, and wound him tightly in
With vines and creeping feelers, tendrils.
Beasts, at his breast and shoulders, rubbed their sides,
While round his neck and arms swung little animals.
When everything alive demanded his attention,
"*Release me!*"

Orpheus cried. But they no longer heard his voice.
In all that gibbering comma shrieking comma cawing
comma mewling comma
Roaring comma barking comma crowding comma
weeping—Orpheus
Could not make himself be heard.

[MISS CUSTIS *writes a little longer.* IGNOTIUS *watches her without expression. The lights go out on them.*

## SCENE VI

*The following scene, between* EURYDICE *and her* AUNTS, *takes place in the hotel room. The light picks them up as they are bustling in and is bright throughout.*

AUNTS Eury!

EURYDICE Pol! Blanche! Robelle!

[*They hug, etc.*

MRS. POLLY It's our own little girl!

MRS. BLANCHE Well, ain't this wonderful!

MRS. ROBELLE [*taking off coat*] Now, let's have a look at you. We haven't set an eye on you for six months . . .

MRS. BLANCHE Eury, you look fine.

MRS. POLLY She don't. She looks a proper sight—
Look at her—all in black—and that hair!
What you been reading, the *Harpers Bazaar*?
You hadn't ought to wear black. Not you.

EURYDICE [*laughing*] Now don't say that. I dressed up
For your visit. [*Pause*] Orphée
Can't be here, you knew that.
He's on the radio this afternoon.

MRS. BLANCHE Eury, fancy Mr. Orpheus
Being so *public* as he is,

Without we ever guessed—
Our little girl!

EURYDICE He wasn't always famous,
Not anywhere as near as this—

MRS. POLLY It's no concern of ours. I'm sure
We didn't come from Florida
On purpose for to get another
Look at Mr. Nibs . . .
It's you we come to see,
Kiddie, and no offense. It don't
Make no difference that *he's* not here.
Sit down here, Eury. Let me take
A look at that hair.

[EURYDICE *sits at her feet.*

MRS. ROBELLE [*inspecting everything*]
Don't take no mind of Pol, she's
Ignorant, that's all, Eury.

MRS. POLLY [*snapping*] Now don't be smart, Robelle!

MRS. ROBELLE I know how big he is.
I read the papers. This article
I read, just yesterday, it said he was
*Astronomical* in the music world.

MRS. BLANCHE Like . . . [*helpful gesture*] . . . a *star.*

MRS. ROBELLE Well *thank you Blanche*—
And so I said, we won't be seeing much of her,
Not even in New York, we won't.

MRS. POLLY [*clucking*] Now, kiddie, when did you last have
A touch-up? Look at that!

EURYDICE Oh, Pol, I'm trying to let it grow.

MRS. POLLY What for! That gold looked swell on you.
Just right, with your eyes.

MRS. ROBELLE He's not long on comfort, is he,
Mr. Orpheus? What's the matter,

Don't you own no *things?* You'd think
With somebody like that, who's
Nationally advertised, and having interviews
In all the magazines—you'd kind of realize it
When you went into his *home*. No pictures!
Nothing! Not even your *belongings*.

MRS. POLLY But, kiddie, when it grows out,
Then what will you do? You can't
Just leave it like that, can you?

EURYDICE I'm going to cut it all off.
I'm going to wear it very short.
[*to* MRS. ROBELLE] You see, he doesn't like a mess.

MRS. POLLY All off! Now, don't say that.
It's beautiful that length!

MRS. ROBELLE A mess! Well, I should think *not*.
You must feel right at home, it's like
The convent, ain't that right, Blanche.

MRS. POLLY Listen, Eury, listen to your aunt:
Don't cut your hair off. Be smart.
You just ain't the type to take up
Like a kid, or have the boyish look.
I don't care who you are, or who you see—
There's no sense giving up entirely,
And cutting off your hair,
That took you years to grow.
And wearing clothes like you
Were some Italian widow that had nothing else!

MRS. ROBELLE [*cheerfully*] Seems like you'd want *something* of your own
To make it homey. How long you been here?

EURYDICE [*close to blowing up*] We do! We have! That's his chair—
Someone gave it to him.
When we go, we'll take it.

[*The* AUNTS *are silent for a moment, sizing. They exchange quick looks.* EURYDICE *is by the window.*

MRS. BLANCHE [*warmly*] I think that piece he wrote,
*The Melancholy Magic of Your Smile*,
Is beautiful. Pol used it for
The Grand Aloha Ho finale at
The end-of-season show, and everybody cried.

MRS. POLLY That they did. Yes, they did.

EURYDICE That makes him very angry, Aunt
Robelle. He only meant it for a
Technical divertissement—then
Someone else put words to it . . .

MRS. ROBELLE I don't know what he meant it for,
But I can tell you Morey Bird,
That's Casey's friend, the sports promoter,
Says royalties alone have run
Into two hundred thousand, sheet releases.

MRS. POLLY That don't mean nothing, Belle.
It goes in taxes, to the Federal.

EURYDICE I'm very happy! He treats me very well.

MRS. POLLY Kiddie, it looks like I spoke
Out of turn. Don't mind your aunts.
It looks like you've got everything
On your mind. Why don't you tell us?
We're all married women, by way of speaking.

MRS. ROBELLE It's none of our affair, Pol.
Not without she asks us.

EURYDICE There's nothing wrong. You all
Jumped on me, and I—

MRS. POLLY [*sharply*] Do you love him, kiddie?

EURYDICE Love him? Love Orpheus? Oh, Pol.

MRS. POLLY That's just to make sure. Now listen here—
It's always very touchy—
For the first year.

MRS. BLANCHE She's right, she really is.

MRS. POLLY Blanche cried herself
To death with Mortimer, nearly.

BLANCHE But all the time we were divinely happy.

MRS. ROBELLE [*rolling her eyes*]
We all of us could tell a long tale.

MRS. POLLY [*enumerating*] Robelle, she's had three husbands,
I've had two, Lord love 'em, also has Blanche.
It isn't like your aunts were inexperienced.
We all will say the same. It's that you're always
Having to learn different from the first you thought,
And make amends.
At first, it shakes you up some.

MRS. ROBELLE Of course, I couldn't say what Blanche says.
To me, they're all the same. With Fred—
He was a dentist—till the day he died
I didn't have no problem. But Maurice,
I knew he wasn't no good from the first,
So I just—paid no attention. Then Casey came,
And he's a sweetheart, but for all of that,
Between the three of them there isn't any difference.
They all got their *ways*, and you get used to them.

MRS. BLANCHE There's always one who's Mr. Right.

MRS. ROBELLE Oh, you can say that. But all I say is,
You take your chances. For me Romance is
Always just around the corner, and never out of sight.
You tell her, Pol.

[*In the following, the* AUNTS *put on a little show for* EURYDICE, *hoping to divert her from something they have seen but are unwilling to recognize. They assume their public, or Entertainment, personalities and throw themselves into the song with spirit, with elaborate gestures and simple but skillfully executed steps. They do not notice that she is sitting hanging her head and looking at her hands, smiling stiffly, until they have finished and are breathless.*

MRS. POLLY Robelle, I'm too old for this.

[*To music.*

We've been blue,
We've all been blue,
But when we were blue,
We knew what to do.

We had a friend,
Handsome and true,
We'd call on our friend,
Our troubles would end,
Our Leopard always knew
Exactly what to do.
Come on, girls.

[*They join her.*

The Leopard was our saint, Saint Leopard!
Gay and inventive.
If we were hesitant,
He was indignant!

MRS. BLANCHE [*with innocent enthusiasm*]
The Leopard was our saint, Saint Leopard,
Gay and ingenious!
Frowning at prudishness!
Charmed by experiment!

MRS. POLLY It was he that watched over us
If some preposterous
Blight to our plans
Might have proved ruinous,
He, Lord of Chance,
Leapt in and granted us
Our animal comforts.

ALL The Leopard was our saint, Saint Leopard,
Gay and inventive!

MRS. BLANCHE We had fun. We picked fruit.

MRS. POLLY Nothing ruined. We picked up.

MRS. ROBELLE [*stepping out, exaggeratedly dour*]
Fruit I ate with *one* was less than fruit.

That fruit was not fun. One should not have picked it.
The Mango less than the Paw-Paw.
The Greengage less than the Soursop.
The Pomegranate had a hole in it.
The Peach was less than the Prickly Pear.
I didn't taste a morsel for another year.

MRS. POLLY AND MRS. BLANCHE For another year!

MRS. ROBELLE But I got over that. I saw him standing
On the green, my Dote, my Batter Up, my Trick,
My Treat, and I crawled out and kicked.
I was thirty, and it was Sunday morning.
Oh, there are always those
Who trick you to suppose—

MRS. POLLY But he knows all of them!

ALL The Leopard was our saint, Saint Leopard,
That's what our Saint was.

[*Laughter. They settle down.*

MRS. POLLY Well, girls, it don't look like
We could make the kiddie loosen up.

MRS. BLANCHE It's just an ACT, Eury.
You remember that.

MRS. POLLY Eury—I'll speak straight.
We brought you up, we hoped you'd meet
An educated fellow. Well, you done it.
But—I don't know. You can hit—
A thing too hard. And when you do,
You ought to know, the crowd—
Out there—catches one, and they don't like it.
You hit too hard, it makes them nervous.
And as for you, the harder something hits you,
You'll blow up. Like day and night, that is—
Throw the wrong lines.
All I mean is,
If I was you, I wouldn't let this Orpheus
Altogether steal the act. I'd keep up
My dancing and get out, sometimes.

MRS. BLANCHE I always thought you danced lovely, Eury.

EURYDICE If I go
Back to that—
That will mean
I've given up. I don't know
How to tell you what it's like . . .

MRS. POLLY Take a poke.

EURYDICE I never know if he knows
When he touches me.
He *is* what he hears.
What he is, he hears. I don't know what he hears—
But what he hears, he does,
And there is nothing you can do for either of us.

[*Pause.*

MRS. POLLY Well, girls, that's how it is.

[*They rise. She hugs* EURYDICE.

You think kindly of your aunts, won't you?
You know we're not so gone on concerts, Eury,
But you think of us sometimes. And we're not
Writers, in our family, but we'll let you know
What towns we're playing in, and what show.
And we'll expect to hear from you the same.

EURYDICE Of course you will.

MRS. POLLY Now all this time we got something to tell you—
Something you ain't heard. It's Blanche.
Blanche is expecting!

BLANCHE Oh, Eury, ain't it awful—
At my age!

EURYDICE Blanche! Oh, no—
That's wonderful!

MRS. POLLY That's why Mortimer ain't here,
He's on the road, all by himself.
It's a great life, and you don't weaken.
Ain't that right, Blanche!

MRS. BLANCHE I'm kinda glad about it.

MRS. ROBELLE And that's the Mr. Plus—
Of understatement! Believe me.
They got him all named. Hyman.

MRS. BLANCHE For Mortimer's father!
Hyman Samuel.

MRS. POLLY And it's a girl, they call her Blanche.
Come on, girls. Let's put this circus
On the road. Goodbye, my girlie. Don't let no one
Hand you a wooden Indian with your change.

EURYDICE I'll be thinking of you, Blanche.

[AUNTS *exit.*

CURTAIN

# Act III

## SCENE I: THE TEMPTATION

JERMYN, IGNOTIUS *and* BERTIE *are circling around* ORPHEUS, *casting, if possible, long shadows on the drop beyond them.* ORPHEUS *sits in a chair, not looking up.*

JERMYN So you see, Maestro,
Why it is we come to you
At midnight. We are all three
Filled with excitement and high hopes for you.
And you'll agree, that had this letter come at four A.M.,
I could not have hesitated to inform you.
Posthaste I called our lawyers, earlier this evening.
Bidding them, immediately, to draft the contract I have here
In my pocket. Then, at eleven o'clock, I picked it up
And came here like the wind.
Consider this, I beg you.
How but for us could you assume so young
This signal honor? Conductors
Many years your senior long for
Such an opportunity as this! At once
So publicly distinguished and a thrilling challenge.

ORPHEUS [*gloomily*] Yes, I know, but—

JERMYN We have, all three, a great respect
For your considered action, but—

IGNOTIUS *Time* is what we do not have!

BERTIE [*impulsively*] Oh, Orfeo, how can you hesitate!

ORPHEUS [*to Bertie*] Because I must have time to think.

JERMYN Consider the soloists alone.

ORPHEUS Think of them.
A hundred,
Waiting to sign, their services contingent on—
Just this, the letter I have in my pocket!

[*Brings it out.*

IGNOTIUS A million dollars!
A million dollars voted us
By Music Lovers Anonymous
To bring to all the world a first-
Class record library. At low cost.

JERMYN And as we told you, this
By our request (for as you guessed,
We telephoned our gratified acceptances
Immediately), this,
Contingent on the leadership
Of that conductor named by us.
And we named—Orpheus!

ORPHEUS Yes.

JERMYN A hundred soloists? A thousand!
Confidentially, you have your choice
Of every major voice in Western Europe!
Ignotius has the contract there—

IGNOTIUS [*reading*] Assigning Orpheus conductor for
Every European orchestra
Contracted to Mozartiana, Long Play,
As well as numerous options on
The property of anyone
He wants! Including various ensembles
For strings and winds, too numerous
To mention, and—

BERTIE Two boys' choirs.

JERMYN Just listen to them.

[*snatches contract*] Evelyn Halogen, oboe and English horn.
Cora Schwartzkopf, percussion!

IGNOTIUS [*reading over his shoulder eagerly*]
Gwendolyn Nemo, mezzo-soprano!

JERMYN Constanzia Pizza, trombone!

IGNOTIUS Septimus Bombo, the master soprano
Of the Lutheran Boys, Berlin!

JERMYN And these just names at random! Listen!

IGNOTIUS Clara Dactyl! Contralto!
On option since April!

JERMYN Boris Erg! Double bass!

IGNOTIUS Kuht Unfarn! Clarinet!

JERMYN Nelli Chopp! At the harp!

BERTIE OLGO VOGELER, ORGANIST!

JERMYN Hans Antz! Helen Boom!

BERTIE AND IGNOTIUS ALBERT ALP, AT THE CONTRA-BASSOON!

[EURYDICE *enters unnoticed and stands at back. The boys fall back and wait their answer eagerly, with tension.*

ORPHEUS [*with emotion*] You have offered me the moon.

JERMYN [*craftily*] All these, and you have not heard the best—
Orfeo. It is—EOHIPPUS!

ORPHEUS [*taken aback*] She? She has agreed?

JERMYN [*smugly*] An unrestricted contract.

ORPHEUS She. The very greatest.
That great, gold voice.

JERMYN [*relaxing*] Yes. Eohippus and a hundred others.
Considering your age . . .

ORPHEUS An honor. Yes. But how can I accept it?
I am committed, you know that—

IGNOTIUS [*craftily*] To what, if not to honor?

JERMYN To what, possibly? You will not be
So long away. The end of May, no longer,
This year—

ORPHEUS The end of May, exactly.
And traveling continually.
Brussels, you said. Vienna. Salzburg.
In the meantime my symphony
Lies in a drawer. No—it must be no.
There is my concerto, promised for February . . .
And, of course, Eurydice.

JERMYN But, Orfeo—

ORPHEUS [*jumping up*] Please, it must be—no.

BERTIE [*in despair*] Orfeo, how can you say so!
We are your friends, who want the best for you!
Jermyn is trying to give you the whole world!

[EURYDICE *comes slowly into the light. They all step back, startled.*

EURYDICE I'm sorry. I didn't want to interrupt.
I know it's business. I'll go out—
And wait until you're finished.

ORPHEUS We are finished. It's all right.
Gentlemen, you know my wife. Eurydice.
Who has been out all evening at the movies.

JERMYN Forgive me, Orpheus. The night is nearly gone.
Those cablegrams must go by morning.
I know that Mrs. Orpheus will understand,
And pardon this intrusion, when
You explain to her the grave importance
Of our errand. You see,
We hang upon your answer.

ORPHEUS You make it very difficult for me, Jermyn!

EURYDICE [*trying to be gracious*]
I'm going to bed anyway.

[*Exit.*

ORPHEUS [*waits till she is gone*]
You offer me the world.
Don't think I am unmoved.
On the contrary,
I am deeply disturbed.
It is my judgment that deters me—I am
Reluctant to turn so completely
From my *own music*, at this time.
And I am young—as you mentioned—
To become a monument . . .

JERMYN [*with a knowing, deadly smile—his trump*]
Very well. It's *simply this*, Orpheus.
Spitsbergen is in Boston. Visiting.
Perhaps you see what this means.

ORPHEUS Spitsbergen!

JERMYN Ye-es.

ORPHEUS [*after a pregnant silence*]
Spitsbergen. You couldn't
Possibly consider him . . .

JERMYN Who else? You force me to it.
He is our next choice.
Confronted, if I am, by your refusal,
I shall, of course, go telephone at once,
Long distance.
He is not *un*aware
That this is hanging fire, being close
To foundation decisions, as he is.
*He* will not sneer at one million dollars!

ORPHEUS Spitsbergen! You can't be serious.
A squalid sentimentalist, who
Persistently misinterprets, even butchers,
Everything he touches!

IGNOTIUS Oh, not always, Orpheus.
Consider the Mizpah music. Marvelous!

JERMYN *He* will not sneer at ten great orchestras!

ORPHEUS You cannot mean this.

JERMYN Indeed we do mean it.
He records for Thoreau, Tito, Black Back,
And Sansouci, L.P.—who are all willing
To release him, if need be, indefinitely.
And just this afternoon we cleared him
With the BBC.
Bertie made the call.

ORPHEUS Just a moment. Eurydice?
[*rattled*] We are going downstairs, to the lounge.
[*to* JERMYN] I *can*not think clearly
In a smoke-filled room.
It has become suffocatingly close.

IGNOTIUS But I opened the windows,
When I lit my first—

JERMYN He has fully recovered, Orpheus,
From the operation on his ear.

BERTIE Oh, Orfeo, come in with us!
We will make history, you know we will!

ORPHEUS [*with a deep sigh*] Very well.

JERMYN What!

ORPHEUS I cannot permit you
To ruin yourselves . . . or to be fools
On my account. Yes. I will.

IGNOTIUS Hurray!

JERMYN You make me very happy.

BERTIE Orfeo, how thrilling!

JERMYN We'll drink to this, at once.

IGNOTIUS At once—we're all too tense.

ORPHEUS Yes.

BERTIE We'll launch a new world in with drinks!

JERMYN And now, just lacking two o'clock,
We know our work has taken root,
And will bear flowers taller than ourselves.
[*All exit. Light dies.*

## SCENE II: NIGHTMARE

VOICE Eurydice?

EURYDICE [*from her bed*] Go away. I don't want to talk.

VOICE You've got to go to the end of the street
And turn back.

EURYDICE I can't.

VOICE You had better.

EURYDICE I shall not go back.

VOICE You've got to.

EURYDICE You don't know. You're dead.

VOICE Do you know who I am?

EURYDICE You're Aunt Blanche's dog.
And you're dead.

VOICE *Why* am I dead?
What's the matter,
Scared?

EURYDICE It wasn't my *fault!*

VOICE Oh, wasn't it!
She told you, didn't she,
To keep me on a leash?

EURYDICE You pulled my hands!

VOICE Ha-ha. We know who let go.

EURYDICE We! Who says so?

VOICE Fidelis is here too.

EURYDICE No!

FIDELIS I am so. And believe me,
Everything you get is
Just what you deserve.
Don't think I didn't know
I was deserted. Cruelly.
Left all alone, in West Palm Beach.
I starved to death.

EURYDICE It's not true! Besides!
I loved you! I looked everywhere!

FIDELIS But not beneath the car.

EURYDICE I did! I did! And you weren't anywhere!

FIDELIS But not—under—the car.

VOICE Come on. You haven't any
Time to spare. You've just enough
To get away from here.

[EURYDICE *comes out in nightgown. She is dreaming.*

EURYDICE Listen, Fidelis, you've got to.
I love you. I never had another—just you.
I'm NOT GUILTY!

FIDELIS Says you.

EURYDICE Ask *him!* He knows I was afraid of him!
I hated dogs! They always frightened me!

VOICE You needn't rub it in.

EURYDICE But you were different!

FIDELIS Well, yes. I was a cat.

EURYDICE And you were *mine!*

FIDELIS All right. Why didn't you find me?

VOICE Come on. You haven't any time.

EURYDICE Not tonight!

VOICE Yes, tonight. He'll never miss you.

FIDELIS Serves you right, too.

EURYDICE Not tonight!

VOICE All right. We'll be back.

FIDELIS Oh, we will, no mistake.

EURYDICE Fidelis!

FIDELIS [*fainter*] Well, what.

EURYDICE Please come back!

FIDELIS What is it now?

EURYDICE You've got to know—
I did love you.

FIDELIS That's just it.
It's not enough.

EURYDICE Love?

FIDELIS Of course not!
I starved, didn't I?
What did *I* care
If you loved me or not!

[*Blackout.*

## SCENE III: NIGHTMARE

*When the lights come up, they are on a table upstage right.* JERMYN, IGNOTIUS *and* BERTIE *are seated around it. There is a fourth chair.*

IGNOTIUS I do wish Orfeo would hurry up.

BERTIE Oh, I'm so glad he signed the contract!

JERMYN He'll be right back. Where is that waitress!

IGNOTIUS It's quite marvelous to see him take control
Of any situation. Who else could keep so cool
Or so precise. Imagine getting reservations
And airplane tickets at this hour of the morning!

JERMYN I told him to entrust those matters to me.
But he, alas, trusts no one but himself.

IGNOTIUS He respects *you*, Jermyn,
More than anyone. One sees that.

JERMYN Do you think so, really?

BERTIE Oh, yes, Jermyn.

IGNOTIUS It's obvious.

JERMYN [*expansively*] How little do they ask of us, the Masters!
And yet without us—it is their secret—
They would be lost! They are like little lambs
Locked in the pasture of their thoughts,
In prospect of their works! Without us—
We, the shepherds—how could the world have access
To these hidden treasures? We tiptoe in,
And find their hiding place, and
Seize upon them!
Where *is* that waitress?

IGNOTIUS Here she comes. At last.

[*Enter* EURYDICE *in her nightgown carrying a small tray.*

EURYDICE Yes?

JERMYN Well, fellows?
I think that we should have champagne
In honor of Orpheus!

BERTIE Of course!

IGNOTIUS Of course!

JERMYN Very well. Waitress,
We will require one, or possibly

Two bottles of champagne, and four glasses.
I would like to see the wine list.

EURYDICE Who's the fourth?

JERMYN [*irritably*] A fourth is joining us.

EURYDICE I'm sorry. I can't take his order
Until he comes. Not even for a glass.
That is, unless you can produce
His draft card.

JERMYN What's this?

EURYDICE You have to prove
He's not a minor, or an alien
Conspiring to overthrow this country.

JERMYN *Really*. Very well, we'll call you when he comes.
In the meantime, *please*, the wine list.
And could you bring some popcorn? I see
The dishes on the other tables.

EURYDICE [*wistfully*] If you could only prove your friend was eligible.
You must have something. A passport picture,
An attestation, notarized, by some
Friendly immigration officer?

IGNOTIUS Really, waitress, that is quite enough for now.
We'll let you know about our friend. Please go.
[*She starts to go and returns.*

EURYDICE I know. You're mad at me
Because I intimated that your friend might be
A foreigner. You mustn't take offense.
There is a certain hostile difference
Between our attitudes, I always sense it—
You foreigners are so defiant, and so proud.
You do cling to your differences so!
That's why you wear your funny hats and coats—
And that hair—

IGNOTIUS Once and for all, waitress,
We are *not* foreigners. Jermyn
Was born in Cambridge, Mass., and this
Is my brother, Bertie, who was
Born where I was, Pigpye, Indiana.

JERMYN This is preposterous.
It always happens, in these places.
One encounters witless
Curiosity and insolence.
Tell her to go away.

IGNOTIUS Yes, now, please!
He asked for the wine list.

JERMYN No! Never mind it.
Just bring a champagne.
Don't *you* choose it.
Ask the maître d'hôtel.
I know you have one.

BERTIE There was, Jermyn, I saw him.

EURYDICE There is, but you can't have him.
You'll have to let me choose one.

JERMYN Heaven forfend! We'll all
Be poisoned.

IGNOTIUS Time is running *out*, waitress.
Can you not appreciate our positions?
We are at your mercy here.
Now, if the situations were *reversed*,
How would you feel about us?
You would wish us to serve you immediately,
And to make no fuss. About your age,
Your clothes, or your face—
Put yourself in our place!

JERMYN You would think very little of us waiters
If we stood and stared, or gabbled and glared,
Or presented ridiculous obstacles—

EURYDICE I'll do my very best!

JERMYN NO!
Your best is *not* enough.
Send someone else. I'm sorry, but
That's how it is.

EURYDICE My best?

JERMYN Would be indifferent.
Just send us someone else.

EURYDICE [*rushing off*] Fidelis!

IGNOTIUS [*seeing* ORPHEUS *approaching offstage*]
Thank heaven, Orpheus appears!

[*Enter* ORPHEUS.

ORPHEUS [*sitting*] I'm sorry.

JERMYN Is everything all right?

ORPHEUS [*cups ear, frowning*] Yes. What's that atrocious,
Faint, but clearly audible distant
Music?

BERTIE Orpheus, you'll never guess!
We have a Mad Waitress!
What fun.

JERMYN [*discontentedly*] She didn't bring the popcorn.
Yes,
One can so easily antagonize
The waitresses of life. Who knows?
One's very looks elicit an
Unpredictable response.

IGNOTIUS [*wringing hands*] The country screams with tensions.
Strong men weep for their mothers.
Peeping Toms weep to become exhibitionists;
Exhibitionists weep to be Peeping Toms.
And every day a hundred thousand
Snap!—and are carried off.

[*Reenter* EURYDICE. *She puts down three glasses on their table. They pay no attention.*

EURYDICE Can I take your order, please?

JERMYN Well, fellows?

IGNOTIUS I still say—and I fear
If we don't make it clear to her,
They'll close the bar—a fine champagne.
It doesn't matter—Brut,
Of any year from '47 on.

EURYDICE From 1947 on.

JERMYN You didn't bring the popcorn.

EURYDICE It's popping. It's almost done.

JERMYN And as you see, our friend has come.

ORPHEUS Thank you, I won't have anything.

EURYDICE [*to* ORPHEUS *as the others pay no attention. Urgently*]
I came because you called.
How could I know you did not really want me?
If you—as I believe—
Have lost your faith,
Then everything I have cannot console me!

ORPHEUS You know, you shouldn't allow
It to matter. I've tried to tell you.

EURYDICE But don't you see? You tricked me!
With my hands in little bags and my head
In a basket, I only came because you called!

ORPHEUS I'm sorry.

[*Enter* WAITER *with champagne.*

JERMYN Observe he hasn't brought the popcorn, either.

BERTIE But the beautiful bottle!

WAITER [*pouring the champagne and emptying their ashtray, matter-of-factly, to* ORPHEUS]
For shame. To put a great bell above your auditorium
And pound the quarters, and by a pet diminutive

Assert a dearness you knew was not there!
You in elaborate brochures sang to her.
She came to you. Now, where is she to go
That has no home? She slept, uncomforted in
Your classrooms, and is soiled and lame!

ORPHEUS I will have no part in this.

JERMYN At last! A toast to Orpheus!
To us—for all the years to come . . .
[*All drink but* ORPHEUS.

WAITER

[*He starts to fill glasses again.*

Well?

ORPHEUS [*impatiently*] I cannot answer for her.
I hadn't understood that that
Was to be part of it.

WAITER Do you, Eurydice,
Become a votary to extradition?

EURYDICE Shall I be innocent by association?

WAITER You shall be gravel,
And grasses will not grow on you.

EURYDICE Oh, yes. I know.

WAITER Eury, Eury, the folly of order
That would not fit the outer, weedy world.
Tangles your fearful, now damaging footfall.
Look behind you and weep for
Your loss of the bright world.
It's a little too late.

EURYDICE Oh, I regret—
I was not cunning, and I came here by idiom,
Forgetting I could forget to understand!
*How do you do*, *ho-hum*, and *Oh*, *Hell* did for a little
while.
But how to put this crooked hunger
That came up out of nowhere and would not be fed?

ORPHEUS I cannot help it.
I have no time.

EURYDICE I'll fix you! I'll go blind!
And not a swallow, however quick,
Shall catch my tongue as I shall
Batten it! Both blind and dumb,
I'll hunger where no light can come,
Or bell can sound!

WAITER [*idly*] The worm has swallowed the swallow,
And the beasts are buried in lime.

EURYDICE Should I grow wands and my arms learn hands,
Honey where my shoulders snap?
How could I call you for your further contentment?

WAITER The lilies lie under quills
That lit our proud shields.

ORPHEUS I tell you, I can't help it.
My time is specified. She'll have to
Bury her dead to her own content.
I have no solution for it.
I have to think about what is important,
You know that. What is basic.

WAITER You heard him.

EURYDICE Oh, yes.

[*Exit.*

WAITER [*shaking the last drop out of the bottle*]
The suns are dead
That we inherited,
They shine like rusty spoons.

[*He exits.* JERMYN, IGNOTIUS *and* BERTIE *rise and gather around* ORPHEUS. ORPHEUS *looks at them, puzzled, as if he were aware that he had been taking part in someone else's dream.*

JERMYN Well, Orpheus, what news?

ORPHEUS Next week, by way of Holland,
Reservations promised.

THE THREE Congratulations.

[*Blackout.*

## SCENE IV

EURYDICE'S VOICE Orphée, is that you?

[ORPHEUS *walks back into their room and stands silently by the couch. He is very tired.*

ORPHEUS Yes. Are you awake?

EURYDICE'S VOICE I don't know.

ORPHEUS [*looking up, almost impatiently*]
How do you mean, you don't know?
[*she doesn't answer*] It's very late.

[EURYDICE *enters and goes to him. He holds her.*

EURYDICE You know, I had a cat once.
I lost it.

ORPHEUS [*still holding her*] Did you dream that?

EURYDICE It wasn't my fault.

ORPHEUS You heard Jermyn, didn't you?
What they said?

EURYDICE About the contract.

ORPHEUS I have to go.

[*She frees herself gently.*

EURYDICE I know.

ORPHEUS [*looking at her*] Sometimes they anger me, also.
How would you like to go to Europe?

EURYDICE You'll take me?

ORPHEUS [*wearily*] Did you think I didn't want you?
Eurydice, I expect you find it

Difficult, sometimes. You realize
This will be no less so.
You'll have to stay in one place.
Probably Paris. I'll be traveling
Back and forth. But there'll be
Weekends . . . we'll go on trips . . .
To the French countryside. Good look at *châteaux* . . .
*[His voice gives out. He is more tired than he remembers having been in his life.*
Eurydice, I'm tired. Oh, so tired.
Let's get some sleep now.
*[Blackout.*

## SCENE V

*The cocktail lounge, as before, but three months later.* JERMYN *is eating vigorously, but the others are drinking. Throughout the scene, they get progressively drunker.*

JERMYN How long since anyone
Has heard from Orpheus?

IGNOTIUS He's perfectly terrible at writing letters.
Only Bertie hears from him.

JERMYN [*darkly*] You mean, he jots a penciled note
On his reports to us. He surely—
Doesn't *write* to Bertie?

BERTIE Oh, no, just because I'm secretary.

JERMYN The time that has gone hence in passage
Seems immeasurable, in months. And yet—
When did he go? In March.
When he gets back,
I must speak to him—of his future.
*Hollywood is waiting.*
One day, I shall persuade him.
Mmmm. *Richesse.* Why not?

IGNOTIUS You don't think they'll tear him up,
Jermyn? He's so intense . . .

JERMYN [*coldly*] Nonsense.

BERTIE This-week-all-week-until-July-sixteenth
He's touring France.
I think Eurydice is with him.

JERMYN Yes.
Ah, well. Our record sales
Are in the millions, as of figures
Collated in the month of May. F.M. reports
On listeners not yet in.
The popular taste achieves new heights.
As Music Lovers Anonymous had hoped.
As for myself, I have been justified
Beyond my keenest hopes, a happy man
Who justly serves both God and Mammon.

[IGNOTIUS *and* BERTIE *drain their glasses and reach for a bottle on the table at the same time.* JERMYN *continues chewing.*

IGNOTIUS That's right, Jermyn.

JERMYN But is this not the curse, Ignotius,
Of greatness—that it must, perforce,
Be victimized by *lesser* spirits?
The butter, please?
It's at your elbow.

IGNOTIUS Exactly . . . lesser spirits? Oh, yes.
Xanthippe.

JERMYN Take, for instance, Orpheus.
Orpheus should not have married.
He is by nature celibate—fanatic—
His whole being, in itself, a poem
To spiritual man.

BERTIE [*from his elbows*] Charlotte Corday?

JERMYN That is *not* the point I'm making.
Bertie. Pay attention. Try to follow.
[*fluently, with sonorous conviction*]
—The painful fact is,

It always happens:
Hero, God, and Warrior
Making this persistent error—
As is written, as is read—
The Hero's bride is always stupid,
The instrument of his Defeat!

BERTIE [*while* JERMYN *is looking around for applause*]
I like Eurydice . . .
Common, but quite a dear, really.
[*coming awake*] Why, do you know, that at this very moment,
She has an aunt that's in the circus?

IGNOTIUS [*waking enough to come to* BERTIE'S *rescue—his brother, after all*]
You put it—so very *well*, Jermyn.
Bertie, don't bring person*al*ity
Into a general Socratic
Discourse. You always do.
Go on, Jermyn, won't you?

JERMYN [*frowning*] What was I saying . . . yes!
In almost every case,
A woman in some way debased
Is the exasperating flaw!
A glance at Literature,
Or to the treasury of folklore,
Confirms our thought:
The great heart suffers,
Pinched in close quarters.
What is extraordinary is
The Hero chooses these himself.
Xanthippe. Yes. Deianeira—
You will recall that bit of business
With the centaur. Hercules,
Her husband, was poisoned.
Juno, a shrew, Eve, Pandora, Psyche,
To mention but a few, whose sneaky
Witless curiosity occurred at home.

All literature is filled with them!
The wonder is, the Heroes wanted them.
Alas! Who *are* these
Lares and Penates? *Devils.*

IGNOTIUS And all those others too.
Officious Dido! or Cleopatra,
*Vain and fat.* One doubts
The charm of Heloise was widely felt.

JERMYN Might I suggest, the more distinguished
Are not *born* at all, of women:
Minerva, now, or Dionysus—
Not born at all but *unstitched*
From the thigh of Zeus—
Caesar,
Or the obvious example
From Shakespeare . . . or
Romulus and Remus!
Who nourished *them* as youth?
Wolves!

IGNOTIUS Wolves!

JERMYN At the moment, I can bring to mind
One instance only of a woman's
Having uttered sentiments both noble and profound
Throughout the Classics—
Ruth, in Sacred Writ.
And I consider it *significant*,
These sentiments, *not* to her husband,
But *to another woman who is going on a trip!*
[*He looks around triumphantly.*

[*tranquilly*] Yes, indeed, we may infer
From all of Ancient Literature,
And certainly, from Life—
Achilles' heel could well be called his wife.

IGNOTIUS Hear, hear!

JERMYN [*graciously*] The term, a picturesque device
Employing art to improvise from life.

[JERMYN *rises, smiling grimly at* IGNOTIUS *and* BERTIE, *who have fallen asleep. Blackout.*

## SCENE VI

*Music from here until the end. A pale-blue light picks out a signpost far upstage, a signpost like a scarecrow tree which spiders have bound into a web. The signs, which point haphazardly, read* LE NORD (ORPHEUS *will go out to the north*), LE SUD (*where they came from*), *and a large, center sign can be seen which says* LAC DES SINGES. ORPHEUS *and* EURYDICE *are lost in a wood in the South of France. The light which lights the signpost is dim and does not show them clearly when they come, wheeling foreign bicycles.* EURYDICE *should stay in shadow.* ORPHEUS *comes on first alone, wheeling his bicycle, sees the signpost and goes to stand before it, striking a match.*

ORPHEUS Exactly as I feared. Twelve kilometers
Off too far, and off the proper road
At who-knows-where. I dare say
Westerly and back, as far as Neuve,
Or Vienne Le Sud. Too far, and then again,
Short of the turn. How could it have happened?

EURYDICE [*coming slowly on stage*]
Orphée, are we lost?

ORPHEUS [*consulting his watch*]
Back at the fork I had a premonition—
This country is, I thought, too large and dark
For Brie. Somewhere we did not watch
The turn, or were distracted, and rode on
And out of the direction. Eurydice,
We have been swallowed up, the trees
Cut off the moon.

EURYDICE Can I sit down?

ORPHEUS NO! Of course not. Did you never climb
A mountain? The moment you give in,

You lose your mind and find you have become
As helpless as a child. If you sit down,
You lose your will and cannot climb
Or even move your hand, then you are done,
One can't sit down, as everybody knows,
Except on the return. We must go on
Until we have no longer need to.

EURYDICE What need?

ORPHEUS Fear of night, or even that
We are unsure. Stop that! Stand up.
You can let go your wheel, but do not
Even rest unless you're very sure
Of being able to get up again
And to go on.

EURYDICE I will. But somewhere near
The Lac des Singes,
A place the trees were cleared,
I hurt my heel . . .

ORPHEUS Three A.M. We may be out by dawn.
It's good by night, I find the sun
Exhausting and make better time
By far by night when it is cooler.
Come on. One cigarette, but don't sit down,
And we'll be on our way.

[EURYDICE *shakes her head, takes a few steps.*

EURYDICE Orphée—I don't know if I can.

ORPHEUS What's wrong?

EURYDICE My heel. I pulled it.

ORPHEUS You're lame? You probably strained
A muscle. You won't feel it, once you're on
Your wheel again. How long ago?

EURYDICE Back the road somewhere,
A place the trees were cleared.
We went by water.

ORPHEUS It can't be helped, Eurydice,
You'll have to do the best you can.

EURYDICE How long?

ORPHEUS Till morning, probably.

EURYDICE And then?

ORPHEUS Until the afternoon, providing
A clear road, the wind behind,
And a cool sun. Come on.

EURYDICE Orphée, my best is not enough.
Let me sleep, please!

ORPHEUS Eurydice! I have engagements
All over France commencing Tuesday. Please,
Don't make me regret we took this trip,
Or found the time to go away a weekend.
Breathe deeply,
Put out your cigarette, and we'll go on.

EURYDICE [*frightened*] Orphée, my hands are cold.

ORPHEUS We're better off for it.
A cutting edge of cold beneath
The morning air, a sense of chill
That stiffens these excessive trees.

EURYDICE [*taking a few steps*] Orphée—

ORPHEUS All ready? Hop! I'll lead as hitherto.
Take heart! It won't be long. You'll
Be asleep in Brie before the afternoon.
And this time, keep pace, Eurydice.
I can't be always looking back
To see if you are keeping up.
Just make this special effort till we're out of here.
[*Rides off.*

EURYDICE [*still standing beside bicycle*]
Orhpée, my hands are cold.
[*to herself*] My hands are cold.

CURTAIN

## Epilogue—Ten Years Later

COCO CRAMBO *sits alone, huddled in a coat, his eyes shut. The ball game is playing behind him.* CHORUS GIRLS *are sleeping at the back. A man is quietly painting a box silver. After a while, the* MANAGER *enters, looks around as if he were checking off an interior inventory, and finally comes over to* CRAMBO. *The* MANAGER *wears an old blue suit, a Hollywood shirt, keeps a cigar in his mouth. This man is* not loud. *He picks his way past a stacked pile of posters.*

MANAGER Say, Crambo.

[CRAMBO *does not open his eyes.*

Say, Crambo! Coco Crambo!

[CRAMBO *opens his eyes and looks at him. He nods slightly. Nobody else looks up or notices.*

MANAGER Didn't ja go out between shows?

CRAMBO [*to himself*] Cold. Hah?

MANAGER Didn't ja go out between shows!

[CRAMBO *wakes fully and adjusts coat, snarling.*

CRAMBO [*slowly and distinctly*] Go out? What for?
I looked out this morning.
I seen it.
This is Union City,
And I seen it. I been here
Sixty-one times since they shut down
New York City, and I seen it.
Ten minutes outa New York, and it
Could be DeButte. Them dirty
Streets. The rooming houses.
The post office. The jerks that live here.

And come to see us. Thank you.
I seen it.

MANAGER Ya listening to the Series?

CRAMBO No.
Say,
If you don't mind my saying so,
Why the hell don't you heat this theater?

MANAGER Ya find it cold, Crambo?

CRAMBO Yes, I find it cold.

[*One of the* CHORUS *wakes up at this and sits up, straining to listen.*

MANAGER Well, I don't know.
It seems just right, to me.
Besides, it ain't up to me.
It's up to the office. Cold.
I wouldn't say so.

[MANAGER *exits, back to his inventory.* CRAMBO *shuts his eyes. The* CHORUS GIRL *gets up and comes over to him swiftly. She sits down beside him.*

CHORUS GIRL I heard ja say that, Mr. Crambo.
And let me tell *you.* Two years ago,
We made out a petition, and we sent it
Upstairs with Rose. That's Rose.

[*Points at sleeping figure.*

We've got to have more heat down here,
It said. There wasn't *never any answer.*

[*Waits, but* CRAMBO *does not acknowledge. So she goes on.*

So we sent someone up! Not just
Anybody, but Florence. Our number producer.
She spoke for us. Rose is sick, she said,
And Shorty quit. Babe has pains in her leg,
And Pat can't move her back. We're all sick
From the cold, she said.

[CRAMBO *does not respond. She waits.*

Well. She went up there,
And the secretary took the paper.
I'll tell them, she said. But you'll
Just have to wait.
Nothing ever happened.

CRAMBO [*after a pause and still not bothering to look up*]
Okay, that's very tough.

CHORUS GIRL Maybe if you spoke about it?

CRAMBO I'm just in the traveling show, kid.
[*After a moment, as his eyes remained shut, she gets up and goes back to the girls.*

CRAMBO [*muttering to himself*]
Gonna tell that agent
Not to book me here, not for
Another winter . . .

MANAGER [*returning briskly*]
Okay, look smart, girls.
Up! They're running off the traveler.
[GIRLS *wake up and stir.*
Ten minutes, you got.
Coco? Ready to wow 'em?

CRAMBO Yes, I am.

MANAGER You comics are always clowning.
[*He makes this as a flat statement.*
Look smart, girls. Where's Lotus?
Where's my feature? Where's
Crystal Flame. Where's Lotus?

ONE OF THE GIRLS Dressing.

ANOTHER GIRL They're all in.

MANAGER She's in her room?
Onstage, girls.
[*Exit.*

[EURYDICE *enters and crosses left to right toward* CRAMBO *and toward her dressing room off right.*

*She is wearing a turtleneck sweater, a dark straight skirt, and a trench coat over her shoulders, but her shoes are stripper's shoes, and her hair is in pin curls under a scarf. She stops short of* CRAMBO.

EURYDICE [*smiling*] Hello—Hyman.

CRAMBO [*comes wide awake and sits up, pleased*]
Oh, it's you! Say
You remembered that, didn't you?
Remembered what I told you,
My right name.

EURYDICE Hyman . . . Well, you see,
I have a nephew Hyman, ten
Years old, on television. So
It isn't likely I'd forget the name.

CRAMBO That's so. You told me.
Been across the street?

EURYDICE Just for a cup of coffee.
I sat and listened to the Series.

CRAMBO That's it. It's all the same.
Union City, Jersey City, Newark.

[*Music beginning elsewhere. The* CHORUS GIRLS *cross stage right, leaving their coats in a heap just off stage left wings.*

CRAMBO There they go. The second show.
You know, I been
Thinking. We talked some,
You and I, this year, and last year,
And the year before, each time
I come here, we had a talk.
And each time I come back
I tell myself you will have taken off
For New York City. That you won't be here.

EURYDICE [*lightly*] Why do you think that?

CRAMBO Well. Your Aunt Blanche.
Or that other one, that owns

The Steak House up in Maine.
Why don't you go and live with them?
There's lots of good work
Other places. Be a bookkeeper
For your aunt. Or a hostess.
They want you, don't they?
Don't they write you, and say so?

[*The* CHORUS GIRLS *pick up their coats and go off, bumping into a stripper who is trying to get "on" stage which is off stage left.*

EURYDICE Yes, they still do.
Once in a while.
I suppose
I'm comfortable, where I am.
Same old apartment.
Same old routine . . .
Crambo,
Are you trying to say something?

CRAMBO Suppose I am.
[*looking away abruptly*] That one went on,
That's Crystal Flame, the feature.
Just a young kid. She came here from
The Western Circuit, she's been on
The wheel now, eighteen months.
I ever mention, Eury,
I once took lessons on the violin?

EURYDICE [*politely*] Is that so, Crambo?

CRAMBO That don't mean nothing to you?

EURYDICE Mean?

CRAMBO My mother, she was Russian—she
Liked the violin.

EURYDICE But you still do play, don't you?

CRAMBO Still play. Yeah, I do.
I play the fiddle in the scene

With the policeman.

[*Two* COMICS *and a* WOMAN *cross to go "on."*

WOMAN What's the matter they don't
Heat this place? Jesus.

EURYDICE I'll see you, Crambo.

CRAMBO Wait a minute, Eury, I got
Something to tell you.

[*But she is off.* CRYSTAL *returns and goes out opposite, followed by* CHORUS GIRL *carrying her "clothes" on a hanger.*

FIRST COMIC Say, Crambo, who's ahead?
Who's ahead in the *game*?

CRAMBO [*not hearing*] Eighteen months on the wheel.

FIRST COMIC Say, Crambo.

CRAMBO [*turning*] You say something?

FIRST COMIC [*seeing his queer look; the others peer at him*]
No. Never mind.

[*They go "on" stage.*

CRAMBO The wheel.

[ORPHEUS *enters. Blinking at the dark and stepping cautiously, he is wearing a black overcoat, hat, carries an umbrella. He removes his hat, on some strange impulse.*

ORPHEUS I beg your pardon—

CRAMBO [*still to himself*] The wheel—

ORPHEUS [*louder*] You are Mr. Crambo, I believe?

CRAMBO [*springing up*] No! Not yet! I told you
Nine o'clock. No, wait—
That's all right—she's in there.

ORPHEUS [*quietly*] You said my wife was here?

CRAMBO I told you nine o'clock—
The show just started—

You got to stand back [*going to him*] there.
I meant to tell you,
They don't let no one in here.
No one. Not in showtime, not
Anytime, not visitors, salesmen,
Anyone. Half of them here has
Grown kids. They can't come.
  See,
I got you in, but—

ORPHEUS  Where is she?

CRAMBO  She's here. You stand there.

ORPHEUS  What is she doing here?

CRAMBO  She likes it—no one ever sees her.
She don't care much particular what she does. She dances.
Sometimes, she takes the lead-off in
The chorus—that's to say, she dances with the rest.
Other times it's features for the house—
She's with the house, permanently,
She don't travel, see.

ORPHEUS  I don't remember that she danced.

CRAMBO  Mister, please stay there. Right there.
You come early. Right now,
  [*listening*] I'm on.
  I hope I done the right thing.

[*Exit.*

[CHORUS GIRLS, *who follow* CRAMBO'S *routine, return.* ORPHEUS *shrinks back almost into curtain.* GIRLS *go to* CRAMBO'S *benches, one holding a Coke. Casual, not seeing* ORPHEUS.

FIRST GIRL [*limping*]  Here, it's cold enough to burn you.
Let me tell you. Listen, Rose,
Do you know what you did? When
You led off the waltz, you led off
On my foot.

ROSE  You didn't do it right. I told you.
You shoulda gone to switchboard, but you went to clock—

No wonder you got hurt.
Flo, get me a Coke
If that's what you're going—

FLO I ain't.

SECOND GIRL Flo is sick. She's going to put her feet up.

ROSE On the *prop bed?*
He won't let you use that!
We all tried it. He's got
A great board acrost it,
So you can't.

SECOND GIRL You can't hardly do no worse than
Ask him, Flo.

FLO I got to put my feet up.

[*Exit.*

ROSE Well, he won't *let* you.
[*to the others*] I wouldn't put my head on that bed,
Let alone lie down.

SECOND GIRL It's clean.

ROSE Don't please amuse me. Them sheets
Have been the same about a million years,
The comics all say that.
They kid the manager about it. He tells them
It looks clean—from the house.
That's all he cares.

SECOND GIRL Clean! I hate them dirty scenes.
The scenes they use the bed in,
They are *foul-mouthed.*

ROSE It's all the same. I just don't listen.

SECOND GIRL I won't be in them dirty scenes.
I said to Crambo, You can keep your speaking lines.
It ain't worth five dollars extra,
Not to me
[*bitterly*] "Call me, in the night,

If anything comes up." He's got Ura
Dis to say that, this week.

ROSE The way she says it
It don't mean nothing. It could be
She was saying, "May I take your order, please?"
Across the street at Jimmy's.

THIRD GIRL Shut up, Rose. Look.

*[As soon as they see* ORPHEUS, *they shrink in toward themselves and away from him. They are startled, not because they recognize him, but because he is a stranger and does not belong there, which cannot happen.*

ROSE Who's that?

THIRD GIRL Look out. He might
Be from the Management, upstairs.

ROSE *[scornfully]* Them fellers never come down here.

SECOND GIRL Rose, it must be that one
From the Blue Cross.

ROSE *[equally scornfully]* Last year
We seen him in the front office.
They wouldn't let him backstage.

SECOND GIRL Look out, that's all I say,
Look out. They sent him in.

FIRST GIRL The *union*, Rose . . . remember?
They'll want to know, up there—
*You* know—They don't want us to join the—

ROSE Okay. Shut your face.
They're not going to find out
Nothing, not from us they won't,
Them *[hissing]* spies.

*[Enter* CRAMBO, *back from his stint. He throws down a prop angrily, pushing the girls aside.*

FIRST GIRL *[excitedly]* Mr. Crambo, *look!*

CRAMBO [*not looking*] You girls go peddle your papers.
This ain't your business.
I know who he is.
He's got *permission.*

FIRST GIRL He ain't a—

CRAMBO You just go about your business.
No, he ain't.

[*Girls start off indignantly.*

ROSE Pay no attention!
He's *ignorant.*

[*They exit.*

CRAMBO I'm sorry, Mr. Orpheus.
Them girls don't understand
Who you are, that's all.
They're very strict here. It's
Everywhere the same. Now Ura Dis
Goes on before the intermission.
She's coming out, you'll see her. Then—

ORPHEUS I understand.

CRAMBO *Do* you? What I mean, you see,
First thing, you see her. Next,
She goes on. Next thing, intermission,
Then, once on again. In that time—
You wait out there at the door,
That's why I told you come *later.*
If they see you standing watching her
Or anybody on stage,
They'll throw you out of here.

ORPHEUS When you came to me—and spoke—
You were not clear, not clear at all—
I still don't understand what—

[SECOND GIRL *returns.*

CRAMBO I told you girls get out of here!

SECOND GIRL *If* you don't mind, Mr. Crambo,
I'm catching for the extra. Ura's
Doing that spot this week, and I'm catching.

CRAMBO [*to* ORPHEUS, *tiredly*] The features got to have
A girl that picks up, that's what
I tell you, *she's*,
This week, got a feature.
[*waving his hands helplessly*] A feature—specialties—
[*to* SECOND GIRL] Okay, just
Stand somewhere else. Go on,
Will you?

[SECOND GIRL *crosses angrily to opposite back corner and sits down.*

CRAMBO [*to himself, a supplication*] I hope I done the right thing.

[*The two* COMICS *and a* WOMAN *enter from "on" stage, and not looking at* ORPHEUS, CRAMBO, *or* GIRL, *but talking among themselves, cross and exit. Enter* EURYDICE. *Her costume isn't particularly brassy. It is pathetic and obviously a makeshift. Regular features buy their own costumes, of course, and these are extremely expensive. House features, or fill-ins, make their own in the interminable waiting periods between dance numbers.*

CRAMBO [*to* ORPHEUS] That's *her.*

ORPHEUS [*stepping forward*] Eurydice.

EURYDICE [*looking around, startled by the pronunciation of her name*]
Yes—Crambo—
[*whispers*] Orpheus . . .

[ORPHEUS *draws a little nearer to her so that they are facing each other at a distance of perhaps eight feet. They freeze into wooden positions with their arms at stiff angles throughout the following.*

CRAMBO [*Coming well forward and sitting on a high stool, speaking into the audience*]
*That's* it. You two get together again.
I won't interrupt. You got twenty minutes,
You have, Eury, to see the light again.
You go off with him. You got a second chance,
You do what's right. If you get out
Of here, I'll feel good. Very good.
You're not getting any younger,
It's no use being proud.
It ain't that I can't keep a secret,
Eury, please to know that. It's just
I heard his concert, and it put
Something in my mind.
    Someone like him
Is different. That's all I'm saying.
From me. From her.
I've got a card here.
        [*Takes it out of his pocket slowly and looks at it.*
My agent prints it up. An ad.
A picture, taken I was younger
Some twenty years. It's all the same,
It don't fool no one.
*Name*: Coco Crambo. Sight and Situation Comic.
Characters and Voice Tricks.
Comedian of Stage and Television.
*Born*: It don't say, Hyman Rosen. Sixty years
Ago in Montreal, a third son. Left school
In grade six, on—financial considerations.
At present, fixed forever, fixed, a Fixed Star.
    Or, a Specialist, it don't say,
In nervous laughter. The audience is looking for
A trick. I do it. I, the Blonde,
And that Policeman. We are Specialists,
We are, in all the forgotten Horrors
Of adolescence.
    The poor, the sick, the desperate,
All the ones that live alone in rooming houses,
They like a dark place (and it don't cost much)

To laugh at what is publicly contemptible.
That's the Girl. That's Hyman Rosen.
And that's the Policeman.

[*Pause.*

[*forte*] Don't think we don't recognize
Jeers, when you jeer at us. We seen
You college boys, slumming in groups of six,
For thousands of years.
Oh, we know you're out there.
We always know which is
Applause and which mockery.
Don't think that we don't . . .
We hear you, we know you, we sense you,
Always. The girls there—they know too
When they are ridiculous. They know
When they're poor, or shabby, or foolish.
    But we are not *artists*. He is.
[*to* ORPHEUS, *quietly*] I know you're different. I, and others like me,
See you, now and then. When you're not watching,
We do. Watch, that is.
    I seen you often,
On the subway. I been going on to Brooklyn
And you get out at Fourteenth, or West Fourth,
Maybe, going all out down to see a friend.
    I seen you look around
You don't see me. I seen you studying
And making up your mind about us,
Us *conditions*. Sitting with our
Interesting faces in a newspaper.
    Well, there's something you don't know.
*We see you.* And we know why you're watching us.
Behind the *Daily News* or *Mirror*, I am
Watching just the same. I know. We are not like you.
But watching from the window of the bar and grill,
Or in the rear-view mirror, in a cabbie's cap,
Or from the sports page—one look—we can tell.
We know, we always know, what you are looking at.
    We *baffle* you.

You wonder why we read the papers that we do,
Or, if you're on the air too long, get up
And turn you off. And get the ball game.
Or we get bitter and won't buy the classy things
You'd like us to, to hang around the house, and you ask
Why do they want that thing on the mantelpiece,
That blue china doll? Or why we won't go see
The shows you think we ought, in any numbers.
    *Maybe, once, we wanted to.*
Maybe, once, believed in you, and looked to you
For something that we knew we didn't have,
And maybe wanted
    Not knowing what it *was*—
But knowing it was different. Might make us
Rich when we were poor, or warm when we were always
Growing colder. Maybe, once, we wanted that—
And maybe not. But we were disappointed.
It didn't work out like you said it would—or
Like we hoped. Oh, no offense. We didn't really get it.
What you wanted.
Or we weren't meant for it, or didn't know the right
  crowd.
That's all right.
    That's all over.
Personally speaking—my mother—
But that don't interest you.
And that's right, you're beyond that. That's why
We respect you. As we do. We don't say much about it.
It don't show. But the hell with you.
I didn't get you here for you. I like the girl.
She don't want to see you, but she ought to.
There's nothing here for her—or anyone—
As far into forever as you look.
    Go with him, Eury.
If you don't believe in something, you dry up.
Go back. Take a try. Go with him. Go his way.
And if you can't be happy, stick your neck out.
Okay, I done the best I can.

[*Exit.*

EURYDICE I know you looked for me. I heard.
[ORPHEUS *tries to speak and cannot.*
[*timidly*] I heard you cried.

ORPHEUS [*tight with anger*] How could you do it to me,
Eurydice,
How? Can you tell me that?
All these years you've let me
Think you dead, all these years—
At first
I suffered horribly. You must have known that,
And known I would. I walked all over Europe
Knocking at doors, asking at inns,
Looking in hospitals, confronting strangers—

EURYDICE I know. I read the papers.

ORPHEUS And even in—houses of death.
Looking at faces laid out on stretchers.
Bodies of children and suicides,
Or bodies without faces—

EURYDICE [*interrupting*] And everyone you questioned, as
always,
Heard you, and cried too, for themselves.
I know they did that. They always did.
I was the love they never had,
But you had had it. And death had taken it
From you and everyone.

ORPHEUS You knew all this, and still
You let me suffer? I looked everywhere—

EURYDICE Not everywhere. Not just behind you.

ORPHEUS Did you go back to Paris?

EURYDICE Yes, finally. To our room.
I was lame. First,
I had to learn to walk again.
Someone found me.

ORPHEUS Someone found you? Who?
I spoke to everyone, to
Every peasant in that district—

EURYDICE Not to every one.

ORPHEUS Who?

EURYDICE I never knew his name.
I couldn't speak his language.
Someone took me somewhere it was warm.

ORPHEUS It was the summer.

EURYDICE I was cold, Orpheus.
I lay there growing colder in the dark
Until a week went by, and then I slept.
I don't know how long.
I don't remember.
Then I came to Paris.

ORPHEUS How?

EURYDICE With soldiers.
I came to our room.
I saw you'd been there.
It was torn apart. But
I found what I was looking for.
Remember? You left my passport—
In the drawer.

ORPHEUS [*suddenly raging*] How could you? How could you?
I don't care. This cannot matter now,
What matters is that you are here,
Alive, my wife. And I,
Despite your cruelty, am also. Once,
I almost died for grief, because of you.
Then I ate nothing and drank no water.
I lost thirty pounds.

EURYDICE [*wearily*] You look fine.

ORPHEUS [*stiffly*] I gained them back again,
In time. Life goes on.
That is its pattern.

EURYDICE How did you find me, Orpheus?

ORPHEUS This is a terrible place, Eurydice!

EURYDICE It was once a church.

ORPHEUS My God, Eurydice, that dog!
That grotesque dog, that lies beside the door!
That growls at all who come up near.
That dog alone is frightening and degrading.

EURYDICE The dog is there to frighten pests.
People who try to get in.
They try, you'd be surprised.
They try to all the time.
No one gets in here by accident.
How did you?

ORPHEUS [*cutting in*] I came to bring you back, Eurydice.

[*She looks at him without speaking, and in this silence some of the others enter, unnoticed.* CRAMBO *enters, hanging back. They hover at the back and at the sides, listening but not clearly seen.*

EURYDICE Perhaps I always thought you'd come,
But then I'd think, they wouldn't let him in,
Not even him, if he knew where to find me.
And then I'd think, what *if* he found me,
Nothing changes. Nothing is different.
And I'd go back to think of nothing,
Not asleep. Not awake. But with my eyes open.
It's been like that. Out there, the audience exists,
But only as a mirror image. All the rest
Is inside out and upside down. We are
The opposites of everyone. Out there,
I think they know that. Sometimes, I listen,
And they sound frightened—
Orpheus, how could you get in?

ORPHEUS What difference does it make?
That man, your fellow. The comedian.
Crambo is his name? At first,

I thought him lying—or some
Miserable creature who had lost his mind—

EURYDICE [*turning to look for* CRAMBO] *Crambo!*
But how?

ORPHEUS He came up to me and asked
To speak to me—I believe he said
He often went to concerts. I was
Conducting, as I do always,
My—my Requiem Mass.

[*Pause.*

EURYDICE [*stepping back*] *My* Requiem Mass.
You ghoul, Orpheus!

ORPHEUS Get your hat and coat.

EURYDICE You take everything, don't you?
Heaven. The holidays. The saints.
You people take
Christmas, to celebrate yourselves.

ORPHEUS Get your coat! I don't care
What you are, or what you've been.
I told you that.

EURYDICE Once I thought
I could keep Holy Days with you.
That was before
I learned to call my saints and angels
By another name—

CROWD Ura Dis, it's time.
You've got to go on.
She's got to go on.

ORPHEUS We're leaving. Don't make me
Speak to you in front of strangers.
Get your things.

EURYDICE I'm coming.

CROWD [*shocked*] She can't go now!
No one walks out in the middle of a show.

ORPHEUS As I have told you, I will take you
Back without questions.
We'll start all over again,
And never speak of what has happened.
The world will joyfully suppose—
I'll tell the newspapers—
You have recovered from a long illness—

CROWD It's time! She's got to on!

CRAMBO Go on, Eury, I'll explain to him.

EURYDICE I'm going.
[*She exits. The crowd closes in around her, blocking* ORPHEUS.

ORPHEUS Wait—I cannot permit—

CROWD Stand back, please.
Get back, mister.
Keep your place.

ORPHEUS I told you I would not permit—

CROWD No visitors backstage.
Who does that guy think he is?
Tell him to mind his business.

CRAMBO [*trying to stop him*] Please be respectful, mister—
Just this once. Just go outside
And wait for her. She'll come with you.
I told you—
[*Music coming up in the distance. Scattered applause.*

ORPHEUS Let me pass.

CRAMBO You *can't* do that—not here!

ORPHEUS [*turning on Crambo*] But I have *come for her!*
This is all over, finished. Can't
You understand? *You have no right—*
[*to crowd*] She is my wife.
[*He breaks through and out. The others break up in knots, break away in twos and threes. Some*

*run off, frightened. Music stops abruptly. A long, sustained roar of laughter in the distance. Catcalls.*

MANAGER [*offstage*] RING IT DOWN QUICKLY!
RING DOWN THAT CURTAIN!

[*Everybody off now but* CRAMBO. MANAGER *hastens in and grabs him.*

MANAGER What is this, will you tell me?
Some guy walked out on stage—
You hear them?

[*There is still laughter and catcalls.*

CRAMBO That's just Eurydice's husband.

MANAGER They grabbed him.
All I ask is, how did this happen?

[*He exits.* CRAMBO *stands looking at his feet. After a pause,* EURYDICE *enters quietly, stands in the wings, hugging a housecoat together. She is carrying the dress she was wearing. That was her "specialty."*

EURYDICE [*after a moment*] I'm not going with him,
Crambo.

[*He doesn't answer.*

What's the matter?
Why should you feel badly?
You didn't know . . .

[*Her voice breaks.*

Perhaps it was better this way.
I wanted him to look at me.

[CRAMBO *looks up, startled, as she cries. It sounds like laughter.*

CURTAIN

# *I Too Have Lived in Arcadia*

A PASTORAL, IN THE PRESENT TIME

There are islands off the south coast of Newfoundland which are all that remain of a French empire in North America. The archipelago is called *Les Territoires des Iles Saint-Pierre et Miquelon.*

The colonial governor lives on St. Pierre, the littlest and most populated of these islands, with a landlocked harbor.

Twenty-five miles away, about five hundred Bretons and Basques live on Miquelon, the largest. Here eighty square miles of green forest, hills and valleys, rivers and brooks are surrounded by wild seascapes. The north Atlantic breakers, which crash on the dark capes and the cliffs, are often one hundred feet high. Connecting Grand Miquelon and Petit Miquelon, or Langlade, is a pure beach, or white reef, eight miles long.

To Langlade have come Damon and Chloris, young anarchists from New York, to breed goats and to live according to their beliefs.

## CHARACTERS

DAMON
CHLORIS
PHOEBE
GEORGES, *a poodle*

## I. DAMON'S BIRTHDAY

DAMON Wind from the North, from Fortune's banks
Nearby in Newfoundland, has cleared the air,
Has chased the fog as far as Nova Scotia
Down the coast—the air is cold and clear.
The sky glitters, windless, down on us
Now, like a vast rose diamond.

CHLORIS Elsewhere the world keeps Christmas,
The guilty world which long ago lost conscience
To its Noma lights, and by a dead tree dances
Around its Present.

DAMON Tonight the frozen bay may heave and crack,
And we expect the snows tomorrow, or next week.
The goats are fed, their coats are clean and thick.
The months have come that go by white and quiet.

CHLORIS We harvested a feast, although we were
Too poor to buy a bag of flour,
Some ours, from hardy seeds—
Black salsify or scorzonēra,
Snow peas and parsnips—but the best
Grew summer-wild around us in the forest.
I put stores by in sterile jars,
Wild strawberries—and red fruit, strange to us,
Called on this island *graine-de-quatre-temps*.
All summer long we looked, and found
Wild celery and spinach growing, mushrooms,
Fiddlehead greens or osmund, and wild turnip.
When autumn came, we harvested the marsh,
Heaped bags with cranberries and currants.
We picked the honey-amber, fat *plat-bières*,

And I found growing, allspice, wintergreen and juniper.
We've even medicines—as violin-wood leaves,
Called *épinettes*, for colds—or yellow-grass,
The tonic *savoyard*, and teas from tonic herbs,
*Thé-rouge*, *faux-thé*, and *thé-de-James*.

DAMON We are rich in these,
And frozen game, and fish, and game birds of the seas:
Rabbit and red fox, eiderduck and wild geese,
And Arctic partridges, here called *perdrix des neiges*.
All these the land has given us and keeps
On ice, against our needs.

CHLORIS Why when we went to catch the sea birds,
Did you mind?

DAMON How did you know?

CHLORIS Because I walked behind you, in the wind.
I had the basket. I saw you drop your hands.

DAMON I'll tell you, sometime.

CHLORIS Here is a love song, for your birthday.

DAMON Sing, then.

CHLORIS Before we met, to take our names,
When you were *aleph*, I was *beth*,
That was before the world—
We had no ways.

Then there were no days and nights,
We lived by artificial lights,
Glow-worms, phosphorescence, plankton—
But there were others.

Things that crept, and hopping things,
Eels, and insects with damp wings,
Frogs that croaked into the silence, fish—
They came and crowded us.

They said, they were in love with us.
But we had no love for ourselves.

We said, "But what can you expect of us?"—
With cold surprise.

DAMON That's how it was, all right.
Sing some more, Chloris.

CHLORIS That's all there is.

DAMON I'll tell you what it is about the sea birds.

They are the queerest.
They're called *le coco* and *le kiri* for
Their cries. They don't come on like ordinary birds
With nests. They want like wild, uneasy scenes.

They can retard. But they won't live with anyone—
It's like they didn't want to get involved with living,
But just the wind, and to and from the Arctic.
They see our windows, and come wailing close.

It's like drowned music, human sounds—I pick out
Notes and phrases and the beat's wild—cold reeds, winds.
I think they're human, and got lost, and know I listen.
They use the sounds I understand. They're cold, and
hung-up.
They want to stop, but they can't ever stop.
We hold. They never hold. They just go there and back.
That's what it is about the sea birds.

CHLORIS We'll never kill them, then, again.
We can eat fish.

DAMON We'll catch them as we can.
It was an old wives' tale.
I am ashamed, to be so simple-minded.

CHLORIS Sometimes, do you look back?
I think you do.

DAMON No.

CHLORIS Then why are you so brooding and so pensive?

DAMON I think of life, and how to live it.

CHLORIS When all that goes before is cold and fresh,
No dark return can touch us.

DAMON The world itself.

CHLORIS Is nothing very much.

DAMON How would you know, when you were hardly in it?

CHLORIS I was. It was a cage until you opened it,
And out I came.

DAMON It was catastrophe, till you came out.
But this is not the same.

CHLORIS It is. I didn't want to come alone.
Who would? Although Sephardic, used to wandering
And nomadic ways, without you I could not have come
Would not have had the reverence or resolve.
Do you love me, Damon?

DAMON I'll answer yes, but after this,
Don't ask.

CHLORIS Now at the close of this, which was
The first year of our providence,
Rehearse our vows.

DAMON Our vows were only to ourselves.

CHLORIS Because this anniversary is precious,
It should be kept, alone, to honor
What belongs to us, and no one else.

DAMON We promised once,
Not loving what we were,
To find regard and honor,
So we came here.

CHLORIS To put behind us
What was there,
And for each other
Have regard and honor
Over all else.

## I Too Have Lived in Arcadia

DAMON We were ridiculous,
Now we are serious.

CHLORIS We were not true,
But now we tell no lies.

DAMON We, that lived as fools do,
Now live as scholars.

CHLORIS We were, as you would say,
The worst.

DAMON Beat.

CHLORIS Bugged.

DAMON Hung-up.

CHLORIS Hacked.

DAMON Dragged.

CHLORIS Accursed.

DAMON We were the worst.

CHLORIS When if we coughed, we lied—
We said we laughed.

DAMON When if we laughed, we lied—
We said we coughed.

CHLORIS I love you and I will, as long as
Betelgeuse can come so close, or
Any other star come nearer.

DAMON And by these Northern Lights,
Called by the natives *marionettes*,
You are the first.

CHLORIS We are the proudest and the best.

DAMON And self-sustaining, where
The cold light pierces languor,
And no fungus, parasite, nor any
Heat-rotten and heat-ridden
Decomposition can come.

CHLORIS Because we chose no slumbering island,
Where the sun was:
Not Antigua, not Ibiza,
Not St. Croix or Desirade,
Not Virgin Gorda, Sigatoka,
Jost Van Dyke, or George Dog—
Or any bargain paradise, as are
The Cocos near Australia, where
Bone coins are legal tender and
The crabs eat coconuts;
Not drowsy Isla-mas-a-Tierra, or
The Seychelles, in the Indian Ocean, either;
Not to the indolent Sese Isles to speak
Swahili to the servants, but to these
Fresh islands of the icy seas, we came.

DAMON Where not to sleep, and spoil in sleep,
But near the Arctic Circle, keep
A vigil to the best for man,
There stateless, godless, and alone,
Supported by our hands.

CHLORIS And may God bless this covenant,
And understand.

DAMON Chloris, you forget yourself.
We are anarchists.

CHLORIS I meant to say, and may our work be blest
By inner strength—may sense of purpose
Make slight the snow and ice.
Then may the storms come,
And we, like Arctic winds, be hard and strong,
Here on these northern islands.

DAMON So it is said. Our life is hard,
And so do we grow hard, the hard way.

CHLORIS Happy birthday.

DAMON It is.

CHLORIS Now do we dare to look back.
Inquiring minds learn conscience as

The diamond does, from darkness.
You are *Le Bateleur*, the leader of the Pack,
And I *La Papesse*—they were the Inquirers,
To whom the sleeping earth was promised.
We are like them, and they like us,
Though oddly dressed,
One as a Fool, the other as a Priestess.

DAMON I see you have put on your party dress.

CHLORIS Why, so I have.

## II. PLEASURES AND PRAISE

CHLORIS They say in town, a spectre has been seen,
Curiously dressed, which in its hands
Is carrying a trumpet.

DAMON Nonsense.
Breed, you goats, and break your backs!
Our banks shall be your beds.
Grow, toss your tails, eat peat and flourish!

CHLORIS You used to play the trumpet.
At the spectre's heels,
A small black poodle follows, which is
Also an eidolon.

DAMON It's probably a tourist.

CHLORIS A tourist, here? On Miquelon,
In winter? Damon! What a comical idea.
All the indigenous say that
Harm has come, and she
Is its dark omen.

DAMON These natives are always crepe-hanging.
I to my goats, you to yours.
We'll spur these ardent animals
To breed, and break their beds, like cannibals.
What are you reading, Chloris?

CHLORIS The history of man, which takes
(approximately),
Three one-thousandths of one percent
Of time upon this planet.
Think of that.

DAMON Let others, then, approaching thirty years,
Write poems. For us,
All of man's fifty thousand years on earth
Are seen in their perspective, just
A week in evolution and our work ahead of us.

CHLORIS Meanwhile we live as Hobbes has taught us.

DAMON Hobbes was the greatest.
By love, we learned his economics.
We subsist
On what we please
To take from under trees,
Sweet barks and nuts.
We eat
Only what is wild and sweet,
And smoke the aromatic grasses.
Sing, Chloris.

CHLORIS We shall live on these,
And make wine, if we please,
Succulently from
The wild pear and the plum
Abounding in this place,
All of which pleasures can refresh us.

DAMON Hobbes was the most, the end, the wildest.

CHLORIS While we, undaunted, prove
This island of our love
A visionary season.

DAMON As Children of the Age of Science, we
Respect the methods of Technology,
As organized by principles of Reason.

CHLORIS But are reminded always,
Of those who tried before, and died for us.

DAMON You always choose these gloomy topics. Who?

CHLORIS The Mammals.

DAMON What did the Mammals do?

CHLORIS Survived for us.

DAMON You mean, they were the Fittest.

CHLORIS Yes!
Once,
It was by no means certain
Who would win, the Others—
The new Amphibians, the Ruling Reptiles,
The Fish—or us, the Animals, when
We contended for control
Of ancient sea and jungle, all of us.
In fact:
Before the Age of Reptiles
In Mesozoic times,
It was by no means certain
Who could win—The Monsters
(Archaeopteryx and Stegosaurus,
Pterodactyl, Brontosaurus,
And others)
Or the Fish. And,
Before the Age of Fish began
(the age of lilylike marine
Invertebrates, of
Ordovician chordates,
Snails and sharks) in
Paleozoic seas, it was
By no means certain any Life
Except the lime-secreting algae,
Protozoa, annelid worms, and
Ancient trilobites of Proterozoic
Waters, could survive,

Or grow up green,
Much less persist upon
That desolate scene
To introduce the separate lung,
The muscular diaphragm,
The stereoscopic eye,
The brain, the heart, the hand, the thumb—
Or could learn to be warm-blooded and to
Bear their young alive!
What was certain was only that
Some things would live, and some would not;
That some would fail, and others would succeed.
The unsuccessful simply disappeared.

DAMON Never mind the ones that disappeared.

CHLORIS They were not the Fittest.

DAMON And life itself, was it spontaneous?

CHLORIS Well, yes. They think it was.

DAMON Tell about Life, Chloris,
And how it started.
Try to avoid the creepy parts.

CHLORIS It was like this:
Before all Life, in Archaeozoic darkness, came
The oceans and the continents, which settled.
Then, as the earth's crust hardened, beating rains
Lashed these emerging plains and thrusts, and washed
The top-most silts and sediments down—which time
Compacted into stone, the eons into rocks, beneath
The ocean.
Then there was no life at all, but just a bubble under
Water now and then. Or here and there, a microcosm.
But all at once, it came. It came from nothing.
It was more simple than the simplest thing,
A single cell, the promise. It was so beautiful!
It was Protoplasm.

DAMON That's how it happened?

CHLORIS Yes.

DAMON Next, *Gloeothece.*

CHLORIS Yes!

DAMON *Ulothrix* and *Oedogonium.*

CHLORIS You've known it all the time!

DAMON Not the grand design. The details.
Go on.

CHLORIS Eventually, when the seas were dense with life,
It happened quite by chance, some organisms—
Little, creeping things like bryophytes—
Struggled to the surface, sensed the sunlight,
Grasped upon some barren rocks, and clambered out!

DAMON Ugh.

CHLORIS Oh, no! They learned to breathe. And these became
Our forefathers, who led the great Procession
To the Land, our common ancestors, whose descendants
Led to life forms infinitely higher than their own.
We are beholden to them! All these
Who left their bodies
Pressed in sandstone, lime and shale
As eloquent reminders.

DAMON So what about the Mammals?

CHLORIS To disregard the tunicates and amphioxus,
Hagfish, lampreys, sharks and skates,
Which led to primitive invertebrates,
To bony fish, to lungfish, salamanders, frogs and snakes,
To Pterodactyls, Archaeopteryx, to modern birds—
*Our* family breaks the tree at just the point
The reptiles got distinguished and important.
We went one way, and they the other.
We took the earth, and they, the air and water.
They took the scaly plates and feathers,
We, the fur and fingernails! and prospered.
At first the platypi and other egg-layers, next

The wallaby and wombat types, marsupials—
Until at last we had achieved the primitive placentals!

DAMON At last.

CHLORIS From these, the Ungulates: Odd-toed (as horse)
And even (pig); Insectivores (as shrews
Or hedgehog); Carnivores (as for example, dog);
And finally, the Primates—us. All these
Achieved success, and by secession passed
The best to first one species, then the next.

DAMON Just one moment, Chloris.
What about the Snail?
There are about ten million times
More snails than *Homo sapiens*, yes?
The snail is primitive.
The snail is dumb.
It has no sex, it has no sense
And no significance. It has no thumb.
But nothing, hot or cold, or dry or wet,
Swamp or tree trunk, bugs a snail.
You have to say, the snail's a great success.

CHLORIS But, Damon, the snail is blind,
And has no life at all!
No one would want to be a snail.
I wasn't counting those whose end
Is livelihood, but only mention
Those whose end is comprehension.

DAMON I'll go along with that.
Here's to the Mammals, then,
Our heroes who, before the Age of Reason,
Endured the worst—
Whose cloven shoes and furry feet
A thoroughfare for Reason beat
Across the Cenozoic years.

CHLORIS And all I have to say,
May we be worthy of the first
Who struck across the highest mountains,

Or to the farthest islands swam,
To form a species of their own,
Where they could feed and cherish them.
And may we charter, too,
A race like migrants who
Pressed to the Galapagos
Despite such dangers to themselves
As we dare not,
There to be separate, remote,
To set their evolution's course
As total strangers.
May we be worthy of the ones
Who founded, all alone,
Ten thousand generations
To claim and imitate their bones
When they had gone!

DAMON They were the Fittest.
Our solemn word, to them,
To those struggling from
The Paleocene to Pleistocene,
Survived, and cast
The Race of Reptiles from the earth
And left this pleasant planet as
Our inheritance.

CHLORIS May we, like them,
Survive, and claim
The unborn of a *reasonable* race.

DAMON Yes.

## III. CHLORIS DISTURBED

CHLORIS The spectres, like shadows,
Cross the polished snow,
And draw in close.

[*Enter* PHOEBE *and* GEORGES.

*C'est-y votre temps ça?*

She doesn't answer,
So is not from here. *Bonjour?*
Nor of France, either.
Speak, if you are spectres—
Do you speak English?

PHOEBE I am Phoebe.

CHLORIS Then, are you a human being?

PHOEBE I am. I am an artist.
Here I intend to write and paint.
Georges, stay by me.

CHLORIS He is your dog?

PHOEBE He is.

CHLORIS You mustn't stay out there.
Come to the fire. Here.
You are like ice, and deadly pale.
No wonder, in the town, they took you for a ghost.

PHOEBE I need no fire.

CHLORIS You are courageous—How could you come so far
Without a road? Here's peat tea with anise.
Take it. It's hot.

PHOEBE Are you Chloris?

CHLORIS They must have told you, in town,
Who lived here, by the forest! Yes,
I'm Chloris now, but born Beth.
Damon was born Aleph. Damon, that is,
Who lives here also. We came a year ago.
And built this house—or rather,
Damon did, and I helped him.
Damon can do anything. He planned
The dry well and the drain, and built them.
He brought the water from the spring,
And laid the pipes. He's an accomplished
Carpenter, an engineer, mechanic, and a master
Electrician! As well as—Please excuse me.

I don't mean to run on. You are welcome,
And for as long as your need is,
Although I don't know who you are.
Why have you come?

PHOEBE To get back what I lost.

CHLORIS You are like us, then! And like us,
Have no doubt taken, for a new life, a new name.
We are not used to visitors in winter—
Not till the late spring, when the snows
Have gone. Then children come from Miquelon
Across the reindeer lichens, and the marsh—
Turned silver, then, and early green, and carmine—
To gather spaghnum, and to look in Langlade Forest
For giant violets!
You are an artist,
You would like it then.

PHOEBE We don't intend to stay that long.

CHLORIS I hope you do! The forest comes in flower
With rosy briars, flax and Venus-shoe.
When summer comes, *nénuphars* float on the marsh ponds.
Why do you neither eat nor drink?

PHOEBE We didn't come to eat and drink.
We have our cans and biscuits. Goodbye.
I have come to the right place.
You'll see more of us.

CHLORIS Don't go! Dressed as you are,
You'll suffer in this bitter weather!
Where can you go? Who are you, anyway?

PHOEBE I am what I am.
I come where I come from.
I get what I want.—Where is Damon?

CHLORIS Damon? Working, where our
Goats are sheltered—but why?

PHOEBE Goodbye.

[*Exit* PHOEBE *and* GEORGES.

CHLORIS She wasn't very friendly. Well.
A stranger, and suspicious, therefore.
How often strangers are!
How strange it is,
I've some constriction in my throat.
I'm dry, and hot.
Why are the walls damp?
They creep with sweat.
I should work,
But I don't want to work. I want to drink,
I want a cigarette. I want to kick my feet
Against the rungs of my chair.
I won't tell Damon,
But I could stare, all afternoon,
At one empty wall. Any failure of the will,
Or fear or any nervousness, angers him.
And so it should, he won't permit them
In himself.
But there are days
You wake up nervous, days you sit and think
Of everything perverse you ever did.
I failed Damon.
I was inadequate, in social situations. Yes.
I sat, and bit my fingernails.
I didn't know a trumpet from a cornet.
In conversation, he always had
To trick me in, as, "Speaking of
Delinquency, my Chloris has
An uncle who is a policeman."
I chewed peyotl, but without success.
I was not hilarious. I wept, instead,
For nearly a week. At visiting hours
In prison hospitals, they said,
"Don't bring Chloris. Chloris isn't any fun.
Come alone." Oh, how patient Damon was!
Many a marriage has been expunged for less.
Why do these fears come?
I know that often, in a woman,
They are expressed as talismans against

Whatever dreadful is about to happen, that
She has presupposed exactly. Then she speaks
To exorcise the fears. But for a man, not so.
What he foresees, he magically reverses—
His most profound suspicions are expressed
As brightest hopes and wishes.
I wonder if that woman will live near?

## IV. DAMON DISTURBED

PHOEBE You don't forget me, I see.

DAMON Of course not.

PHOEBE You know my hands, my face—
These hands, Damon—as if
They were your own. These lines,
Traced here upon the palms, could be
The same you traced yourself.

DAMON I wasn't the only one.

PHOEBE Say, at least, that if you shut your eyes,
They are there, that on the lids
Configurate in pinwheels, darting circles.

DAMON They are that close, that they could be
My own palms.

PHOEBE And so close, why did you drop them?

DAMON It was time.

PHOEBE Did you suppose, that as you dropped my hands,
Your lids could drop, and I should vanish?
But I was there—the pinwheels and the circles—
And pressed against you in the dark.

DAMON You did, from time to time. And I woke up
Thirsty, and tossed in my bed.

PHOEBE And Chloris? Did you tell her that?

DAMON I love Chloris.
I despise weakness.

PHOEBE I see. Perhaps, what you call
Imperfect, Chloris could not love.

DAMON She could. I wouldn't want her to.

PHOEBE Why not?

DAMON I had enough of that, with you.
I put you out.

PHOEBE Yet, you wake up in want . . .

DAMON I admit it.

PHOEBE And drink water, and lie awake,
And think, you would give up
Everything you have, if
For a night with me.

DAMON I get over it.
I live with want. There are
Around me all of its species.
Yours is the least important.

PHOEBE Perhaps. But if you want me,
It's not too late.

DAMON Late? That isn't it.
The question never was the moment
That I made a choice. It was no accident
Of getting there half-past the hour,
And missing you because you stood
Somewhere else, in some place unappointed,
To search the faces there, in case
I hadn't got the message. It wasn't that.
You knew I was distraught.
You must have known it. You had my heart,
Or you were close to it. We had gone on
Too long, but neither tried to extricate
The other. Need and hunger were
Too close, to give the other up.
In some part, we despised each other,
But there warned us always,

That unthinkable alternative,
To be alone.

PHOEBE Is that all it was?
Think back.

DAMON I was your servant.

PHOEBE I found you.
You lay abandoned, in
The bubble of a crater.
Your eyes, wide open,
Looked at nothing.

DAMON At that time, there wasn't anything.
You picked me up. You kept me.
You were pitiless, it made it easy.

PHOEBE It wasn't so bad, was it?
Think about it.
Nights,
From midnight on, we heard
The sounds we liked. We danced,
Alone. We listened—
Certain voices on the radio
Whispered private jokes
We understood. We taught
The dog. His barks and wails
Echoed us. When light came up,
And crossed the railroad tracks,
We drew the shades.

DAMON But days, I wanted to be dead.

PHOEBE Only at first.
You warmed, and then you worked.
I did all that. Then came
The rest.

DAMON It came, it was too easy
When it came. In you,
I had escaped contempt. At last,
I learned it for myself.

In the world I want, there will be
No victims, like I was.
In the world I want, there will be
No waste, no thought of death,
No dread, no wilderness.
There will be monuments, in all
The forests and the empty spaces.
And when I made that choice,
I broke with you.

PHOEBE The break was false.

DAMON I love Chloris.

PHOEBE I know you best.
I know what Chloris cannot know.
I know your worst.

DAMON It's dead. The worst is past.

PHOEBE It lives. Did you tell Chloris,
Here is a half-face, a heart
Stripped from its visking, a half-heart
Which half beats? Or did you dare to admit
What still exists?

DAMON I told Chloris what I was.
I told her what I wanted for myself.

PHOEBE Did you tell her also, what I nursed?

DAMON I told her I was nursed,
I told her what you were—and
Cut it short, to spare us both.

PHOEBE Us? You liked it, well enough.

DAMON You forget. But I do not.
You bled where I kicked you.
I told you once, that you were rotten.

PHOEBE I covered your face from the flies.

DAMON I need no mask now.

PHOEBE We ate worms until we found each other's arms.

DAMON And knew worse.

PHOEBE Your breath is sharper.
You are not unmoved.

DAMON Get back, you are too close.

PHOEBE Nothing has changed. Tell Chloris, Damon,
That, before your time, you lived your life—
And what your life was, you are. Tell her!
Point at your flesh, and show her where
I was, and she will see there, left over,
Little more than lungs and a finger.
So much, have I had of you.

DAMON You've had nothing of what I am now.
You're a trick, no more than that, a shadow,
Standing in the ways of views I like to look at
While I work. I can look up now, and see them.
Breakers are near that come, unbroken, from
Across the ocean, to crash on the cape rocks.
The forest's dark against the snow—
You're going now. The valley will be quiet.

PHOEBE Look at what you like! Before you looked,
You were committed. You are your life.

DAMON My life is now my life with Chloris—
Our life is what's ahead of us.

PHOEBE Perhaps! But you have *lived* your past.

DAMON I don't look at you. I don't see you.
You do not exist.

PHOEBE We'll see.

## V. DENIALS

CHLORIS Damon, who is that woman?

DAMON Woman? What woman?

CHLORIS Damon, there was a woman with you—
Just now, on the west path.

DAMON At the railing? The fence blew down,
And I was there to fix it.

CHLORIS Damon, I saw you speak to her!

DAMON There was no woman. No one.

CHLORIS There was. I saw her—

DAMON You could have seen my coat,
Caught up and blowing in the wind.

CHLORIS No! Not your coat. A woman
That has come before.

DAMON It stands to reason, doesn't it,
That if there were someone,
There'd be footprints?
There are none.

CHLORIS Footprints? Where the ice has frozen
On the snow, like glass? The wind that
Whirls upon it would cover any tracks!

DAMON What is this, Chloris?
Don't you trust me?
There was no woman. No one. No dog.

CHLORIS I spoke of no dog!

DAMON You are distraught.
I said what you said. Word for word.
You slept, you dreamed, and
You forgot you slept.
Let's go back to work now,
Let's forget about it.

CHLORIS Damon, how my head hurts!
Was it that? Could it be that?

DAMON You stay awake at night,
And nurse these fantasies.
That's why your head hurts.

CHLORIS I dreamed last night—but
That was very different—I dreamed

The goats were sick and lay about
Their pens. I woke up, I spoke
Your name but nothing I could do
Would wake you. I had to talk.
Damon—shrug me, spite me,
Strike me too, but
Wake up when I need you!

DAMON I can't resolve these dreams of yours,
These ominous anxieties. You ask too much.
I have enough, to combat spectres
Of my own. From now on
Say only happy things, or what is useful.

CHLORIS Damon, what is happening to us?

DAMON My fears—I keep them to myself.
I don't tax you.

CHLORIS Lately, we have been like this
Too much, dissatisfied and anxious—
You, more than I, are drawn into yourself
And always angry. I want to speak,
But you won't—speak, why—can't we talk about it?
You turn from me, I haven't forced it,
But now for love, I ask to be returned
That am removed. What have I done?

DAMON Nothing! You have done nothing.
Never mind. Let me alone.
It's this winter, this endless winter.
Let me alone, I tell you.

[*Enter* PHOEBE *and* GEORGES, *who sit.*

PHOEBE I've heard that you two disappeared
To start a sort of ideal community. Tell me,
Is this it?

CHLORIS Not yet.

DAMON What?

PHOEBE It's rather dreary, isn't it?
Or don't you mind (I understand

You were some kind of student) not being—
How would I put it?

GEORGES *Pas à la banche?*

PHOEBE Not very hip. That's it. Not making it.
But Damon was quite different.
He always said, the heart
Of everything that happens
Was the spot for him.

GEORGES *Une autre fois, il était le plus sauvage.*
*Une autre fois, il creusait tout.*

CHLORIS *Creuser? As creuser un trou?*

GEORGES Ha-ha. *Sans pic.*

CHLORIS Why does the dog speak?
Damon!

DAMON I hear nothing. There is no one here.

GEORGES *Un trou—c'est le plus fou!*
*Quelle femme carré! Non*, chick,
*Pas de trou.*

CHLORIS Answer them, Damon—
I know you hear!

DAMON You are out of your mind.
There is no one there.
Let me alone, I tell you.

GEORGES *Creuser, comme bêcher, mais*
*Bêcher san bêche. Est-ce-que tu bêches?*

CHLORIS This dog's barks and sounds
Open my wounds. I know the speech
And where it leads.

PHOEBE I'm not an anarchist, myself, I like a
Centralized society, if I'm to be
At center. Don't you care?

CHLORIS Do you mean, what do I care for?

GEORGES *C'est fabuleux, Ho-ho, un trou . . .*

PHOEBE I mean, for the contemporary scene,
For new directions, bold experiments,
Offbeat expressionism—and the Dance.
Perhaps you never had advanced opinions?
Some take no active interest in the arts.

CHLORIS Damon, when will you speak?

DAMON I am not listening.
Look at my hands, Chloris,
There is a book in them.
Your fantasies are your problem.
Scenes like these, I simply do not listen.

PHOEBE Why can't you understand him, Chloris?
This man, so facile and so various, an artist
Cut off from everyone who could sustain him!
No wonder he produces nothing—he has
No stimulation—no support!

CHLORIS How have you the right to say this?

PHOEBE Who else is there to say it?
I was, perhaps, surprised
To find no work in progress.
He played three instruments.
He wrote the most amusing compositions.
He was the most progressive—insolent,
Bold, ironic, clever, new. We all said so.
As for his painting, he was on his way.
Everybody knew him. He knew everybody.
Another one-man show—but who can say?
Now he casts his contacts all away.
It's always true it isn't you, it's who you know.

GEORGES *C'est le plus vrai.*

PHOEBE And, Chloris, how much worse
For those who must produce originals—
Who must at any cost avoid the trite—
To be cut off, like this! Can you expect him

To be informed, and estimate his competition
In this awful, God-forsaken place?
Nature, after all, abhors a vacuum.

CHLORIS That doesn't mean what you think it means.

PHOEBE What?

CHLORIS It means,
Our atmosphere permits no perfect emptiness,
But rushes in, with close to fifteen pounds
Of force for every inch of surface.

PHOEBE What a hopeless pedant you are, Chloris!

CHLORIS It means,
Because the air itself is heavy, nowhere
Exists in nature, that is, without pressure.

PHOEBE A schoolgirl, that's all. We'll be back.
This may be easier than I thought.
[*Exit* PHOEBE *and* GEORGES.

DAMON It's this winter, this interminable winter.
This snow. The wind forever in our ears
Which howls, and howls, which beats the trees
And tears them down. It shrieks all night.
You sleep, and dream of bad things. Days,
You wake up chilled, and look out
Into nothing. Nothing. Nothing ever happens.
We are divorced from everything and everyone.
We have no fun at all.

CHLORIS Damon, how can this be happening to us?

## VI. DAMON'S FEVER

CHLORIS [*to the sea birds*] You, *pic-épeiche* and *l'hirondelle*,
We are mortal, and we are in danger.

You were born remembering passage, channels in the wind,
You could warn. Snow birds and sea swallows, warn him.

Beams from your wings could heal,
Shoot, as you wheel and circle.

All of you that follow the Great Circle, call to him.
He is like you. He could hear, if you called.

Spell him, as you next cry out.
Save him, for Damon is mortal.

*Le coco*, call, and you, *le kiri*, call his name,
Confine his yearning. Comfort him.
Call to him to keep what he has.

[*Enter* PHOEBE *and* GEORGES.

PHOEBE To who do you speak, Chloris?
No one listens.

CHLORIS To the sea birds.

PHOEBE I thought I heard prayers.
Do you pray?

CHLORIS Not prayers. Petitions.

PHOEBE Then, are you bankrupt?

CHLORIS We are not.

PHOEBE Why is Damon asleep?

CHLORIS He was up all night.

PHOEBE How odd it is—he waits to sleep, as if
For you to wake and get up from his bed!

CHLORIS He is sick.

PHOEBE An infection, perhaps?

CHLORIS An old sickness.

PHOEBE He is feverish?

CHLORIS It won't last.
The climate here is good for it.

PHOEBE I'm glad to hear that.
And to see that

You are vexed, and vacant, and
Out of your depth.

CHLORIS I'm all right!
Why did you come?
Why did you have to come?
Before you came,
He wanted to be still.
He went down,
All the way to the beginning,
Down until he touched.
Then, for the first time,
He reached for what he was, and waited.
He knew he had to wait.

PHOEBE Why wait? When he was making it
Right where he was?

CHLORIS Leave him alone! He'll begin again.
And when he does, he won't be wrong.

PHOEBE Leave him alone? I want the best
For him, you know! I'll give him just
A whispered warning of the *famine of no fame*,
A breath of calliope from the bandwagon.

GEORGES *Écoute. Elle est la plupart.*

CHLORIS I know you, Phoebe, and that you are no stranger,
And what you are to him. He knew you very well.
I saw your name, the first time,
Written on a wall. The second,
Heard it called in warning
By children on an empty dock.
After that, I always looked
At what was written out
On walls and doors and sidewalks,
From fear, or in protest.
But I never thought
That what was scrawled for all to see,
Was there addressed to me.
You are not Phoebe.

You were never Phoebe. I know now
That it was your face, at the broken window,
Behind a match flame, that watched us go.
"Hurry," Damon said, "or she will hate you."
He never told me who it was,
But later, when a letter came,
I learned your name, and I rehearsed it.

PHOEBE What do you know of me?

CHLORIS They called you Gummi Strümpfe, in the city.
You must be Gummi Strümpfe still.

GEORGES *Est-ce-que tu piges?*

PHOEBE You don't know much.
You never will.
I don't give up.
I'm not through yet.

[*Exit* PHOEBE *and* GEORGES.

CHLORIS She knew quite well of Damon's fever.
She was here yesterday.
How dared she come? Perverse creature!
I'll mend Damon's shirt, and forget her.
He sleeps heavily.
I always break the thread.
Neanderthal woman could sew as well as I do.
Why does he lie that way?
Something is unnatural, as if—
—Damon, are you asleep?
Of course he is. He doesn't hear me.
I've no thread but the black, but I'll use it.
Here it is.
Why should he breathe like that?
No, this sleep's not sound! He could be chilled,
He's thrown his blanket down.
I'll cover him.
Damon?
DAMON!

DAMON Why do you cry out?

CHLORIS *You've been awake!*
All this time, you've been awake.

DAMON I was asleep.

CHLORIS Your eyes were open.
Your face was—

DAMON Was what? Say it.

CHLORIS Changed.

DAMON What about it?

CHLORIS You weren't asleep, you were just—
Damon, what were you staring at?
*What was it?*

DAMON I don't know what you're talking about.
Chloris, get me a glass of water.
I'm burning.

CHLORIS Yes.

DAMON When I was a child, I willed the world.
I said, I'll rule by a tower I'll build.
I will be any-er than anyone.
That was when I was a child.
Then I ruled, for a while, by a tower of force,
By a turn of force, till I lost it.
I have no money. I have no good suit.
Even to be magical isn't it.
You have to—Chloris?

CHLORIS I'm back. Here, drink this.
*I was so frightened.*

DAMON Frightened of what?

CHLORIS It wasn't your face.
Damon. Take me back. Talk to me.
Talk to me about her.

DAMON *Her?*
Oh, listen, Chloris.
You bug me. You really do.

You hack me with these ideas of yours.
Forget them, will you?

CHLORIS I've tried to.

DAMON Why are you looking at me?
Stop looking at me.

CHLORIS If there were a doctor—

DAMON I don't need a doctor.
I'll get better in my own way.
Get back, you are too close.
Go sit somewhere else.

CHLORIS [*to herself*] But if *she* is not true,
Neither is this.
No snow bird or sea swallow could call.

## VII. DAMON RECOVERED

DAMON I don't know why I never opened them,
When they came. I didn't.
I put them in this box—here it is.
But now I have the time to really dig these
Hilarious messages from my old friends.
What's this. Ruby writes on paper napkins,
"You can't get in the Old Place for tourists
Who expect to be degraded." Crazy.
Here's a card from Arpad—

[*Enter* PHOEBE *and* GEORGES.

CHLORIS A lady's notepaper I saw and she
(So help me) seventy-seven—no monogram—
A little picture of a bird cage with the door wide open,
The bird already out, escaping somewhere.
No address, either. It said, engraved:
*Qui me néglige me perd.*

GEORGES *Alors*

DAMON Arpad is talented, but what a chick he has.
One Saturday in August took all her clothes off

At the beach, in front of all of us. I wouldn't
Look at anyone undressing, but I looked at her.
"No one has ever looked before," she says.
I looked. She asked for it.
That was Arpad's hung-up chick.

CHLORIS Funny notepaper.
Next to neglect, need.
Next to need—nowhere—
Not far from the cage door.

DAMON What are you saying, Chloris?

CHLORIS I'm talking to myself.

DAMON Talent, yes, but what a Wig he is.
Since I am—aesthetically at least—
A Marxist, once I criticized his things,
"Form, like, follows function," I reminded him,
And do you know that crazy Arpad
Flipped, he broke my nose.

GEORGES *Maboule.*

DAMON Who was this, Chloris,
That had the notepaper?
Why are you mumbling to yourself?

CHLORIS The bird, the bird took off and disappeared.
So did the Dawn Horse, cloudy Eohippus,
Who galloped past primeval bogs to bark,
And scratch the ground for edible remains
Preserved there from a previous age of ice—
Dear little horse! No bigger than a standard poodle,
Eating bryophytic fossils . . .

GEORGES *Qui me néglige me perde?*
*Tu te perds, alors.*

CHLORIS *S'il vous plait, ne me tutoyez pas.*
The Brontosaurus
Stand and watch, their pale, already weedy eyes
Are hurting them, and their unmanageable crusted limbs.

They pray for conservation, while the great, winged monsters
Twitch and molt, unbalanced and resentful, in the primal trees
Which can no longer bear their weight, or hold them. In the quiet,
The fungus creeps out of the forest, for its time has come.

DAMON Scenes like these, I question them.

CHLORIS But to go back to Mrs. Palmer—it was her
That had the notepaper—for a moment. Ancient and invalid,
She crowded, full of rage and shock and stroke, into
The final bed, where had the family put her. And there
Shrugged up to look at traffic going North North West
On Fresh Pond Drive beneath her window, she said
"Myself you never cage." Then losing touch
And eye and tongue she lay alone until, just as
The family thought she would, she died.
I was her nurse.

DAMON Scenes like these, I simply do not listen.

CHLORIS But who has tears for frantic pterosaurs, for flying reptiles
Who beat the trees and scrabble to hold on?
Who can preserve their hollow bones, which once
Permitted them to heave their monstrous birdlike bodies
Up, and at the sinister ocean swoop,
With thirty feet of gleaming wing to dip
And pierce the Mesozoic fish with pointed beak!
The hollow bones must crust and snap,
They are so hopeless! Hangers-on,
With never any more to come, no more of them again.

DAMON That's their problem.
And Mrs. Palmer?

CHLORIS Yes.
She joined the ghostly choirs of pterodactyls,
And borne by them upon their beating wings rose upwards,

Beyond the nearer stars, beyond the envelope of nitrogen,
Beyond our atmospheric rim—to sit alone, unvanquished.
It's always cold, there. The nights are loud with crushing.
There is no light—but when we meet, we'll know,
Although our bodies are below, and by
An elephant femur or rhinoceros ulna, lie
Undifferentiated in a pit, until
The workmen come and roll us out of it.

DAMON This Mrs. Palmer, Mrs. Death, can serve—
You brought it up—to illustrate
Our difference, which is
That some say *mortal*, others *human*.
I say human.
I'm getting up, and going for a walk.

[*Exit.*

CHLORIS Damon, Damon, don't leave me alone!

PHOEBE So. Chloris.

## VIII. REASON NOT ALL

PHOEBE He turns to me. He twitches.
There are rats in his mouth.
He's coming back, Chloris.
He always does.

CHLORIS Why have you done this, Phoebe?
What you come from was,
For him, a prison.

PHOEBE So he would have had you think.
It seems, they need to say this.

CHLORIS They? In all the world, there is
No one like Damon.

PHOEBE How little, Chloris, do you understand
Recidivists!

CHLORIS The *fittest?*

PHOEBE Oh, yes, they're sharp. They are the most.
They say they want to get away,
But they don't want to. I make it with them.
I'm quite tolerant. I put up
With their ways. When they go out
At night, I know for what. Their eyes
Are dry and hot, that cast the red beam that
I come by—in to see the fun. Believe me,
The earth comes to life when they are angry.

CHLORIS You have others! You don't need him.
Not Damon.

PHOEBE He likes me.

CHLORIS But you are black, and jealous, and no longer pretty!

PHOEBE I am the City.

[*A silence.*

PHOEBE I was his Nurse.
I fattened on his senses.
I know what he is.
I raised him, from
A shifty little Romulus, to this!
And when the time had come,
I gave him all of Rome to walk on.
When he grew up, he gave me this dog.
Darling, bark for us.

GEORGES *Insecte.*
Lady, not to eat and not to love
And to no purpose but to live it up
And have a ball, was I brought into life.
The plot grows sad, no longer good for laughs,
*C'est une espèce de rat-de-cave.*

PHOEBE He barks. The dog is tired.
Be quiet, Georges.
Chloris, use your common sense!
By *this*, could you expect to keep him?

CHLORIS The choice was his.

PHOEBE It still is.

CHLORIS We built a house, a house which stands,
Of dwarf firs, cypress, spruce and birch,
We've thirty goats, two sheep, and sheltered pens
In which they sleep—all these are his.
And lambs! We are expecting lambs.

PHOEBE He lied, maudlin Chloris.
He doesn't want these things.
He lies, he doesn't want your lambs.
He is mad. In me his madness is.
He plays. I taught him what he plays.
In bistros and in black cafés, I
Kicked his table-tops. All Rome was ours,
As, after hours, I took his trumpet home.

CHLORIS We are not bound, except by conscience.
I trust him.

PHOEBE Then, if you trust him—
I am not too late.
What we are from is dark and sick,
Its flesh is black. Its heart
Is eaten out. Yet no one weeps for it!
Why? We eat the rats instead.
Chloris, this was your mistake:
You don't admit we keep our secrets.
We *like* the rats.
They can be quite exciting.
As for sickness, where it breaks,
Go look! The place is crowded always.
Consider this, next time.
You had your fling. You were around
For better than a season. Time enough
To know the score, and time enough
Not to be unreasonable about it.
Think about it. It's not so bad, is it?

CHLORIS No more or less than you,
I am his mistress.

Let him choose between us.

PHOEBE Yes, indeed.

## IX. DECLARATIONS

CHLORIS Damon—

DAMON Don't speak. I want to talk.
I've walked. I've let the words
Come in my head. I want to get them out.
We have to do what's best.
We have to do what's right for us.
Yes? We have to do what works.
So I thought—

PHOEBE Damon, had you thought that Chloris,
If left alone, if by herself—
Might write? She could have talent.
I like the way that she expresses things.

CHLORIS Now she whispers to him, there is justice
For a bent line, if he wants it—
Non-Euclidean geometries of tension, for
Lines disguised, which are described
As the expedient. She means,
I would do well enough alone. Damon—

DAMON Don't speak. Not yet.
I walked
To town. That boat, the *Miquelon*,
Has come with mail. Tomorrow it returns.
I didn't know the boat was in.

CHLORIS Damon, listen! Look up!
The birds are coming back!
The sky is flocked with wings!

DAMON I told you, the boat has come.
The birds follow, for whatever reason.
I stopped, in town.
There are storm warnings. I asked

If they should sail on schedule, even
With the *coup-de-poudrin* promised.
And at that time, although I had no reason,
It occurred to me to ask them—

CHLORIS Damon, stop, look up!
I see his red beak, his red claws!
Look how *le kiri* flies above us!
Don't tell me, look first!

PHOEBE Ask what? What did you ask?

DAMON Let me finish, Chloris.
I asked
If there were also passage.
They will sail, and they have passage.
Chloris,
I have been upset.
The future worries me, and what
Could happen to us. There are
A thousand things I left unfinished
In the city, opportunities
I never took, advantages I should
Investigate in person, contacts
To establish, people I should meet.
I thought, if I could take this trip,
I could attend to all these matters.
I am sick with shadows.
I can scarcely stand my thoughts.

GEORGES *O, ça par example.*
There is seldom anything as sad as this,
Which is why, as we will see, no one admits
To what is taking place, but waves excitedly,
And smiles, and lets his parting words—those
Hopeless reassurances—get tossed into the wind.

PHOEBE Georges! To heel.
We will be going.

GEORGES *Je suis au talon, madame.*

DAMON But then I thought, will Chloris understand?
Or will she look to find, in this,
Something more serious than it is?
There's no reason for you to be upset.
To be unhappy about a little business trip
Would be ridiculous. It will be best
For both of us, we'll have a chance
To think about ourselves—and act upon
Our problems, which are very human.
Everybody has them. I'll be back
When everything has worked out,
The late spring or the summer.
It won't be long! A season or two,
That's not such a long time.
    So that's that.
Now, what about the sea birds?

CHLORIS Why were they flying north so early,
So early, and in such variety?
I wanted you to look.

DAMON I couldn't look.
I had to speak first. It was
Prepared, you see, in fixed sequence.
You wanted to interrupt.

PHOEBE It's better not to be articulate,
As she is. Chloris is glib.
How much better to
Turn to the exact it is,
Than to admit the circumstances.
Have you your ticket?

CHLORIS Damon—

PHOEBE Damon, it's too late
For you to gape and hesitate!

DAMON Chloris—

PHOEBE Your visa has run out!
You must redeem it. Hurry up!

DAMON It's so late. I must work fast.
First, to see the mayor—
Chloris, can you understand?

PHOEBE And must the mayor wait forever
With a red stamp in his hand?

DAMON Later. We'll speak later.

[*Exit.*

PHOEBE So. Georges, we're on our way at last.
I had nothing against you, Chloris.
Nothing whatever. I'm sorry
That anyone had to be squashed, but—
Someone always is.

CHLORIS Phoebe, if I were absolutely certain
What you were, if I were sure
That you exist at all, and as a creature,
And you were not, in part, what was disastrous
In myself and self-inflicted, as an illness,
Then—

PHOEBE What would you do?

CHLORIS I would throw myself at you, and try to tear out your eyes.
I would set fires against you and cry out alarms.
I would go to St. Pierre and tell them, there, what you were.
There, they would hear, they would sound the public drum.
I would convince them to denounce you, and to cast you out.
All of our fierce dogs would come and chase you out.
I would cry, "Bitch! bitch!" until everyone had heard me.
All this, if I could be certain.
But you see, I have never been sure.

PHOEBE Then we'll go out like spectres,
Georges and I, to take our place
By Damon's side, and in his time—
And let you make of us what you please.

GEORGES Goodbye, Chloris.
At another time, perhaps—

PHOEBE Georges.

GEORGES *C'est ça.*

[*Exit* PHOEBE *and* GEORGES.

CHLORIS Perhaps we have become like cave creatures,
Who, being blind, can only the blind beget.
Sight is becoming useless. We are turning black.
Well,
We will sweat now, like shuddering mountains
Struggling to grow in the millions of long time.
But squashed in the heart of us, surely there are footsteps
Of all the monsters who kept us alive.

## X. AFFIRMATIONS

DAMON Well, I'm off.

CHLORIS Soft this, which is my last to you.
Remember once we held hands, to lead
Each other through the alleys? Remember
The jealous neighbors, who watched the way
We went, and spoke from broken windows?
They said, "*You cannot have this.*" But you laughed.
And said, "I've signed my name at last—
And taken back my rightful name as God."
"Why not be just a man," they said, "and then
You wouldn't have to be a god." But we fled
Because their tongues were black, their veins
Stuck from their skins. You said, "By my side
Chloris is, who joins me. She and I are on
Our way to find the *Fête Champêtre* beyond
The City Limits." You said, "We'll find
The dancing eagles, where every corner of the forest
Is filled with muguette, gentian, cardinals and lilies,
There to observe harmonious birds that feed each other,
Tipping their barley-corns and berries beak to beak.
*Only there can we work.*"

Damon, if it wasn't that—
It was sometimes like it. I'll wait,
Whatever name you take.

DAMON Whatever name I take?
*So that's what you think, is it?* Oh, no.
Not I. Not Damon.
That won't happen.
How could Damon be resigned to snap at flies,
To foolish barking—a god who has become a dog?
I don't forget the sun-machines. I claim them!
No, Chloris,
Not a god, not a dog, but something in between—
My right is to the power and pride. I want them.
I'll always want the things we talked about.
I mean to have them! But I don't know when.
I want to claim them at a time I want them.
When it comes, I'll write you.
I won't change my name again.
Sometime, I'll grow into it.
Don't make me say too much.
And don't you say too much. Let's keep composed,
And make of this leave-taking what it is, the words
Of friends before a holiday trip. Why not?
I'm glad you play along, and do not weep,
Or beat your head—I saw you do that, once,
And was embarrassed.
How much better it is
To smile and kiss, like *this*.
Goodbye, Chloris.

DAMON [*to himself*] I have always been honest with her.
And if not Chloris, there'll be someone else.
Someone else to dream the honest island.
I'll find the final place with someone else,
And live there honestly. But not this year.
It could be next year, or the next—but now
I go to apprehend these multiple desires,
These bolts and streams which were too soon put down.

I'll go and play my trumpets in the town.
Phoebe understands.

[*Exit.*

CHLORIS It is finished.
The boat crawls back, the island promises
Are already jeweled fishes, that swim the air,
And in an hour vanish, as the sun shifts.
The hills of love grow small, seen from the ocean.
Goodbye, Damon.
I'll look out to the mainland,
Sometimes. And I will not smile.
I was at fault. I was too serious.
All we can do for each other is to this purpose,
To keep the sand beneath our feet, which tears
Away from us, and guts the shore.
We can do more, but not for love.
We do it by ourselves.
Oh, Mrs. Palmer,
Take care of everything, and I shall come.
You and I will have our season, when,
Deaf and dumb as diamonds,
We'll share the final mine!
We'll meet again,
Beneath the beating wings of gleaming creatures,
Released from all their earthly cages,
Who were beyond their time.
Picking our way
Past obsolete, exanimate compass points,
Past human artifacts—the clocks, chronometers,
Sprawled over all the frozen forest—
Past our ancestral bones and scales, we'll come.
It will be time.
And North North North, we'll point for home.